Franchising 101

THE COMPLETE GUIDE TO EVALUATING, BUYING AND GROWING YOUR FRANCHISE BUSINESS

ASSOCIATION OF SMALL BUSINESS
DEVELOPMENT CENTERS (ASBDC)
EDITED BY ANN DUGAN

DEARBORN™
A **Kaplan Professional** Company

This publication is designed to provide accurate and authoritative information in regard to the subject matter covered. It is sold with the understanding that the publisher is not engaged in rendering legal, accounting, or other professional service. If legal advice or other expert assistance is required, the services of a competent professional person should be sought.

Associate Publisher: Cynthia A. Zigmund
Acquisitions Editor: Mary B. Good
Senior Managing Editor: Jack Kiburz
Interior Design: Lucy Jenkins
Cover Design: DePinto Studios
Typesetting: Debra Lenyoun

Printed in the United States of America

10 9 8 7 6 5

Library of Congress Cataloging-in-Publication Data

Franchising 101 : the complete guide to evaluating, buying and
    growing your franchised business / by the Association of Small
Business Development Centers (ASBDC) : edited by Ann Dugan.
        p. cm.
    Includes index.
    ISBN 1-57410-097-1 (pbk.)
    1. Franchises (Retail trade—United States—Handbooks, manuals,
etc.   I. Dugan, Ann.   II. Association of Small Business Development
Centers
HF5429.3.F718   1998   98-14310
658.8'708—dc21   CIP

CONTENTS

Part II: Acquiring Your Franchise

Part III: Managing Your Franchise

The mere fact that you have opened this book indicates that you are thinking about, or are committed to, owning a franchised business. Your readership also indicates a desire to be successful in your enterprise. You have no doubt heard that thousands of people have found franchising to be a satisfying and profitable way to own their own business, but you probably also have heard far too many horror stories about people losing their life savings in a franchise relationship gone awry. You are reading this because you want to be a part of the happy, not sad, statistics that tell the story of franchising in the United States.

When the editor and contributing author of this book, Ann Dugan, approached the national leadership of the Association of Small Business Development ment Centers (ASBDC) about developing this book, we asked ourselves if the world really needed yet another book on how to buy a franchise. After examining shelves full of "how to" books, we found that most publications lacked an honest critical appraisal of the pros and cons of franchising. Many books examine franchising from the perspective of people with opportunities to sell. We wanted to look at franchising from the perspective of consumer awareness, realizing that protection-educated consumers make better, more informed choices.

The ASBDC is a partner agency of the Small Business Administration and offers one-on-one counseling and educational programming to the small business community through more than 950 centers in colleges and universities around the country. Many individuals seeking our free, confidential counseling are interested in the purchase of a franchise but really do not understand what that encompasses. We believe that it is our mission to help individuals walk through the various opportunities, understand the differences, and assist in the analysis of the market for the particular products and services of the franchises under consideration. Ultimately, by going through this type of process the franchisor and franchisee will enter into a mutually satisfactory relationship. This book provides a guide for your use in conjunction with the investigative process developed by our Small Business Development Centers across the country.

Let us journey together towards your success as a franchisee!

—Woody McCutchen
Executive Director, ASBDC

ACKNOWLEDGMENTS

Providing franchising seminars around the country for SBDCs as well as others, I often have been asked about a book to complement the material I was providing. My standard reply was that I just did not have the time to write a book.

Early in 1997, I ran into yet another franchisee involved with a poorly developed franchise system who did not know what to do next. I asked him, as I always do, why he had picked this particular franchise. He gave me the answer that I have heard time and time again from all parts of the country: "I could afford it and the salesperson told me that if I didn't jump on the opportunity someone else was interested. I didn't have time to really investigate what I was getting into."

I knew the time had come to write a comprehensive manual that could assist the potential franchisee that I was not reaching in my seminars as well as a manual for SBDCs to use in assisting clients interested in the area of franchising. I decided to enlist a group of renowned franchising experts who I had come to know from around the country to become the authors of this book. I am most grateful to these individuals for their time and dedication to this effort, and for sharing their years of valuable experience. Hopefully, our collective effort will help those interested in purchasing a franchise in making the best, most informed choice. These authors are Joseph Lamble, Cheryl R. Babcock, Howard Bassuk, Harris J. Chernow, Keith J. Kanouse, Richard Rosen, L. Seth Stadfeld, Kevin Yeanoplos, Thom S. Crimans, Janice Dwyer, Ronald Noll, Lance Winslow, and Charlene Gross. In particular, I also would like to thank Harris Chernow for his invaluable contributions as an author and his assistance during the editorial process.

I also would like to express my deepest gratitude to the many people who supported this endeavor and whose ideas contributed to its success:

- To the leadership of the ASBDC, including Greg Higgins, Sam Males, Hank Logan, Jim King, and Woody McCutchen, whose encouragement, support, and willingness to assist came at critical times in the process and was greatly appreciated.
- To Robin Nominelli and Danielle Egan-Miller of Upstart Publishing Company for their support and encouragement through the long process of writing a good book. In particular, I want to thank Anne Basey, a writer whose editorial assistance was critical in developing a common writing style for 13 diverse writers.
- To those around me in Pittsburgh who had to live through the daily struggles of writing and meeting deadlines. My assistants, Davinna Pearson and John Dobransky; my family, James, Maria, Eleni, Larisa, Kerry, Jamie, Katie Dugan; my parents, Bob and Lil Meyers; as well as many others too numerous to mention, for whose patience I am always astounded. Last but not least, my grandmother Marie Lang of Brunswick, Georgia, who taught me much about life, and because of knowing her I am truly blessed.

—Ann Dugan

INTRODUCTION

This book is designed to help you decide if franchising is right for you, and whether now is a good time to buy. If you decide to press on, you will find everything you need to guide yourself through choosing the right franchise opportunity, given your skills, interests, and aptitudes, to preparing yourself to succeed as a franchisee and businessperson.

At the outset, we ask that you not fall in love with the first opportunity you see, throw caution to the wind, and sign on before you have completed the analysis outlined in this book. You are considering the opportunity to be self-employed, but you are hedging your risk by perhaps becoming part of a group of people who are in a franchise. The word *franchise* implies that these individuals are all working together towards a common goal: to promote the brand name with all its identifying marks, logos, colors, and motto and to deliver the same products and services to the public in a uniform and consistent manner. In an undeveloped franchise system, these goals are not present. In the worst case, a franchisor is or salesperson's primary goal is to sell something to an unsuspecting investor and then disappear.

This book will help you choose, acquire and manage your franchise. Part I, "Choosing Your Franchise," will help you distinguish a good opportunity from a poor opportunity and find the one that fits best and is most likely to make you money in the market under consideration.

Part II, "Acquiring Your Franchise," leads you through some of the details of the beginning stages of your franchise purchase that often are overlooked, misunderstood, or ignored by those new to the world of legal contracts and long-term business commitments. This section will be particularly useful to those that find themselves in areas without attorneys or counselors familiar with franchise law. In these cases, take this section to your attorney so he or she can better assist you in your understanding of the documents of franchising.

Although this book is far too short to tell you everything you need to manage your franchise, Part III, "Managing Your Franchise," will get you off to a good start. Oftentimes, even the best of franchisors are not equipped to teach every franchisee all they need to know about business management. Most franchisors offer approximately two weeks of training. This short period has to concentrate on the technicalities of the franchise product or service and only briefly covers business topics. We put our experiences in these chapters to round out your initial education as a new franchisee.

This book gives you all the tools you will need to make a good business decision in the selection and purchase of a franchise. If you follow the advice of the experienced authors presented here, who have witnessed franchisees experiencing the joys of success as well as the agonies of failure, you will certainly be well on your way to achieving your dreams as a business owner.

Now let's start our class in Franchising 101!

Cheryl Babcock of Minneapolis, Minnesota, is the director of the Institute for Franchise Management and the chief operating officer of the Society of Franchising at the University of St. Thomas.

David H. Bangs, Jr., of Portsmouth, Hew Hampshire, is the author of numerous Upstart books on small business, including the bestselling *The Business Planning Guide.*

Howard Bassuk of San Diego, California, is the founder and president of FRANNET.

Harris Chernow of Philadelphia, Pennsylvania, is an attorney and member of the law firm Heller, Kapustin, Gershman & Vogel.

Thomas Crimans of Louisville, Kentucky, is president of FRANNET Midamerica and LedgerPlus.

Ann Dugan of Pittsburgh, Pennsylvania, is the director of the Small Business Development Center and the Family Enterprise Center at the University of Pittsburgh Katz Graduate School of Business.

Janice Dwyer of Cleveland, Ohio, is an insurance broker with the firm of Luce, Smith & Scott.

Charlene Gross of Arlington, Virginia, is a franchisee and consultant to the Small Business Administration.

Keith J. Kanouse of Boca Raton, Florida, is an attorney in private practice as well as the primary author of the fair franchising standards of the AAFD.

Joseph Lamble of Indianapolis, Indiana, is the chief operating officer of FRANNET in the mid-central states.

Ronald L. Noll of Malvern, Pennsylvania, is a CPA with the firm of Noll & Company and a franchisee of Triple Check.

Robert Purvin of San Diego, California, is an attorney and founder of the American Association for Franchisees and Dealers.

Peter Rainsford of Ithaca, New York, is an internationally known consultant on restaurant and hotel management and a professor at the Cornell School of Hotel Management.

Richard Rosen of New York City is an attorney and principal with the firm of Rosen, Einbinder & Dunn.

L. Seth Stadfeld of Boston, Massachusetts, is an attorney and partner with the firm of Brown & Stadfeld.

Lance Winslow of Los Angeles, California, is the founder and franchisor of the Car Wash Guys national franchise.

Kevin R. Yeanoplos of Tucson, Arizona, is a CPA/CVA and partner in the firm of Moran, Quick & Yeanoplos.

PART 1

Choosing Your Franchise

Purchasing a franchise is a major life decision that requires careful deliberation. Unfortunately, many people spend more time investigating the selection of a penny stock than they do investigating a franchise opportunity—even though a franchise will tie up enormous assets for many, many years.

Part I, "Choosing Your Franchise," will help you make your decision the outcome of a sound and logical process. The following chapters will help you evaluate your own interests so you can select a franchise that fits you and your lifestyle and will help you achieve your financial and personal goals. It will also help you investigate franchise systems thoroughly so you can be assured that the franchise you ultimately select is a bona fide opportunity.

After all, just because a franchise system appears on the "Hottest Franchises" list in an entrepreneurial magazine doesn't mean it is a good opportunity for you. It *does* indicate that the franchisor has talented sales people. But can it really make you happy?

There are three ingredients to success in business: passion, commitment, and intimacy. You need to be passionate about your business and look forward to being there every day—and your family, friends, and others surrounding you also need to be appreciative and supportive. You also need to be committed to your business in good times and bad. If you are only committed during the high moments, the bottom will be very, very low. Finally, you need to become intimate with your business and your industry and have your finger on its pulse at all times. You cannot afford to be an unimpassioned observer on the sidelines. You need to understand your business and industry so well that you can recognize trends early: anticipating increases in sales so you can build momentum in your own store, and recognizing the signs of a lull early enough to batten down the hatches and do what you have to do to weather the storm.

It takes diligence to sift through opportunities until you find the right one. This section will help you find a business that can be a life, not just a get-rich scheme.

CHAPTER 1

Franchising: Yesterday, Today, and Tomorrow

Robert L. Purvin

Franchising in America has a stellar reputation. Fed by studies that suggest 95 percent of all franchised businesses are successful* and industry claims that in franchising "you are in business for yourself, but not by yourself," franchising has fueled the get-rich dreams of thousands of wanna-be small business owners. But like the California Gold Rush of 1849 and the great bull stock market of the late 1920s, perception can be quite different from reality.

Common Franchising Myths

By exploring a number of the common myths about franchising, you can learn about the dynamics of the franchising relationship and avoid some of the stumbling blocks that affect franchisees.

Myth #1: Buying a Franchised Business Is a Guarantee of Success

When done right, franchising can be a method of business expansion without peer in the annals of commerce, but it is no panacea for business success. Although some franchisees forge successful businesses and amass fortunes, others lose their life savings. Those who succeed combine a proven recipe of careful planning, proper financing, and hard work with a modicum

---

*International Franchise Association, Franchising in the Economy, 1991; and the Department of Commerce, *Franchising in the Economy, 1984–1986.*

of good luck. Those who fail lack some or all of the foregoing and usually have presumed that buying a franchised business would ensure success and cover all sins of omission.

But franchising by itself is not a guarantee of success. Franchise a proven product or a proven method of service to a hardworking and well-financed franchisee in a prime location and you are likely to have a real winner. But a poorly conceived franchise program with a new or untested product or service, perhaps without all the bugs worked out, franchised to a poorly financed and trained operator will most likely spell disaster, and quickly! The reason is that franchising is a method of commercial cloning, and it is as easy to clone a poor concept as a successful one—perhaps even easier.

In brief, franchising is a method of product or service distribution. Many businesses distribute their products through wholesale distributors for ultimate sale in retail stores. In these situations, how a product is marketed is generally left up to the retail dealer. When a product or service requires more control over the distribution process, companies producing such products frequently develop their own retail outlets. But the capital required to develop a chain of retail stores can be staggering and can limit the growth of the enterprise. By franchising, a company can grant or license rights to the business to a local entrepreneur who uses his or her own capital, management, and good will to develop the distribution outlet. As a result of cloning, companies can grow at a very accelerated rate while exerting substantial control over the distribution process.

Commercial cloning can lead to success—but success, like beauty, is in the eye of the beholder. To a franchisor who profits on every dollar of sales, a store is successful as long as it is open. Consequently, early surveys of franchising companies claimed that all outlets that remained open were "successful" even though franchisees had sold out at a loss or remained open in the face of mounting losses. Indeed, recent studies that measured the profitability of franchise owners found that *in the current market* franchisees as a group are less profitable than independent businesses that are not franchised.* This is not to say that franchising cannot increase your odds for business success; the simple lesson is that all franchises are not created equal.

Myth #2: Franchising Is a Form of Business Ownership

Franchising is *not* a form of business ownership. In fact, sometimes franchising conveys no true ownership to the franchisee at all.

Who owns the franchised business depends upon the franchise agreement. The franchisor may retain or convey ownership depending on the deal. As a general rule, the more mature the franchise enterprise, the less true ownership is conveyed. In most modern franchises, franchising represents only the license to operate the franchisor's business for the term of the franchise agreement; the right

---

*Dr. Timothy Bates, "Franchise Startups: Low Profitability and High Failure Rates," *EGII News* (Dec. 1993), p. 9.

to own the business ends with the franchise. In other words, a franchisee may not have the right to stay in business after the franchise ends.

Myth #3: Franchising Is a Protective Relationship in Which the Franchisor Looks Out for the Best Interests of the Franchisee

In most modern franchise relationships the franchisor has very few duties to the franchise owner. Indeed, this is a source of many complaints from franchise owners, who expected their franchisors to protect the value of the franchised business. But generally speaking, companies engaging in franchising are intent on increasing market share for their business. They are not necessarily committed to the financial success of their franchisees.

Myth #4: You Get a Proven Operations System with a Franchise

Myth #5: Franchising Provides Franchisees with Established Product or Services

Myth #6: The Franchise Comes with Complete Training

Myth #7: Franchising Guarantees Market Penetration and Mass Marketing for the Good of the System

While all or some of these important ingredients to a successful business may be present in many franchise systems, these are not qualities of franchising per se. When these benefits are present in a franchise system, they are qualities present in a successful business enterprise that also happens to have employed franchising as a method of distribution.

Franchising: The Reality

The reality is that franchising is a method of product and service distribution that is governed by a contract. This distribution method is utilized by successful and unsuccessful companies. Indeed, recent studies have suggested that more than two-thirds of companies that engage in franchising will themselves fail within 5 to

12 years.* These findings are in stark contrast to industry claims of 95 percent success rates and demonstrate that buying a franchise cannot in general deliver all of the benefits attributed to franchising.† *If the franchised product or service is good, if there is an established value to the trademark, if there is a sound business plan behind the franchised program, and if the franchise agreement has fair protections for both the franchisor and the franchisee, franchising can be the answer to all of your business dreams.*

The Franchising Marketplace and the Franchise Relationship

In the end, whether or not a franchise is successful boils down to two ingredients: a relationship and a contract. Franchising is a relationship between a company that wishes to franchise its business—the franchisor—and a person who wants to purchase and operate the franchise—the franchisee. In a positive relationship, franchisor and franchisee strive to create a win-win situation by trusting each other and pursuing the mutual goals that ensure success for both parties. In a negative relationship, these characteristics are not present. Even though the relationship is guided by a contract, it has changed over time, especially as the demand for franchise opportunities has surged.

For more than 30 years, there has been an unprecedented bull market in franchising. With more than 3,000 franchise opportunities on the market at any given time and a growing population of eager consumers set on entering the world of business ownership, today's franchise marketplace is a frenzied place. An attorney at the U.S. Federal Trade Commission cautioned a few years ago that a "buying frenzy for franchise opportunities had reached such a state that consumers would buy anything called a franchise, no matter how bad the deal."

In the face of this staggering demand for franchise opportunities, franchisors have been able to write their own ticket and dictate the terms of the franchise contract and the franchise relationship. Only recently have franchisee groups begun to fight to regain a balanced franchise relationship by demanding rights and protections that characterized most franchise agreements and relationships 30 years ago.

In short, the quality of the franchise relationship is market driven. The nature of franchising and the franchise relationship changes as the franchising marketplace changes, just as the stock market goes up and down depending upon investor confidence and demand. Like all markets, the franchise marketplace is driven by the laws of supply and demand, the principles of marketing, and the public's perception of the quality and value available in the market.

---

*Compare a study by the American Association of Franchisees and Dealers in 1993, which found a franchisor failure rate of 69 percent over a five-year period. Professor Scott Shane of MIT reached similar conclusions in a study released by the Small Business Administration in 1996. The AAFD Study was conducted and published by Robert Purvin in 1993.

†Scott A. Shane, Mass. Institute of Technology Hybrid Organizational Arrangements and Their Implications for Firm Growth and Survival: A Study of New Franchisors, 1995.

To understand the franchise relationship, it is imperative to appreciate that the current nature of the relationship reflects the current market. The relationship between franchisors and franchisees is directly related to what consumers are willing to buy and what franchisors are willing to sell. This distinction is important to your analysis and evaluation of franchising for several reasons. The quality of franchise opportunities shifts based upon what consumers are willing to buy. Whether you like franchising or an independent opportunity will depend on whether your particular demands are satisfied. Although franchising as a method of small business ownership has clearly proven itself many times over, franchises offered in the current marketplace may not be worthy of investment. Most important, educated consumers, willing to say no to unfair franchise opportunities, will inevitably cause a shift in the market, giving rise to a more acceptable product.

In today's bull market, the franchisor has the upper hand in the franchisee-franchisor relationship. But that has not always been the case. Understanding the franchising marketplace, how it has evolved and current market conditions, will help you evaluate whether you want to participate in franchising—and what kind of relationship to pursue with a franchisor.

If you are like most consumers, you are sensitive to prices and quality when you shop. Because you have been buying oranges for years, you have a clear sense of good and bad quality and good value in pricing. You've probably developed the same sensitivity in other product categories, such as computers, office supplies, and automobiles. Before you decide to purchase a franchise, you need to develop the same yardstick for value in the franchise market. A short history of the franchising marketplace can help.

The Franchise Marketplace: Yesterday, Today, and Tomorrow

Franchising has its roots in feudal times, but the first commercial retail franchise is reputed to be the Singer Sewing Center, developed by Isaac Singer in 1858.* After Singer invented the sewing machine, he encountered two significant obstacles in bringing it to market. Consumers had to be taught how to use the new invention before they would buy, and Singer lacked the capital to manufacture his machine on a mass basis. Once Singer seized upon the idea of selling the rights to local business people to sell his machine and train users, his enterprise expanded rapidly. Fees for the license rights helped fund his manufacturing, and because each franchisee was self-financed, Singer was spared the expense of hiring each center's manager.

---

*Robert Purvin, *The Franchise Fraud: How to Protect Yourself Before and After You Invest*, Chapter 2 (New York: Wiley, 1994 1-7). The concept of franchising, even in a commercial context, goes back to at least 12th-century Europe, but the Singer model and a few others will serve our purposes.

The Singer model had been copied in several industries by the turn of the century. Coca-Cola was able to expand nationally by shifting the burden of manufacturing, storing, and distributing its product to local businesspeople who acquired bottling rights. In 1921, when the U.S. population was a mere third of its present size, there were more than 2,000 Coca-Cola (Coke) bottlers. In exchange for assuming risks at the local level and providing the capital for Coke's expansion, Coca-Cola franchisees were granted exclusive marketing and distribution rights in their respective territories.

The introduction and mass production of the automobile early in the 20th century fundamentally changed franchising as well as American culture. As Henry Ford introduced the assembly line and the age of mass production, methods of mass distribution also had to be devised in order to sell, fuel, and service cars and provide affordable, familiar places for drivers to stay during their travels. Franchising met all of these needs. Automobile manufacturers that spent enormous amounts of capital to tool their assembly lines were able to develop retail distribution networks using capital provided by independent dealers. Oil companies like Standard Oil and Texaco granted franchises to mom-and-pop convenience stores and repair mechanics across the country. Travelodge and its franchised Sleepy Bear trademark were household symbols by the early 1940s. The success of these early examples of commercial franchising led to the explosion of franchising in the 1950s and 1960s.

A closer examination of these early franchises demonstrates significant differences between the early franchises and the modern franchises sold today. For starters, early franchisees had a much better contractual deal than their modern-day equivalent. To induce a franchisee to sign on, franchisors usually guaranteed an exclusive territory or a protected market. Most franchises were signed either in an at will arrangement or for an indefinite term, often to the franchisee's advantage as the local business established a local identity and goodwill through personal service. As long as the franchisor wanted to have a presence at the franchisee's location, the franchisee had significant bargaining leverage.

Early franchise agreements were fairly short documents that dealt more with pricing and terms of payment than with the terms of the relationship. In the early days, franchise agreements were silent about who owned the location, the phone number associated with the business, and whether the franchise owner could stay in business after the franchise had terminated. In addition, these early franchises were not generally royalty based but were dependent on the franchisee's buying and reselling the franchisor/manufacturer's goods. Both sides benefited from healthy margins and fair prices to keep volume up and a healthy distribution network in place. And if the franchisor did not deliver quality goods and fair pricing, the franchisee could terminate the relationship, even change brands.

Although the simplicity of the franchise formula and contract in the first half of the century usually favored the franchisee, this was not always the case. Franchisees often became captive markets for their franchisor's product lines, and their profits were often squeezed by their franchisors, especially in tough times. Automobile manufacturers required their dealers to stock inventory as a condition of maintaining the franchise. In the first signs of what we now call franchise system encroachment, oil companies began to develop company-owned service stations that directly competed with their dealer networks. In response, automotive and gasoline dealers developed national trade associations to combat manufacturer practices that were deemed abusive. And in each industry, dealer protection laws were developed both at the state and national level to address various industry issues.*

A look at the first 100 years of commercial franchising reveals some interesting observations. Many, if not most, early franchises involved the distribution of products, dominated by automobiles and related goods and services (e.g., gasoline service stations), beverage sales, especially beer and soft drink distribution, and convenience store networks, such as 7-Eleven, Ben Franklin, and Western Auto. Product franchisors did not charge royalties based upon gross sales; franchisors made their money instead from the wholesale sale of products to their franchisees, which then sold them at retail.

Perhaps most important of all, most early franchisors did not attempt to control the look and feel of their franchisees. Although early retail franchises could be identified by a common trade name, they were free to establish their own business style. The roadside gasoline station did not have a common look or feel; neither did each motel, auto dealer, or convenience store look the same, or even offer identical service from one outlet to the next.

Indeed, most early franchisees were true independent contractors, entitled to run their business as they saw fit. But all that changed in the 1950s when Ray Kroc recognized the "cloning" potential of franchising to repeat a successful formula and launched business-format franchising as we know it today.

It is a story that has been often told but bears repeating. Ray Kroc, in his late 40s, was a fairly successful salesman selling milkshake mixing machines. One of his accounts was a very successful hamburger stand business in San Bernardino, California, called MacDonald's, which sold 15-cent hamburgers by the bag as well as a very high volume of shakes and fries. Captivated by the singular success of a business so simple to run that most of its employees were part-time high school students, Kroc reasoned that he could exactly replicate the MacDonald's business system and repeat its success all over the country. Kroc believed, quite correctly as it turned out, that by carefully controlling and repeating the business format that became McDonald's, he could achieve predictable success time and again.

The success of McDonald's is the stuff of legends, and Ray Kroc has been compared to Henry Ford for bringing the assembly line to the fast-food industry. But Kroc did more than put the *fast* in fast food. He invented the concept we now call *trade dress* to encompass not just the look and feel of a business's decor but every detail of the way a business is conducted. For Ray Kroc, every aspect of how to run a McDonald's franchise became part of the system in order to ensure that the customer's experience in every McDonald's would be the same everywhere, everyday.

---

*The Petroleum Marketing Practices Act, enacted in 1978, was intended to prevent petroleum manufacturers from cannibalizing their dealer networks by prohibiting oil companies from establishing vertical monopolies. In the automobile industry, the Automobile Dealer's Day in Court Act was passed in 1956 for the purpose of guaranteeing due process to retail automobile dealers from alleged abusive practices involving both encroachment and inventory requirements.

Kroc's theory proved so successful that it spread throughout the franchise industry. In the 1960s, gasoline service stations began to adopt a uniform trade dress and standardize the methods of delivering services. Convenience stores, motels, and flower shops began to standardize not only their store designs but their service methods. Even car dealerships, hotel properties, and restaurant chains caught on to the advantage of business cloning.

Some business-format clones succeeded, such as Kentucky Fried Chicken, Holiday Inn, Taco Bell, and many service station conversions. Others, like Howard Johnson's Motor Inns, Bob's Big Boy Restaurants, and Shakey's Pizza, enjoyed initial success but floundered because they failed to control quality and uniformity throughout their system.

To ensure uniformity of quality and service throughout a franchise system, franchisors had to exercise substantially more control over their franchise owners. Thus, those relatively simple franchise agreements began to lengthen and extend the reach of the franchisor's authority to virtually every aspect of the business. Because uniformity seemed to ensure success, franchise buyers accepted these contracts. But in the name of protecting the trade name, trade dress, and the system, franchise agreements became more restrictive and one-sided. Indeed, in the view of many experts, the modern franchise agreement severely stretches the legal requirements for an independent contractor relationship. In some instances the Department of Labor, the Small Business Administration, and the Federal Trade Commission have denied franchisees recognition as small businesses because the franchisor exercises total control over the business enterprise.

But the buying public continued to buy, and the franchise marketplace offered no resistance to increasingly onerous terms that continued to creep into the modern-day franchise agreement.

The Modern Franchise

The typical franchise agreement of the mid-1990s is a very different proposition from its predecessor of 50 to 60 years ago. That 3-page agreement has grown to 50 pages or more, and the franchisor now usually dictates every aspect of the enterprise. Most agreements bind the franchisee to very specific terms, and renewals, if granted, are conditioned on the franchisee's promise to sign a renewal agreement on whatever terms the franchisor may later decide to impose. In the interests of uniformity, the franchisee usually agrees to adopt (and pay for) any required system changes, including products offered, trade names used, and trade dress required.

Because franchising has enjoyed such enormous popularity, most franchisors have granted limited market protection—or none at all—to their franchise owners. Because it is the system that is franchised (not merely the right to distribute a product), most franchisors now charge rent (in the form of some kind of royalty) on the right to use the name and the system. With no contractual limits on how many stores a franchisor can open and because royalties are earned on each dollar of gross sales (with no consideration to the franchisee's profit), franchisors and their shareholders are focused totally on system sales. Too often franchisees claim that their franchisors are not sensitive to the franchisees' need to have suitable profit margins to be successful. Indeed, many franchisors claim they don't even measure their franchisees' profit margins, and are therefore unable to predict profitability to prospective purchasers!

A curious aspect of the modern franchise is that very few franchise agreements are negotiable. Franchisors argue that the need for uniformity within their systems coupled with the impracticality of having differing agreements with scores, or hundreds, or sometimes thousands of separate owners makes it impossible to individually negotiate franchise agreements. Moreover, the enormous popularity of franchising, and the impression franchisors have given that the streets of the franchising community are paved with gold, have created a franchising marketplace that does not demand negotiated franchise agreements. Buyers are convinced that one-sided franchise agreements are "industry standard" and thereby acceptable. Besides, buyers reason, if they don't take the offered franchise and its one-sided agreement, the franchise will simply be grabbed up by the next willing buyer. As long as there are buyers standing in line with pen and cash in hand, the franchise marketplace will continue to deliver franchise agreements that protect only the franchisor's interests.

The Good News Future

Although the concept of a fair franchise agreement is still somewhat a myth, there are exciting signs that the marketplace is beginning to change for the better. In the past few years, franchise owners have begun to object to the more onerous features of franchise agreements and relationships. Growing numbers of franchisees are organizing into effective franchisee associations that offer support, a collective voice, and bargaining clout. Most franchisors initially resist such organizing efforts, but many of these groups have been recognized by franchisors. As a result, we are beginning to see franchise agreements that have been collectively bargained. These agreements achieve greater balance between the franchisor's and franchisee's interests yet preserve the need of uniformity for the entire franchise network.

The American Association of Franchisees and Dealers

Organized in 1992 to encourage fair franchising practices, the American Association of Franchisees and Dealers (AAFD) represents thousands of franchisees across the United States. It supports same-system franchisee organizations and helps foster negotiated franchise agreements. It has adopted the Franchisee Bill of Rights reproduced in Figure 1.1 and published *Eight Things to Look For in a Franchise*. In 1996 the AAFD adopted its Fair Franchising Standards, which are being circulated among franchisors and their lawyers to raise their awareness of what constitutes a fair franchise agreement. It also now offers accreditation to franchisors who comply with the AAFD standards by earning the Association's Fair Franchising seal. The Seal is awarded to franchisors that recognize an independent franchisee organization and offer a franchise agreement that has been collectively bargained and ratified by over 50 percent of its current franchisees.

Where necessary, the AAFD supports franchisee grievances, and sometimes lawsuits, to draw attention to franchisee claims of abuse by franchisors. The AAFD also actively supports franchisee concerns about federal and state legislation affecting franchising, providing a growing voice of franchisee interests.

All of the AAFD's efforts are designed to help the franchising marketplace demand a fairer, more balanced franchise agreement and relationship that is, quite frankly, more franchisee friendly. As franchise owners and buyers become more aware of practices that are detrimental to them and begin to demand fairer practices, franchisors will modify their programs to meet the demands of the marketplace. The result will be negotiated franchise agreements and relationships that balance the legitimate interests of franchisors and franchisees, and deliver what the AAFD has termed *Total Quality Franchising!*

As this workbook goes to press, the AAFD has accredited a half dozen franchisors that have earned the AAFD's Fair Franchising Seal for having a negotiated franchise agreement and high franchisee satisfaction according to independently conducted surveys. More franchisors are being considered as the marketplace begins to dictate and demand negotiated franchise relationships.

Your Future in Franchising

As this chapter has made clear, franchising is *not* an automatic win/win situation. But by understanding the importance of being a careful and demanding buyer, you will be able to use the balance of this book to select, finance, and operate a franchise that suits your interests and aptitudes—and can support you comfortably.

As you begin your journey, be cautious, careful, and demanding. Here are some helpful hints:

- Limit your search to franchise systems that recognize and work with an independent association of its franchisees. A strong franchisee association recognized by the franchisor means there is a mechanism in place for solving problems that inevitably arise in the relationship.
- Study and use the Franchisee Bill of Rights shown in Figure 1.1 as well as the AAFD Fair Franchising Standards. They will help you understand the need for balanced franchise relationships and provide a standard by which to judge the franchise agreement offered to you.
- Assemble a "Dream Team" of advisers to help you understand your business requirements and get you going in the right direction. Your team should comprise a knowledgeable franchise attorney, accountant, banker,

FIGURE 1.1 American Association of Franchisees and Dealers Franchisee Bill of Rights

The Franchisees of America, representing the best of the American entrepreneurial spirit, hereby recognize and demand a basic minimum of commercial dignity, equity and fairness. In recognition thereof, the Franchisees of America do proclaim this Franchisee's Bill of Rights as the minimum requirement of a fair and equitable franchise system.

- The right to an equity in the franchised business
- The right to engage in a trade or business
- The right to the franchisor's loyalty, good faith and fair dealing, and due care in the performance of the franchisor's duties, and a fiduciary relationship where one has been promised or created by conduct
- The right to trademark protection
- The right to market protection
- The right to full disclosure from the franchisor
- The right to initial and ongoing training
- The right to ongoing support
- The right to marketing assistance
- The right to associate with other franchisees
- The right to representation and access to the franchisor
- The right to local dispute resolution and protection under the laws and the courts of the franchisee's jurisdiction
- A reasonable right to renew the franchise and the right not to face termination, unless for cause
- The reciprocal right to terminate the franchise agreement for reasonable and just cause
- The post-termination right to compete

The American Association of Franchisees and Dealers has developed the Franchisee Bill of Rights and works to promote awareness and acceptance of it among the franchising industry and the general public.

and business consultant. Your local Small Business Development Center can assist you in identifying individuals for your team.

As you launch your franchise journey, remember: a successful franchise search takes research, research, and more research. Start by researching yourself and your interests. Then look at the market and the economy. What kind of business is right for you? What kind of business is right in today's environment? Once you begin to narrow your choices, your research begins in earnest. Find out all you can about the franchise opportunity you are investigating. And one last caution: if a franchisor claims that it does not provide essential earnings data regarding the opportunity you are investigating, *run, do not walk, to the nearest exit.* Do not accept statements like "We are prohibited by law from disclosing economic data." Such statements are simply not true. The only information franchisors are prohibited from disclosing is false information. Think about it. Then go on to the next opportunity. In the end you will be able to "Just say no" to unfair franchise agreements.

CHAPTER 2

Do You Have What It Takes to Be a Franchisee?

Joseph Lamble

Not everyone is cut out to be an entrepreneur. And not everyone will make a good franchisee.

Being a franchisee is not the same as being an entrepreneur. Like an entrepreneur, a franchisee is responsible for his or her business 24 hours a day—but the qualities that make a franchisee successful may make an entrepreneur champ at the bit in a franchise system. This chapter will help you understand the differences so you can evaluate the suitability of franchise life *before* you commit yourself to purchasing a franchise business.

Let's start by looking at what it takes to succeed in business regardless of the type of business you choose to start or purchase.

Do You Have What It Takes to Be in Business for Yourself?

Some characteristics are prerequisites for launching a business, whether you opt for a franchise or decide to operate independently. Owning and operating your own business takes motivation, maturity, money, knowledge and experience, strong family support, tenacity, and an even temper. Let's look at these qualities one at a time.

Motivation

Motivation is the "fire in the belly" that feeds the will to forge ahead no matter what. It's commonly found in people who have worked hard on the job but never quite felt fulfilled—the folks who find themselves saying—"If

I owned the place I'd . . . ." That desire motivates people to start their businesses and stick to them through good times and bad.

Maturity

Motivation gets you going; maturity helps you persist as you work long hours without complaining, get along with your personnel, handle money responsibly, and handle crises with patience and good judgment. All these challenges take maturity—the wisdom to accept the hard work and occasional setbacks it takes to make your dream a reality. As a business owner you must be a dreamer and a realist. You need to set goals and plans to achieve your dreams while being realistic and planning the attainable. You need to accept your limitations as short-term handicaps and hunt for ways to grow beyond them. That's maturity.

Money

Starting a business takes money. You must be willing to look honestly at your money situation and determine how much you can put into your business. With your family you must determine what portion of your net worth (the value of all you own minus what you owe) you are comfortable in investing and which of your assets you will convert to cash to meet the liquidity (what you can convert to cash in 30 days) requirements that your bank or franchisor may impose. You also need to determine whether the business you are considering can provide enough income—especially if you are accustomed to a high income.

Knowledge and Experience

To gain the confidence and loyalty of staff and customers, you must provide a quality product or service in a first-class manner at a competitive price. That means knowing your business and your industry inside and out. But that doesn't mean you have to open a business in a field you know (and possibly dislike) just because you think that is all you know.

You might very well elect to open a business in a hobby or field of interest in which you have experience. Hiring tradesmen or experts is another way to get the required know-how. You can't be expected to be an expert in every job, so you must bring in people who have the necessary expertise.

For franchisees, franchisor training is a source of knowledge. Because franchisors know that how well the new owner applies their system depends on how well the new owner is trained, they invest significant time and money in training programs that teach expertise in their industry and, more particularly, expertise in the way they operate. But franchisor training doesn't cover everything. While training may cover the nitty-gritty of a particular service system, the franchisor may leave general business and management principles to you. Be wise: take a personal skill inventory. Evaluate your level of competence in such fields as finance, marketing, accounting, human resources, operations, and advertising. Know your limits, and when you reach them, find a way to expand your knowledge.

An Even Temper

A business owner or franchise needs to be able to make decisions logically and with good judgment. That means handling pressure, conflicts, and crises calmly and thoughtfully. If you are impulsive, you may make poor decisions. If you are hotheaded or have a quick temper, you may alienate customers and employees alike, putting your business at risk.

Tenacity

"Stick-to-it-iveness" is a must for any business owner or franchisee. When a job needs to be done, an employee needs feedback, or a customer needs special attention, you will need to see that it gets done. When faced with setbacks, you must draw on your experience and maturity to make the best possible business decisions. It takes tenacity and determination to weather the bumps on the road to success!

Family Support

Strong family support is invaluable to a franchisee—particularly when family money helps finance the business. You need to build support for your idea among your family members, whether or not they will be your working partners.

Your family needs to understand that your business will come first for the next several years—that your hours will be long and irregular, that you may miss meals and social events, and that, in general, you will have less time for family members. Your family also needs to know your income will not be steady. You won't be paid until all other expenses have been met. Some months that may be very little indeed. And even during good months, you may use your income to build cash reserves. A business is not a bank account that can be accessed at will. Make sure everyone is willing to live with the conditions of self-employment before you embark on your venture.

Do You Have What It Takes to Be a Franchised Business Owner?

Joining a franchise system can be greatly beneficial. For starters, you get a tremendous amount of help from experts in the business: trainers, site specialists, money people, and operations people. You can also call upon other trained franchisees, who have a good deal of wisdom to offer.

You also get a blueprint for success—a blueprint that is the result of years of making mistakes, correcting them, and making sure they're not made again. You spent your money for a system that works in other areas, and the franchisor must assist you in delivering the successful system to your location.

Finally, you can develop solid business friendships with other franchise owners by working on regional committees or talking at franchisee meetings. These friendships can last a lifetime because in all likelihood you will run into these same people (and their families) for years to come.

But not everyone is cut out to be a franchisee. Being a happy owner in a franchise system requires a personality that enjoys working as part of a team. If you don't like teamwork, a franchise may not be for you. Succeeding in a franchise system also requires adhering to an operations manual and certain established procedures. If you're the type who resents following a set program and would rather create your own, you may not be as happy as those who enjoy the rewards gained from going by the book. If your favorite phrase is "If I ran this business, I'd . . .," you may want to give franchising a pass.

Even developing business friendships is hard for some people—yet franchisees need to develop and nurture cordial and respectful relationships with other franchisees and the area managers who help franchisees carry out the program's brass tacks. Those relationships are motivated by the mutual desire to operate a system as profitably as possible.

Let's take a closer look at some of the qualities required of the successful franchisee.

The Ability to Live with the Franchisor's Game Plan

People often say that in franchising you are "in business for yourself but not by yourself." True enough—but this benefit is double-edged. As a franchisee, you are not alone. There are professionals to consult with and plenty of resources to fall back on when difficulties arise. On the other hand, because you are purchasing a system that is already in place, you have a very limited ability to change it. That may rub an entrepreneur the wrong way.

True entrepreneurs love to innovate, to find new niches and new ways to do things. People who question things, want to change the product line or a product color, or do things their own way may not be happy in a franchise system.

A happy franchisee wants to follow the game plan that is in place and doesn't mind taking directions. When he or she sees room for improvement, the franchisee speaks up but isn't disappointed when the suggestions are not implemented.

In short, a franchisee needs to be able to accept things as they are. If you're a person who spends lots of energy on things as they should be, you may not be cut out for franchising.

The Ability to Tolerate Differing Points of View and Accept Consensus

Franchise systems are rife with opposing viewpoints. As a franchisee, you'll have a chance to express your opinion—but so will everyone else. It takes patience and tolerance to hear all sides and to live with a consensus decision that, while maybe the best for the franchise as a whole, isn't the one you would make on your own.

The Ability to Be Corrected and Take It Gracefully

It is in the franchisor's main interest to make sure everybody is following the game plan and staying in line. If the franchisor thinks you need to implement the system more diligently, or believes you are ignoring certain practices or even taking your franchise in another direction, you'll hear about it.

If you have a hard time accepting suggestions or criticism, franchising may not be for you.

A High Level of Trust in the Franchisor

To succeed in franchising, you need to believe in and support your franchisor's system and policies. After all, franchisors make money from royalties, so it's in their interest to help franchisees build the largest possible business. Your franchisor will search constantly for ways to help you achieve that potential, often developing new approaches or policies for you to implement. As a good franchisee, you'll accept policy changes in the spirit they are intended—even when your reaction to the new policy is —Who thought that up?" or "How can I possibly. . .?"

The Ability to Communicate

Franchisees communicate often and openly with the specialists at the home office. The more franchisees share their experiences, the better the franchisor headquarters can offer ideas and assistance. You will need to work closely with field consultants who can share their broad knowledge of how other outlets are operated and provide solid information from trusted and valued associates.

The Maturity to Live with Your Franchise Agreement and Abide by Your Operations Manual

All franchisees in a system follow their franchise agreement and operations manual as they conduct their business. Living by the same rules means you and your colleagues are building the system using the same blueprint. But now and then, some franchisees feel a little stifled by always "going by the book"—especially when it appears to prevent a franchisee from implementing a great new idea.

It takes maturity to follow the rules and maturity to try to change the system from within. But the system grows by adopting good ideas and discarding bad ones. It may take time, but a great new idea just may eventually be adopted if it benefits the entire system, not just a single store or area.

Attributes of the Entrepreneur versus Attributes of the Franchisee

* An entrepreneur is very courageous, a franchisee more cautious.
* An entrepreneur is highly independent, a franchisee more open to guidance.
* An entrepreneur is a visionary, a franchisee more methodical.
* An entrepreneur accepts higher risks than a franchisee.
* An entrepreneur is normally somewhat of a loner, a franchisee more readily interacts with the franchisor and fellow franchisees.

Are You an Entrepreneur or a Franchisee?

Before you elect to purchase a franchise, take a long, hard look in the mirror and answer the question posed above: Are you an entrepreneur or a franchisee? If you're an entrepreneur trying to shoehorn yourself into a franchise, you may be in for an unhappy, unprofitable journey. But if your personal characteristics appear to match those of a successful franchisee, then by all means forge ahead in your search for a profitable, compatible franchise.

When you have chosen an operation that seems ideal, take another look in the mirror and ask yourself why you're taking such a big step. Before you sign anything, be sure you understand

* why you chose the business you are purchasing;
* why you are confident it is the best choice for you;
* that you did not choose it just to satisfy your ego;
* that you did not choose it just because it was glamorous;
* that someone else did not talk you into it; and
* that you really are prepared for the bad days and the hard work that come with every new venture.

When you know you chose your business for the right reasons and in the right way, you are ready to set out on what could be the most rewarding venture of your life!

CHAPTER 3

How Do You Find the Right Franchise?

Howard Bassuk

It sounds trite and simplistic, but it's true: finding the right franchise starts with *you*.

Successfully starting your own business requires you to balance many personal and business considerations. While it's important to affiliate yourself with a franchise company that is a leader in a strong, vibrant, and growing industry, it's just as important to choose a business that matches your skills, ambitions, dreams, and work habits.

Far too many would-be franchisees fall prey to a fast-talking salesperson and literally buy the first franchise they see. Then there they are, the proud owners of a fast-food restaurant—except they dislike teenagers and working at night.

Chapter 2 explained the importance of determining whether you are cut out for franchising before committing to a franchise business. Assuming that you have discovered that franchising is for you, this chapter will help you review your talents and skills in order to select the franchise that is most complementary. It will help you accomplish the following four steps involved in choosing a franchise:

1. Decide what *you* want.
2. Develop a three-tiered strategy that permits you to enter and exit your franchise as well as operate it profitably over the long run.
3. Determine what you expect from your franchisor.
4. Research opportunities.

20

Decide What You Want

The most important question to answer when you are selecting a franchise: *can this franchise fulfill my business dreams?*

Answering this question takes plenty of self-examination. To choose the business that is right for you and that will fulfill your business dreams, you must know yourself, your skills, and your dreams and aspirations inside and out. That's why it's important to begin your process of selecting a business by analyzing yourself.

First, catalog your own personal strengths, weaknesses, skills, and personality type. Be honest, and be brutal. Be sure you can answer the following questions:

- What do you want to achieve in your business?
- What type of business will best allow you to maximize your skills?
- What sort of quality of life do you want?
- How will this investment affect your finances?
- How will this investment affect your family?
- Are the rewards of succeeding great enough to balance the chance that you could lose your entire investment?

Next, consider individual preferences that could affect your final choice. For instance:

- Do you prefer a business that has a lot of employees or just a few?
- Do you like wearing suits to work, or would you prefer a business that is more casual?
- Do you want a business that is open only five days a week or one that can do business every day of the week?
- Are you a morning person or a night person?
- Do you like to work with people, or do you prefer to work on your own?
- Are you comfortable selling a product or service, or would you rather be supported by a system that helps send customers to you?

Take a few minutes and make a list of the things you really enjoy. Compare that list with the business you are considering. Will it *really* make and keep you happy? Look beyond appearances. For example, an avid golfer might want to buy a golfing supply store. Sounds like a match—except that retail hours will require a severe cutback on greens time. You want to pursue an opportunity that is compatible with your personality and your skills.

Use your answers to these questions to create a model of the ideal life and the ideal business. Compare your model of ideal life and ideal business to every franchise that you investigate. By doing so you can compare different business opportunities, not only with each other, but with their fit to you.

A comprehensive model gives you another advantage: a clear goal of what you are looking for. When you know what you're looking for, you'll find it faster—

and you'll be much less likely to stray haphazardly into a franchise that looks good on paper but doesn't help you achieve your dreams.

Develop an Entry Strategy, a Long-Term Strategy, and an Exit Strategy

Once you have painted a picture of your ideal business, start to create a strategic model with three tiers: a entry strategy, a long-term strategy, and an exit strategy.

Your entry strategy allows you to get into business safely and establish a business beachhead. It includes finding and purchasing a business and getting it off the ground without running out of business working capital or personal living expenses. You must also be able to do certain jobs that later you can delegate to others.

Your long-term strategy is your overall "success" strategy. Here you map out what your long-term business should look like, do for you, allow for you, and provide for you. This strategy takes into account not only your pragmatic life needs but also your dreams, ambitions, and values. Ask yourself what you would like your business and personal life to be like if, after five to eight years of working hard, you are successful. Every business you seriously consider purchasing should not only allow you to safely enter into the world of business ownership but also reach your dreams over the long run.

Your exit strategy lets you consider what will happen when you want to sell or pass on your franchise. Most people aren't thinking about getting out of business before they get into business, but they should! Business can be cyclical, and there are many reasons why you want to leave a business behind. Your needs and circumstances may also change.

Do you want to create a family legacy and pass your business to your children? Do you want to sell all or part of the business after you have built it, or create an ongoing cash flow? Each of these is an exit strategy. It's worth reflecting about what you will need economically from a business to secure your future. How easy will it be to sell the business you are buying? Do businesses in this industry sell for high premiums or low? Can your business be run by just about anybody? If you are the only one who can make your business work and you are leaving, your departure will certainly affect the value of your business.

Even though, during the franchise research process, you are primarily focused on your entry strategy, it is important to factor your long-term and exit strategies into your decision-making process. Keeping all three strategies in mind as you research opportunities will help you make a sound decision.

Once you have developed both your personal/business model and your three-tiered strategy, you are ready to consider on what you can expect from a franchisor.

What to Expect from a Franchisor

Before looking at specific franchises, determine what you expect from a franchisor. Different people want different things. Some want a lot of structure, whereas others prefer a less structured franchise that offers more freedom. Some buyers want to be part of a large, well-established franchise system, whereas others prefer to be "in on the ground floor."

Consider your own tastes and preferences, but be realistic. Don't expect the franchisor to do the day-to-day work required to run your business. It's your job to work hard and make your business succeed! However, if a franchisor can't meet certain standards, you should not seriously consider becoming a franchisee in that system.

Here are some of the things to look for in a franchise system that you consider.

A successful system that can be easily transferred from the franchisor to the franchisee. If the system is not successful or proven, why should you as a franchisee pay for it? Don't let someone learn a business on your fees!

A company that is committed to franchising and is vitally interested in distributing its products and services to its ultimate customers. Avoid companies that are more interested in selling new franchises than supporting them, or that sell products through several channels, such as grocery stores, company-owned stores, or nontraditional outlets like college cafeterias and airport concessions. You don't want to compete against your own franchisor!

Answers to your questions before you buy. A franchisor should spend the time required to answer all your questions *before* you sign an agreement. Certain legal restrictions may prevent a franchisor from answering some of your questions, but all others should be dealt with to your satisfaction.

A sense of compatibility with your franchisor and its vision. You should like your franchisor and feel that the franchisor's vision of the future conforms to your own. It is very important for you to believe in the future plans of the franchise. Businesses need to change to stay competitive, and it's important to feel comfortable with the direction you are going.

Strong name recognition and/or excellent growth possibilities. A strong trade name is one of the most important ingredients of a franchise system. It's best to select a franchisor with a well-established trademark, although in some cases the greatest growth opportunities are found in younger systems. But no matter how well known the company, a franchise should produce and market quality goods and services for which there is an established market demand.

A fair franchise agreement. It's no surprise that most franchise agreements favor the franchisor. The franchisor has taken a risk and developed a business that you are asking it to teach you. In return the franchisor will want to be protected and will want to control certain parts of the system. But the street should run both ways. Look for a franchise system that grants you unlimited rights to renew (called an evergreen clause) as well as the right to sell or transfer your franchise easily and fairly. Most important, find a franchise that recognizes your equity rights in the business that you are going to work so hard to build.

Assistance in finding a location that is suitable to your needs. Legally, many franchisors are afraid to insist that you take a location that they have found. Conversely, many are loath to let you pick a site on your own. Look for a happy medium: a franchisor that works actively with you to find a location and gives you several choices. Find a site that you and the franchisor like rather than one that only one of you believes in.

Excellent training. Franchisors typically assume that you have no prior independent ownership experience, so they offer training that covers business in general as well as specific business. Other franchisees can tell you whether the training they received helped them enter business with the fewest possible problems and glitches. If it didn't help, find out what else they wish had been offered. Check to see if the franchisor has a real commitment to current and future training, too. What happens if you or your employees need additional training? Training should be available for a reasonable rate or at no charge at all.

Franchisor visits. Your franchisor should visit you and help you at your location after you have opened for business. You benefit because you can tap your franchisor's expertise. Your franchisor benefits because it gains a "feel" for your territory that will be invaluable if or when issues or problems arise.

A partnership with your franchisor. Your franchisor should think of you as an associate, a partner, and a customer. Investigate its attitude toward the franchisor-franchisee relationship by talking to other franchisees. Check to make sure the franchisor is "franchise friendly." Look for companies with good relationships with its franchisees. One good sign is a strong advisory council that has negotiating leverage with the franchising company or is represented on the franchisor's board of directors. That's a good sign that you will be a team member whose voice is valued.

A strong orientation toward the future. It's not enough to have a system that works well today and has succeeded until now. Businesses, like the world around them, constantly change. When they don't, franchisees become dissatisfied. Your investigation will identify franchisors with little propensity to change. Steer clear of them, and look for a franchisor with a clear vision of the future—a vision that you can endorse.

A solid record of keeping franchisees in business successfully. Some franchisors will move heaven and earth to help you succeed. Others will assist you should you decide to sell your business. This kind of support takes the kind of financial resources usually associated with a long-standing franchisor. Although buying into a younger franchise structure can be a good decision, be aware that younger franchisors may have neither the resources nor the experience needed to help you if you get into financial trouble.

Adequate human and financial resources. Too often franchisors, like other growing companies, are short on money, people, or both. A younger company will obviously not have the resources of a corporate behemoth, but you must still make sure that your franchisor has the resources to do the job properly. If a franchisor is on shaky financial ground or lacks the resources it takes to open outlets in multiple, geographically dispersed locations, gain market penetration, and build a brand name, don't buy it.

A franchise unburdened by litigation. Even though litigation isn't necessarily a bad sign, look closely if your investigation determines that a franchisor is involved in litigation. Be sure that the litigation will not affect your ability to do business and that it is not so overwhelming that the franchisor must concentrate more on defending itself than on growing its franchises. Also, look for patterns to the litigation. The same kind of suit filed again and again may indicate weak areas or even suggest that the franchisor does not deal with franchisees in good faith. Be especially wary of any lawsuits that jeopardize your ability to use the franchisor's trademark.

Technology and communications that keep you ahead of the competition. Do not underestimate the importance of technology. If a franchisor is slow to embrace new technology, you could suffer.

Selectivity in awarding franchises. Just as the quality of employees affects (or even determines) the quality of a corporation, so does the quality of the franchisees in a system affect the overall quality of that system. Younger franchisors may not have enough experience with their franchisees to know who performs best in their system, but more mature franchisors certainly should.

A franchise system that "validates" well. Validation here means that most of the franchisees in the system are happy with their choice, successful in their business, and would recommend the franchise to you. As you investigate franchise systems, look for franchisees who are satisfied. When you do, seek out a few franchisees who are doing extremely well, a few who are doing extremely poorly, and one or two who have failed. As you talk, compare yourself with the most successful and least successful franchisees in that system and ask yourself who you are most like.

If you are like the most successful franchisees, that is a strong recommendation that you are looking at a good fit for you. If you are more like the less successful franchisees, don't buy that system. Even though most franchisees are doing well, there is a good chance that you won't.

Not all of these issues may be significant to you; other issues that matter more may not be listed here. The point is to ask yourself what *you* are looking for from a franchisor, and then choose a franchisor that helps you get it.

Once you know what you expect from a franchisor, you can start investigating franchise opportunities.

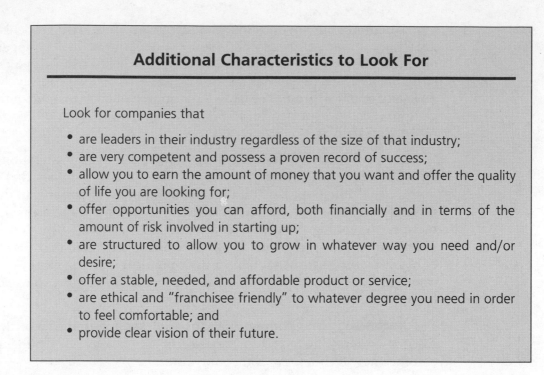

Additional Characteristics to Look For

Look for companies that

- are leaders in their industry regardless of the size of that industry;
- are very competent and possess a proven record of success;
- allow you to earn the amount of money that you want and offer the quality of life you are looking for;
- offer opportunities you can afford, both financially and in terms of the amount of risk involved in starting up;
- are structured to allow you to grow in whatever way you need and/or desire;
- offer a stable, needed, and affordable product or service;
- are ethical and "franchisee friendly" to whatever degree you need in order to feel comfortable; and
- provide clear vision of their future.

Research Opportunities

Always, *always* research a franchise before you purchase it. Too many people let their wallets chase their hearts into a foolish purchase, and then they wake up unhappy when a little research could have prevented a disaster!

Try hard not to limit your research to only one franchise even if you are pretty sure it's the one you want. It's better to compare and contrast two or three franchise systems with your established personal and business models. Better yet, before you buy compare a few franchises that are in totally different industries. A great way to do this is to disguise each business's name and then compare their attributes to your ideal model business. You may find that some franchises that you hadn't strongly considered are much better suited to helping you achieve your personal goals than ones that you originally preferred.

Don't research too many opportunities at a time. Your research should be intensive and extensive, but it won't be if you are looking at more than two or three businesses simultaneously. Less is more. Do more research, but look at fewer businesses at the same time. If a business does not meet your personal and professional model, reject it and select another. (Sometimes a company's sales literature tells you enough to eliminate it.) Repeat the process until you have found one that matches your model. Remember, the business that gets you to your goal fastest, easiest, cheapest, and best is the one that you should most seriously consider.

A Four-Step Plan for Selecting a Franchise

For best results, follow a research plan. The following four-step plan, developed by Howard Bassuk and Franchise Network's (FranNet) Gerald Moriarty, will help you do a thorough and complete job of researching franchises you may want to acquire.

This plan requires you to *read* the offering circular, *question* franchisees and the franchisor, and *visit* stores and corporate headquarters to uncover information that will help you make your decision. It proceeds in four steps summarized in the box below.

Before you begin, assemble an *experienced* team of professional advisers, including a franchise attorney and an accountant. They can help you answer technical questions and will be a useful sounding board throughout the research process.

Step 1: Read the offering circular and interview franchisees and the franchisor.

- Compile questions for the franchisor.
- Compile questions for the franchisee.
- Ask questions in telephone interviews with eight to ten franchisees.
- Take notes and compile additional questions for the franchisor.
- Check your interest level.

Step 2: Review your questions and repeat the process.

- Review your notes.
- Put aside questions that have been answered sufficiently.
- Add new questions that your notes inspire.
- Answer your new questions by interviewing eight to ten more franchisees.
- Take notes and jot down any additional questions for the franchisor.
- Call the franchisor for answers to franchisor questions.
- Check your interest level.

Step 3: Visit franchise locations.

- Make a list of results you want from each visit.
- Visit several franchises and take careful notes.
- Ask franchisees lots of questions, especially "Would you do it all over again?"
- Check your interest level. If you can see yourself in this business, go to step four.

Step 4: Visit the home office of the franchisor to obtain first-hand impressions of the franchisor's staff.

- Compile specific questions for the major players: officers and the managers of training, finance, operations, marketing, and customer service.
- Have an accountant determine the franchisor's financial strength, and ask your franchise attorney to review the Federal Trade Commissions Uniform Franchise Offering Circular (UFOC) and the franchise agreement.
- Set aside plenty of time to review all of your notes as well as the attorney's and accountant's conclusions, and decide whether this opportunity is for you.

Step One: Read the Offering Circular and Interview Franchisees and the Franchisor

An offering circular is a document that offers basic information about a particular franchise system. Federal law requires the franchisor to give it to you at your first face-to-face meeting or at least ten days before you are required to sign a franchise contract. It covers 23 topics that are related to the franchise and includes a sample franchise agreement.

As you read, compile two lists of questions: questions you would like to ask the franchisor and questions you would like to ask other franchisees. Highlight technical sections that you may want your attorney to explain.

Next, interview franchisees to glean "inside" information from the people who run the business on a daily basis. *There is no one better equipped to tell you what you need to know!* If you approach them tactfully, the majority of the franchisees will be very forthcoming.

Use the telephone at this stage of the research process and commit to yourself completing eight to ten telephone appointments with franchisees in the system you are considering. View these as structured interviews and spend time preparing your call. Don't expect the franchisee to stop everything to talk to a stranger. Rather, introduce yourself, explain that you are researching the franchise, and ask when it will be convenient for you to call back. Let the franchisee know you will pay for the call. Prepare a list of questions and jot down others that occur to you during the interview. To help you focus on the most important items, rank your questions by priority, dividing them into A, B, C, and D categories. Take complete notes of each interview.

During your research, you will want to list questions for the franchisor. Your conversations with franchisees will also inspire questions. Write these on a separate sheet. When you complete the first round of interviews, call the franchisor to get answers to these questions. Again, take careful notes.

When you have read the circular and spoken to franchisees and the franchisor, check your level of interest. Are you still interested in the franchise? Is your interest growing or declining? If you decide to continue your research, then go on to step two.

Step Two: Revise Your Questions and Repeat the Process

Take a look at your notes from conversations with franchisees. If eight to ten people gave the same answer, chances are you have learned all you can regarding that question. Set aside the answers for later analysis and add any new questions prompted by your previous interviews.

Using your new list of questions, complete eight to ten additional telephone interviews with franchisees. Again, take careful notes and add to your list of questions for the franchisor. Then call the franchisor with your new list of questions. Take complete notes.

Still interested? Then go to step three.

Step Three: Visit Franchise Locations

Plan to complete three or more visits with franchisees in their place of business. Prepare by making a list of what you want to learn before you go. The franchisees will know you are a serious person by the amount of investigation you have already completed. Thanks to that research, you are prepared to learn a great deal more. The unspoken questions you are asking yourself: *"Can I see myself doing this business? Will I like it? Is it what I have been looking for?"*

Keep in mind that local franchisees may have mixed feelings about helping you. They may see you as a resource for growing the business *or* they may see you as a potential competitor for a future location!

Take along your spouse and any other family members who may be involved in the purchase. Prep them ahead of time so they can take notes and help you look for hidden signals in the workplace. All of you should try to determine whether the franchise is a happy environment. What is the body language of the franchisee and employees? Are there any signs of tension? If so, what is causing them? Ask employees about their feelings about the job. Be sure to ask the franchisee, "Would you do it all over again?" Pay attention if franchisees repeatedly say no.

After completing the visits ask yourself: "Am I still interested?" If so, go to step four.

Step Four: Visit the Home Office of the Franchisor to Obtain First-Hand Impressions of the Franchisor's Staff

Arrange to visit the home office of the franchisor. Schedule appointments with all the key players: officers as well as managers of training, finance, operations, marketing, and customer service. Treat these as formal interviews and plan what you want to learn.

The franchisor's staff will be sizing you up, but you should be sizing them up as well! You want to find out whether these are the kinds of people you want as your senior partners.

Still interested after visiting the franchisor? Then hire two qualified professional advisers: an experienced franchise attorney, who can review the offering

FIGURE 3.1   A Typical Timetable

Number of Weeks	Steps to Be Taken
1–26	Locate businesses that seem attractive to you.
2–4	Use the four–step method to investigate each franchise opportunity. Visit several franchisees; call many. Know what you're getting into and make sure it's a good investment for you.
2–6	Have your attorney and CPA validate the various documents while you write your business and marketing plan and determine bank requirements.
2–8	Get a commitment from your bank for the funding.
4–24	Get your site and take the franchisor's training. A restaurant or a retail store will take longer to locate.
2–3	Buy fixtures, equipment, and inventory while remodeling takes place.
2	Prepare the preopening setup and begin employee training.

circular and franchise agreement, and a qualified accountant, who can review the financial strength of the franchisor and advise you about the economic opportunity. Caution: you hire an attorney for his *legal*, not his business, opinion. If you need a business adviser, hire a business consultant.

Armed with a mountain of information and impressions, and the advice of an attorney and an accountant, you are prepared to decide: "Is this for me?" Whether the answer is yes or no, you can be confident that you carried out an intelligent and diligent investigation.

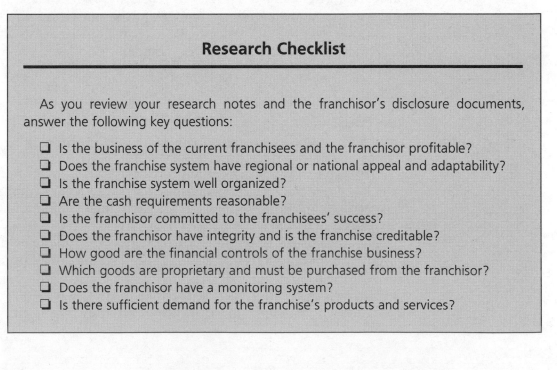

Research Checklist

As you review your research notes and the franchisor's disclosure documents, answer the following key questions:

- ❑ Is the business of the current franchisees and the franchisor profitable?
- ❑ Does the franchise system have regional or national appeal and adaptability?
- ❑ Is the franchise system well organized?
- ❑ Are the cash requirements reasonable?
- ❑ Is the franchisor committed to the franchisees' success?
- ❑ Does the franchisor have integrity and is the franchise creditable?
- ❑ How good are the financial controls of the franchise business?
- ❑ Which goods are proprietary and must be purchased from the franchisor?
- ❑ Does the franchisor have a monitoring system?
- ❑ Is there sufficient demand for the franchise's products and services?

How Long Will It Take?

Researching, selecting, and opening a franchised business takes time. Don't rush! Allow yourself time for each step, from the selection of your business to its opening. A typical timetable is shown in Figure 3.1.

From the time you select a business, it can take at least 24 weeks to open a business that is not site-intensive, and up to 48 weeks for one that requires an optimal site. Any number of items may cause delays: equipment could be slow to arrive; contractors could be delayed; your loan could be tied up. The bottom line: *don't rush.*

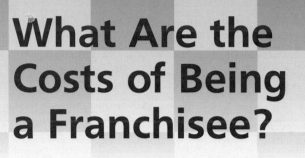

CHAPTER 4

What Are the Costs of Being a Franchisee?

Kevin R. Yeanoplos

Before you can select a franchise, you need to determine how much money it will take to acquire it—and whether you can afford it! The answer usually depends on whether you are buying an existing franchise location or starting a brand-new one.

In general, starting a franchise is very much like starting a business. The only costs that are unique to franchising are the franchise fee, the royalty payments, and the national advertising fee. But you can easily discover these costs as you talk to existing franchisees in the systems you are investigating. Although some franchisees may be less than forthcoming about dollars and cents, you will certainly be able to find some who are willing to supply real numbers.

By the way, there is no automatic correlation between a franchise's acquisition costs and how profitable it will later be. The investment needed is merely an index of how much it will cost you to get it started, not how good that business will be once it is running. It is often possible to buy a business that is less expensive than another yet outperforms the more expensive one, and better meets other parts of your personal and business strategy!

Franchisee-Franchisor Arrangements

Franchisee-franchisor arrangements generally take one of three forms: single-unit purchase, multiunit purchase, or area developer. In a single-unit or multiunit franchise, the franchisee typically pays a one-time franchise fee plus a monthly royalty for the right to operate one or more franchise units. An area developer is a franchisee who pays the franchisor for the franchise rights in a certain area. The franchisor agrees not to award franchises to anyone else in the protected area as long as the franchisee agrees to open a certain number of units in the area within a certain amount of time. The greater and more protected the territorial exclusivity, the more a franchisee can expect to pay.

Estimating Earnings

Whether you are buying an existing franchise or starting one from scratch, you will need to estimate earnings in order to project your costs and income. Without a base to forecast gross sales, it's impossible to determine if a franchise can eventually meet your personal income goals.

A handful of phone calls will help you determine how much to allocate for equipment, rent, inventory, and utilities—but ferreting out information about sales and earnings will be harder. That's because most franchisors don't want to make claims (on paper, anyway) about the net sales and net profits of existing franchises. Their reticence stems from fear that they will be sued if a particular franchisee's business doesn't match their claim. However, some franchisors may divulge the performance of franchisor-owned stores or provide an anonymous listing of franchise gross sales without any comment in writing. Franchisees may also be willing to share these figures.

But if a franchisor or franchisees are unwilling to provide sales numbers, you can determine average sales per outlet by using this four-step formula:

1. On the franchisor's financial statement in the franchise agreement, find the line labeled "royalty payments."
2. Take the total number of franchise outlets in the system and subtract any corporate-owned stores as they don't pay royalties.
3. Divide the royalty payment figure by the number of non-corporate-owned franchise outlets to determine the average royalty payment per store.
4. Divide the average royalty payment per store by the royalty rate listed in the franchise agreement. The result is the average gross sales per store.

Use the average gross sales per store to build your forecast for the location you are considering. Remember, this is only a starting point. Be sure to do a best-case, worst-case, and average-case scenario.

Starting a Franchise from Scratch

Whether you are buying an existing location or starting from scratch, it is vital to remember a very simple maxim: you have to spend money to make money.

Invest too little and the franchise operation will never reach its potential. Invest too much and you may not effectively utilize resources.

It's important to estimate your costs as accurately as possible. If you underestimate them and run out of working capital six or eight months into your business, you'll discover that it is very difficult to go back to the bank for more money. And if you can't get the money, you may find yourself cutting corners in important areas: instituting changes that reduce your product's quality, cutting employee wages or hours, or limiting advertising expenditures. Opting for these desperate measures reduces your potential to grow and generate new sales. It's a little like finding yourself in a plane that is in a downward spiral that is hard to pull out of. Without more money, you are likely to hit the ground.

To avoid this nightmare, overestimate costs and use a conservative figure for gross sales. Doing so will help ensure that you have enough money to hire staff and purchase sufficient product, enough to take advantage of discounts for bulk inventory purchases, and enough to increase advertising and promotional activities that generate new sales. You will be able to move forward, secure in the knowledge that a comfortable cash cushion lies between you and emergencies.

Although every franchise has a different cost structure, it is important to cover each of the categories below in your estimates. If you omit something, you may paint yourself a rosy but inaccurate picture of your true costs. Before you commit to buying a franchise, take the time to educate yourself about the capital requirements for start-up. Plan on the following start-up requirements:

Cash. Set aside enough cash to cover one to three months of operating expenses. Your franchise may not be profitable for the first six months, and you will still need to pay each month's operating expenses. When it becomes profitable, it's still a good idea to have the cash on hand for unforeseen circumstances. Instead of salting away cash, some franchisees obtain a short-term line of credit to finance short-term cash deficiencies.

Inventory. Whether it sells products or services, every business needs start-up inventory. While a service franchise may only require office supplies, a franchise selling products will need to invest in opening inventory. Without the product, there is nothing to sell! As you decide how much inventory to purchase, consider

- the lead time required for obtaining new inventory,
- how quickly inventory is sold (called "inventory turnover"), and
- the shelf life of the inventory.

Inventory for a fast-food restaurant may need to be purchased every few days, where as a seasonal gift store may only purchase inventory twice a year. To find out how much you expect to invest in inventory, ask other franchise owners what they typically spend. You can also find inventory benchmarks for various inventories in a publication from Robert Morris Associates (see the appendix for the address).

Equipment. One reason franchise start-up costs vary so widely is because equipment needs vary dramatically from one franchise to the next. Equipment that is specific to a franchise may be expensive and will have a very limited resale market. To keep costs down, consider looking for second-hand computers and office equipment.

If you are considering a franchise in an industry whose technology is changing rapidly—printing or signmaking are two good examples—be sure to investigate the franchisor's equipment package very carefully. Talk with other equipment suppliers to compare prices and confirm that the franchisor is offering the very latest equipment. If it isn't, consider acquiring equipment from another source. You don't want to lock yourself into equipment that is out-of-date!

Consider leasing equipment instead of buying it. Buying equipment allows you to expense all or a portion of the cost in the year of purchase—and to enjoy the sense of "owning something"—but leasing may lower your monthly payments and allow more financing flexibility or permit you to replace obsolete equipment. Over time, however, the tax benefits of leasing and buying are roughly equal.

Building and improvements. Whether you rent your location or purchase it, building and improvements can be one of your highest start-up costs. Where the franchisor retains the ownership of the physical facilities and leases them to the franchisee, rent will be a major expense item. When you own the real estate, you will need to factor in the cost of preparing the site for your business. If you rent, you will also have to cover the cost of interior modifications. To make sure you correctly estimate leasehold improvements, get two or three construction estimates early in your location search and use them to make your decision. Say, for example, that the franchise you are considering requires three-phase electricity to power its equipment. A site that already offers such electricity will be cheaper in the end than a site for which three-phase electricity must be installed. Up-front construction bids will help you choose the most cost-effective location as well as help you estimate how much you will need to customize your location.

Professional fees. To prepare your franchise properly and prevent headaches, heartburn, or worse down the road, enlist the services of a franchise attorney, a franchise accountant, and an experienced insurance agent. Remember the old adage, "An ounce of prevention is worth a pound of cure." Think of franchise professionals as physicians who keep your franchise healthy, and don't cut costs in this important area.

Franchise fees, royalties, and national advertising costs. Plan on paying between $3,000 and $60,000 to the franchisor just for the right to use the franchise name. This franchise fee is a one-time, up-front fee paid on signing your contract with the franchisor. Fees vary from industry to industry: A franchise printing outlet may cost in the neighborhood of $25,000; fast-food operations typically run between $7,500 and $12,000, with the exception of such well-established brands as McDonald's, Burger King, Wendy's, and Kentucky Fried Chicken.

A higher fee does not necessarily mean a higher quality franchise, and a lower franchise fee is not necessarily a better buy. Your fee helps cover the franchisor's marketing costs as well as the costs of consultants, brokers, real estate experts, and trainers that the franchisor provides for you. If the fee is too low and the franchisor doesn't have the funds for training, follow-up, and support, you will have saved nothing and probably cost yourself your business!

In addition, you will pay weekly, monthly, or semiannual royalties based on a percentage of gross sales *and* a 2 to 5 percent fee to cover national advertising for building your system's brand name. The fee does not cover your local advertising, an expense that comes from your own marketing budget.

Time. Time is a very real cost of starting a franchise. It takes time to construct your location and to hire and train employees and management. It can take several months before an employee is efficiently contributing to profit. And even though your franchise may have a recognizable name, it can take months or years to establish a clientele. Be sure to factor in time when determining the cost of starting your franchise.

Buying an Existing Franchise

Buying an existing franchise offers several benefits. For starters, the franchise will have an established clientele. In addition, the necessary equipment, leasehold improvements, and building are probably in place and operating. Because the business is up and running and has presumably passed its breakeven point, you can probably expect better profits and a larger owner's draw than you could from a start-up business. Also, the existence of financial records makes it easier to forecast future sales and profits. Because the bank can also examine real records instead of estimates, the financing process may be faster, too.

If you are considering buying an existing franchise, look at the following factors to determine the price you will pay.

Financial statements. If you are buying an existing location, you should be given complete information about the outlet's financial results for the last three years. (This is typically found in internal accounting records and tax returns.) Those financial statements should demonstrate that you can anticipate a reasonable return on the investment required and that enough excess cash is being generated to service the debt payments and provide you with a reasonable income for 50 hours of work a week. Financial statements will also help you determine the franchise's performance and its potential for increased profitability.

Be suspicious if someone is not able to provide you documentation of financials because he or she claims it is a cash business and the records don't reflect cash under the table. If you can't document the difference between what the person says the business makes and what the records say the business makes, turn down the opportunity. Not only is the person cheating the government and the franchisor but is probably about to cheat you.

Lease terms, including renewability. You can expect to pay more for an existing business if it has an assumable lease with favorable terms, especially if the lease does not expire for several years. If the lease expires shortly, you should determine the expected terms for the lease renewal. Enter discussions with the landlord early.

Franchise license terms and renewability. Typically, initial franchise agreements are written for 10 to 20 years with various renewal options. A franchise whose agreement expires in 2 years is less valuable than one whose agreement is in force for 12 or 15 years because of uncertainties related to renewal of the franchise.

Age of the franchise. If you are buying an older existing franchise, the capital expenditure requirements for continued profitable operations can be substantial. The physical condition of the franchise is a very important element to consider when buying an existing franchise. The franchisor may require that specific capital reinvestment occur periodically.

Location. Expect to pay more for a franchise located in a crime-free, upscale area than one in a high-crime, inner-city environment—even if both outlets have the same sales volume, rent structure, and profitability.

Time. Pay less for a business that requires you to be present 7 days a week and 12 hours a day to be profitable than for a business that requires less of your time.

Cash flow. A franchise's ability to generate cash is an important factor in determining its value. The more you pay for a franchise, the sooner you should be able to recover your initial investment.

When it's time to talk price, talk to an expert. Valuation formulas tend to be industry specific, and you want to use one that is standard in the franchise's industry. The franchisor may know which formula is most appropriate.

Can You Afford the Franchise?

To determine whether you can afford to purchase a particular franchise, look at the total package. What will you need to open the doors, keep them open, and support yourself and your family? Answering the following questions will help you decide whether you have enough for a particular franchise opportunity.

Do you have the necessary liquidity? Liquidity is the cash you need to make a down payment on your business. Do you have enough savings or assets that you can convert to cash to pay for 25 to 40 percent of the total amount required yourself?

Will someone finance you? Will you be able to find a lender to finance the balance of the cost of acquiring and opening the franchise? Do you have certificates of deposit, real estate, or other property that can be used as collateral for a loan? The riskier the industry in which your franchise will operate, the more collateral a bank or lending institution will insist on. In the worst-case scenario, it may demand dollar-for-dollar collateral.

Can you line up sufficient working capital? During your first year of operation, you will need a significant amount of working capital—a cash cushion you can draw on to cover expenses as the franchise's income fluctuates. Your need for working capital will severely restrict your ability to take money out of the business. Therefore, you need another source of income to cover your personal expenses. If your spouse has a job, great. If you are the sole source of income for your family, then factor your expenses into your projections. If you don't allocate money for your personal expenses, then you will be robbing Peter to pay Paul. To keep up with your personal rent or mortgage, you may take funds that would be better spent on marketing activities or payroll, thus crippling your business's ability to grow and prosper. Make sure your working capital includes enough money for the salary you need.

Making Your Decision

If you decide you can afford to purchase a franchise business that your research indicates is an excellent and sound opportunity, begin to move ahead cautiously. Read Chapter 12 to acquaint yourself with the lending process and to identify sources of money. Shop around for the best financing deal. Examine all the possibilities before choosing the one that makes sense for you.

Plenty of people will offer you advice. Listen to and consider the advice of experts, but beware of well-meaning outsiders who are not informed or experienced enough to give you good advice. As the saying goes, consider the source. Remember, it is your life and your business. If someone has something valid to say, listen. Otherwise, ignore it.

If you have followed the steps in Chapter 3, you will have enough information about franchise systems to make a very educated decision. Take care to invest as much time and energy in determining whether your own sources meet the challenge of franchising. Avoid overextending yourself or placing your personal assets at risk. If you can't afford the business or the numbers don't look good, don't buy it.

CHAPTER 5

Is There Demand for Your Franchise and Its Products?

Cheryl Babcock

Remember how every episode of the original *Star Trek* television series began with Captain Kirk proclaiming that he was about to "boldly go where no one has gone before"? That phrase suits franchisees as well as the crew of the *Starship Enterprise.*

Whenever an entrepreneur prepares to launch a new franchised business or a franchisor introduces a new product or service, a new idea is launched boldly into the business galaxy with the expectation that riches will follow. But there's a problem. Marketers of unprecedented products rarely ask themselves why nobody else has undertaken the mission before. If they did ask, they might discover that, like the folks who brought us the swine flu vaccine, they have come up with a solution for which there is no known problem.

The point here is simple. Good ideas are not enough. You need somebody to pay you for that idea, which means you need to have a way to market it. For proof of how hard that can be, think about Texas-based Bounty of the Sea, which tried to convince the world to eat tuna hot dogs! The company's premise was simple. Almost everyone likes hot dogs, and almost everyone knows that fish is healthier than the stuff found in frankfurters. So why not create a hot dog made out of tuna fish?

Jerry Grisaffi started Bounty of the Sea in 1987 after discovering a Costa Rican invention that could take fish meat and shape it into forms traditionally reserved for other meats, such as bologna, breakfast sausages, and hot dogs. The process removed the fishy smell and left a healthy white meat that took the place of fatty, calorie-riddled beef or pork. Grisaffi thought that tuna-based foods would be perfect for people on restricted diets and a natural for health-conscious America.

His market research and taste tests showed that 84 percent of the people who sampled the tuna fish hot dogs liked them. But there must have been a big gap between getting someone to say nice things about a product they got for free and getting them to purchase it, because tuna hot dogs are not a staple in the supermarket refrigerator section!

The moral of this story is simple: Before you offer a product, think about how it will be received and how you will market it. No matter how technologically perfect your franchisor's idea is, if you can't figure out a way to sell it, you're better off never ordering business cards.

The Value of Market Research

Before you decide to buy a franchise, you need to determine the extent of the demand for its products or services. Market research can help you. By systematically collecting, analyzing, and interpreting market data, you can uncover key trends and form a better understanding of the franchise's market, customers and competitors. Those trends and insights can help you answer such questions as the following:

- Who are my customers?
- Who are my potential customers?
- What kind of people are they?
- Where do they live?
- How often do they buy my products or services?
- What models, styles, colors, or flavors do they prefer?
- Why do or don't they buy from my store?
- How do the strengths of my product or service match their needs and wants?
- What hours do they prefer to shop?
- How do customers rate my business versus the competitors?
- Which advertising media are most likely to reach them?

Perhaps more important, market research can help you uncover important market information about a particular franchise so you can make an educated decision about whether to purchase it.

If your research shows that demand is sufficient to support and grow your prospective franchise business, then you can use the results to help find an ideal location and develop a start-up marketing plan. Because this information is also an essential part of your business plan, investing in market research *before* you buy will help you discover and organize information for prospective lenders.

And if your research reveals that customer demand for a franchise product is declining or nonexistent, you'll avoid making an expensive, heartbreaking mistake.

Using Market Research to Explore Franchise Opportunities

The four-step plan for selecting a franchise outlined in Chapter 3 uses a combination of telephone interviews and site visits to gather information about franchise systems you are considering. By following this process, you are essentially conducting primary market research, which means getting answers directly from a customer, a fellow franchisee, or a supplier.

As Chapter 3 recommended, interview a wide variety of franchise system representatives. Talk to existing franchisees in several areas of the country as well as franchisees who have left the system. Ask them what their customers are like. How old are they? What are their demographics? What are their favorite products, and why? Use open-ended questions that encourage in-depth answers.

Secondary research should also play a role in your investigation. Secondary market research comes from published information such as census data, surveys, and government statistical information. Even the franchisor's audited financial statements can be considered secondary research. For other sources of secondary data, see the box below.

Three steps will help you investigate the state of your intended market and determine demand for your franchise:

1. Conduct an industry analysis that reveals the health of the industry you are considering.
2. Conduct a market analysis that indicates whether there are enough consumers in a particular area for you.
3. Review the data and draw your conclusions.

Secondary Data

Secondary data are abundant, inexpensive, and easy to find. Try these sources:

- Professional journals, trade magazines, reference books, government publications, and annual reports of public corporations abound with data.
- University or community libraries are excellent sources for publications.
- Small Business Development Centers (SBDCs) are located at over 950 colleges and universities and offer a variety of information about the marketing, legal, financial, and accounting aspects of business expansion as well as state and federal business assistance programs.

- County government agencies can supply census tracts that show population density and distribution. Read them to discover who lives in the areas you are looking at and what population trends indicate about the area's future.
- Trade associations offer a wealth of information, including industry and market statistics, books and reference materials, and membership directories that identify key industry personnel.

Local chambers of commerce or business development organizations can supply information that is pertinent to your research. Contact them for

- demographic reports on the local, regional, and state level;
- relocation and site selection assistance;
- maps of major trading areas showing the major areas of commerce and reflecting the population's spending habits; and
- informational sessions on networking, managing, financing, or developing a marketing plan.

Trade associations, franchise research services, and market research sources are listed in Appendix A.

Step One: Conduct an Industry Analysis

Every franchise operates in an industry that has a direct impact on the way the franchise conducts its business and on its potential for success. McDonald's operates in the fast-food industry; Jiffy Lube operates in the automobile services industry. Some franchises operate in more than one industry, like quick-print franchises, which operate in the printing industry and the marketing industry. Industries are constantly in flux. New consumers and competitors enter the marketplace; old technologies are replaced; new methods of reaching customers are discovered.

Before you decide to purchase a franchise, you need to understand the big picture of its industry. By conducting an industry analysis, you will learn how rapidly an industry is growing and how long it is expected to thrive. You will discover its strengths and weaknesses, pinpoint its opportunities, and confirm whether you are about to join an industry that is robust or one whose prospects are dwindling.

You can gather primary field data on the industry by talking to the following people in the industry as well as outside it:

- *Customers* can provide clues to satisfaction with the industry and the product or service supplied. If you get lots of complaints, listen to them. Be tough-minded as you determine whether this franchise is giving the customers what they want.
- *Suppliers and distributors* are in an excellent position to comment on the financial strength and market practices of major firms in the industry and to assess the demand for an industry's products and services.

- *Employees of key firms in the industry* will be able to provide information about potential competitors.
- *Direct and indirect competitors* can tell you about the intensity of competition for customers. If three major competitors are sharing a market, is there room for a fourth? Are they acquiring new customers or merely fighting over existing customers? Visit trade shows to quickly identify major players and assess the strength of their market strategy.
- *Current franchisees* can also share their perspectives on where the industry is headed.
- *Industry experts* who report on particular industries for the media can provide global information and identify major players and issues that may affect a franchise.
- *Attorneys, accountants, and other professional service providers* who work within the industry are also knowledgeable sources.

Acquaint yourself with basic industry knowledge *before* you meet with key industry figures. The people you want to interview are busy and may not want to take the time to bring you up to speed. *Do* demonstrate your knowledge of the industry and show a genuine interest in it. *Do* be considerate of the person's time. If you make an appointment, start and end it on time. *Do* offer the person a summary of the results of your analysis. Follow these guidelines, and you will begin to gather a great deal of information as one interviewee refers you to another, and so on.

Secondary sources are also a vital part of an industry analysis. Use them to gather statistics on sales, products, and prospects as well as information on key figures in the industry. Don't let the magnitude of available facts overwhelm you. Your goal is not to write a formal report on the industry but to learn enough through research and interviews to confirm that it is the right place for you to be.

In the end, your industry analysis should tell you the following:

- Current size of the industry
- Industry growth potential
- Geographic concentration
- Industry trends
- Seasonality
- Profit potential
- Sales patterns
- Typical gross margins on products
- Major players and their product lines and market strategies
- Channels through which products reach end users
- Typical buyer behavior
- Technology
- Major suppliers
- Economic environment
- Regulatory environment
- Sociopolitical environment

All of this information will be useful when you develop your market analysis and, as you prepare to open your business, develop your marketing plans.

Conducting an industry analysis is an important part of the due diligence that goes into a sound franchising purchase decision. Skip it, and the consequences may be dire. You may find yourself owning equipment that will be obsolete in a matter of months—or, worse, find yourself locked into a 20-year contract in an industry with 3 years to live. Before you sign any franchise contract, you need to evaluate the industry and make sure that your franchisor is aware of, and planning for, industry changes. After all, the only sure thing in business is change.

Step Two: Conduct a Market Analysis

If step one reveals the health of an industry, step two confirms whether there are enough target customers in a particular area to support a profitable business.

The industry and your franchisor have probably identified a particular demographic segment as target customers for its products and services. Your job is to make sure that demographic segment resides and makes purchases in the general market area you propose to serve. A market analysis or market feasibility study will tell you whether there is potential demand—that is, enough target customers—in your market to sustain your business. If there's a match, great. If there's not, think twice about this opportunity. The most ideal products and services in the world will go unnoticed if there aren't enough potential customers.

To conduct your market feasibility study, compare a reasonably detailed profile of your typical customer with statistics on the population to determine how many of those consumers live in the market area you are considering. Your customer profile will emerge as you conduct your market research. Franchisees can give you first-hand descriptions of typical customers; your industry analysis will yield insights as well. Secondary data from the U.S. Department of Commerce and other sources offer a wealth of information on the buying patterns of Americans in relation to particular businesses. They can also reveal the characteristics of the market area you are looking at.

Visits to existing franchises in similar markets can also tell you a lot about your prospective customers. You can draw many conclusions merely by observing customer buying habits during your visits and confirming your observations with franchisees.

All of this information is pertinent to your market analysis. For example, industry studies may show that males 18 to 38 are a growing market for your potential products or services, and visits to franchisees in other areas confirm this. Now, determine the number of 18- to 38-year-old men in your market area, and compare their buying habits to the locations you have in mind. Does your proposed site match the target market's traffic patterns? Is it nestled among stores offering complementary products that appeal to the same group? If research shows that your product is an impulse buy and will do best in a high-traffic mall, that's the kind of location you need to look for. Don't settle for a strip mall instead of a shopping center, or your business may be doomed. If what you need isn't available where you are looking, don't pick a second location. And don't locate a business targeted to mature adults in a neighborhood bursting with young adults. Use the insights generated by your industry analysis and your market research to evaluate the appropriateness of every location you consider.

Questions to ask about your proposed market area

- What type of neighborhood surrounds it?
- Who lives there?
- What is the area's household income?
- Is the population growing or declining?
- Are the families young with children or are they older families whose children have moved on in life?
- How many of your desired target customers live in the area?
- How many target customers live within five miles of any location you are considering?

Analyze your competition

Your industry analysis should reveal which companies would be your direct and indirect competitors in a particular business. Look for them as you conduct your market analysis. List all of the competitors located in your prospective market radius. Then shop them. Visit each one several times and answer the following questions:

- What does each one do well? What does each do less well? In what areas do you think your franchise can do better?
- Who are the customers? When do they purchase? How many visit on weekdays? Weekends? Holidays? Do they visit during the day, evening, or night?
- What is its peak hour? What is its slowest period?
- Extrapolate the competitor's sales by learning its prices and then multiplying by the number of people who leave with packages during a particular period. Enlist family and friends to help log customers during different parts of the day, and do the math once you have a good sample.

Step Three: Review the Data and Draw Conclusions

Listen to your research. Kenneth L. Bernhardt, professor of marketing at Georgia State University, says that initial research for the ill-fated DeLorean automobile showed a large demand for a specialty sports car in the $15,000 to $20,000 range. But DeLorean ignored the research, adding features that resulted in a $25,000 price tag—and ultimate failure.

It's a good bet that DeLorean turned his back on his research because he loved his own product so much he couldn't be objective about it. *He* wanted those features, and he could offer them; why wouldn't others embrace them?

Sadly, many would-be franchisees make the same mistake. They are so delighted with a system and so eager to feel a part of it that they dismiss the hard facts turned up in research—or they skip research altogether.

Pay attention to your research. If an industry analysis and a market analysis reveal a major flaw—insufficient demand, a looming industry change that threatens to cause an industry shakeout, or strong competition that is likely to launch an expensive counterattack if you enter the market—think twice about your investment. Because if you can't sell your product, you won't succeed.

On the other hand, if the numbers and the trends look good, consider your research results a green light, and move ahead to find the exact location within the market under scrutiny.

Understanding the Four Ps of Marketing

Four elements play a role in a customer's decision to buy a product: product, price, place, and promotion.

These four Ps of marketing are variables that can be mixed, matched, and manipulated to create an unbeatable blend of attributes that is sure to attract a customer. Take a fast-food hamburger, for example. To appeal to a teenager, the *product* has to be tasty and conveniently packaged. The *price* has to match the teen's spending habits while still allowing the restaurant to make a profit. The *place* where the teenager purchases the hamburger needs to be somewhere along his or her regular route. And the hamburger must be *promoted* in a manner that catches the teen's attention—probably not in a copy of the *Reader's Digest*.

Your franchisor will already have made many of these decisions for you. The product is the cornerstone of most franchise systems. It has been extensively tested, and if you are buying into an established franchise, it has a strong track record in other units. In most cases, franchisees are responsible for maintaining product quality rather than developing new products. While antitrust laws prohibit a franchisor from dictating a specific price for its products, the franchisor will probably suggest a pricing structure. Your franchisor will have many suggestions about how to deliver the product or service in an appropriate place, but selecting the location is your job. So is promotion. The franchisor will provide some support, but most local marketing and promotion decisions are yours.

Market research is a critical element in achieving the right mix of product, price, place, and promotion. What you learn about the industry and the customer from market research and your franchisor will dictate where to locate your unit and how to select promotional vehicles. Ultimately, you will use your research to develop a concrete marketing plan to guide your promotional efforts and build sales in your new franchise outlet.

The Four Ps of Marketing

Product

- What is the physical product?
- What additional features/accessories are needed?
- What are the functions or uses of the product?
- What services need to be provided?
- Does the customer expect guarantees or warranties?
- How should the product be packaged for shipment?
- How should it be packaged for the consumer?
- What images should the product project?
- What brand name should be used?

Price

- What price is needed to make a profit?
- What price will customers be willing to pay?
- Who determines the price customers will pay?
- Should discounts and allowances be provided?
- Should coupons, rebates, markdowns, or sales be used?
- Should credit be extended to customers?
- How should the business respond to competitor's prices?

Place

- How will the product reach the customer?
- How will products be handled, stored, displayed, and controlled?
- How will orders be processed?
- Who will be responsible for products that are damaged or not sold?
- What kind of traffic patterns fit the buying patterns of target customers?

Promotion

- What information do customers need?
- Should promotions be informational or persuasive, or merely reminder messages?
- Do all customers need the same information?
- What combination of advertising, personal selling, sales promotion, and publicity is needed?
- Will mass or individual promotion be most effective?
- What media should be used?
- How often must information be communicated to franchisees and customers?

CHAPTER 6

Choosing a Location

Harris Chernow, Keith J. Kanouse, and Richard Rosen

In today's competitive marketplace, location is as important as your name, your company colors and logo, and the products and services you sell. In fact, it may be even *more* important. For if your location is wrong, your name and products won't matter because your customers won't be able to find you. And that's why the old canard about real estate is true: in selecting a home or a franchise, what matters is location, location, location!

Your location can spell the difference between success and failure to your franchise. With a good location, success will come easier. A bad location will hamper you again and again. Sadly, franchisees with bad locations based their decision on these three criteria:

1. "It was available when I was looking."
2. "It was the lowest-price location."
3. "It was near my home."

Even though availability, price, and proximity are issues to consider, many other criteria need to be taken into account. To find the best location, your market research should dictate a long list of criteria that you must use to evaluate each potential location.

The type of franchise you are purchasing will, of course, greatly influence the location you choose. For example, a fast-food restaurant with an adjacent parking area and a drive-through window will require a different kind of location than a franchise offering home-cleaning services. The former may be freestanding, whereas the latter may be located in an office building.

Franchises that rely on impulse purchases need to be located within shopping malls with heavy foot traffic. Other franchises need to be located in areas where the local demographics meet the specific needs of the franchise. For example, a day care center franchise would probably not do well in a Sun Belt retirement community.

Choosing a location is a marketing decision. If you've done your market research, you know something about your customers. You know who they are and when, where, and how they buy your product or service. Now you need to find a location that fits your customer profile and complements its buying behavior. If your product is purchased in conjunction with errands to the grocery store, doctor, or dry cleaner, then your location needs to be somewhere along your customer's path. An expensive, high-visibility location may not be important; in fact, a service business that works on-site at a customer's home can probably save money by locating its headquarters on the owner's dining room table.

Some franchisors can help you find a suitable location. They may give you certain criteria or even dictate exactly what types of locations you may consider. For example, an automobile dealership may be required to secure a large free-standing location on a major thoroughfare; a high-visibility clothing store may be urged to set up business in a regional shopping mall; a dry cleaning franchisor might steer franchisees to strip malls. In most franchise systems, the franchisor has the right to approve a franchisee's location.

Franchisors have different approaches to choosing franchisee retail locations. Some will do the legwork themselves: their real estate experts will pursue and investigate potential sites until they have found a location which they feel is suitable for you. Most franchisors, however, will require you to seek out your own location and then submit it to the franchisor for its approval.

This chapter summarizes the criteria and issues to consider in choosing a location for your fledgling franchise outlet.

Evaluating Your Location

Consider the criteria described below as you compare and evaluate potential locations.

Accessibility and traffic patterns. Is it easy to exit and enter into traffic? Are there divided highways, difficult intersections, major road construction, or other impediments? What time of day is traffic heavy? Where is traffic going? Are people shopping or merely commuting to neighborhoods where they can purchase your product or service from a more convenient store? If the location is in a newer neighborhood, what kind of developments and traffic changes are planned for the future? In an evolving area, today's choice corner may be tomorrow's forgotten cul-de-sac.

Visibility. Is visibility important to the success of your business? If you've done your market research, you know the answer to that question. If your product is an impulse item, then you need to be where customers can see you and say, "Oh, I need one of those." But if your customer will come to you in the course of doing errands, you may need to give less weight to visibility and more weight to how well your business complements others in the vicinity. Visibility comes at a premium. Don't buy it if you don't need it.

Hours of operation. Do the hours of your location match the needs of your customers? You may not want to be the only store open at 8:30 PM in an area that is shuttered by 6:00 PM unless you have a good reason. A dance studio, for example, might want the daytime visibility of an early-to-close area but the convenience of a parking lot that is uncrowded during its evening classes. Again, this is where knowledge of your customers and how they shop can really pay off.

Parking layout. Determine how much parking you need, and select a location that offers it.

Public transportation. In urban settings, access to public transportation can be more important than access to parking. Such access is less important in suburban settings where virtually everyone owns a car.

Neighborhood development. Is the neighborhood stable or declining? Talk to local authorities, business groups, and others in the know to determine the economic trend.

Competing outlets. Are competing businesses located in the immediate vicinity? If so, the good news is that your location is attractive; the bad news is that you'll have competition. If you aren't far from another outlet in your own system, you may benefit from group advertising and immediate name recognition.

Size. Do you require space for selling, storage, or maintenance of equipment? The larger your space, the higher your rent, electricity, insurance, and maintenance. The franchisor may recommend or require certain square footage. Don't rent more than you need!

Lease terms. Look for a lease whose term matches your franchise contract but can be renewed in shorter increments. Too long a term and you may find yourself paying rent for a business that no longer exists. Can you get a 2-year lease with three 3-year options to renew, creating in effect an 11-year lease? Or, a lease with yearly renewal options? With a professional, carefully examine the options before signing a lease. See Chapter 10 for an in-depth discussion of how to understand and negotiate a commercial real estate lease.

Financing Your Location

In some instances the franchisor will negotiate the lease for the franchised location directly with the landlord and then sublet the location to the franchisee. (Still, you *must* have the lease and sublease reviewed by your attorney to protect your interests!) Most franchisors require the franchisee to negotiate and enter into a lease directly with the landlord. The franchisor's sole involvement with the lease may be as a guarantor or, as is usually the case, it may have no involvement at all.

When you are the lessee, your credit will have to stand on its own in qualifying for a retail location. When the franchisor takes the lease and sublets to you or "guarantees" your lease, its credit will be scrutinized. If you agree to a sublease, insist on a provision that requires the landlord to notify you of any default by the franchisor and give you the opportunity to cure the default so that you may preserve your right to remain in possession of the premises.

While most franchised retail outlets are leased, hotels, large stand-alone restaurants, and some other types of franchises own their property. When you are required to purchase a location, your costs of ownership (including land acquisition) will be greater than the initial costs of leasing. Your investment will also make it difficult or impossible to move if your location turns out to perform poorly. The wisdom of a decision to purchase should be confirmed by extremely thorough market research.

Get Professional Help

Negotiating a commercial lease is tricky, and it's no business for neophytes. Get professional help. Hire an attorney or a commercial real estate specialist who does not represent the interests of the landlord to review the lease and highlight areas that are negotiable. See Chapter 10 for more on working with professionals to negotiate your lease.

Constructing Your Location

Once you have chosen your location, your next concern will be constructing it. Some landlords will "build your location to suit," whereas others will require that the franchisee (or the franchisor, as the case may be) undertake all of the construction itself. You should obtain an estimate of construction costs before entering into a lease so you know approximately what your costs will be.

High construction costs are one reason it pays to select a location carefully. After all, dollars invested in remodeling or leasehold improvements can never be retrieved if you find you must leave your original location. In fact, you'll have to spend the same amount or even more to make your new location workable. Before you sign a lease for a property that requires extensive modification, make very sure it is a location where your business can flourish.

Get a Work Letter

If the landlord is doing some or all of the construction at your location, you will need to negotiate a work letter that sets forth in detail what the landlord's and tenant's responsibilities are with respect to the construction. If the landlord is to construct or demolish walls, install new electrical outlets, run a water line to the premises, or provide a new air-conditioning unit, the work letter will set out the specifications. Because the work letter is really a part of the lease, the lease should not be signed until the work letter is fully agreed upon and incorporated into the lease by reference. The work letter should also include a clause penalizing the landlord if it does not complete its work in a timely manner.

Before you negotiate a work letter, retain an architect or a reliable contractor to advise you on the proper specifications for your premises. The landlord may suggest that you use its architect or contractor, who is familiar with the premises. Nice try, but use your own. You want someone on *your* side. In many instances, it is appropriate for your architect to prepare plans for the construction for your landlord's approval before the lease is signed. Once the lease is signed, many a tenant has found a previously friendly and cooperative landlord to be somewhat intransigent when construction arrangements are discussed. Rule number one is "get it in writing" before you sign the lease.

Hire a Contractor

To properly construct the premises, you or the franchisor—whichever one is responsible for the construction of the premises—will have to hire a contractor. Make sure that the contractor is reliable (recommendations are helpful) and request a completion bond to ensure that you will be compensated if work is unreasonably delayed. Never start work until there is a written contract between the contractor and the tenant. If possible, try to get the contractor and its subcontractors to agree to a waiver of the right to place a mechanic's lien on the premises if payment is delayed. Your landlord may require a lien waiver before work commences. For a large job, add a clause requiring payments only upon your architect's confirmation that work is progressing properly. Hold back at least 10 percent of the payment until the job is fully completed and approved by your architect and by the landlord.

Licenses and Permits

Both your lease and your contract with your contractor should indicate who is responsible for obtaining building permits, use and occupancy permits, business operation permits, and other local licenses and permits. Your lease with the landlord should contain a representation that local zoning as well as the landlord's certificate of occupancy allows the use contemplated. Your contractor should provide and display all building and construction permits, and your franchise agreement will undoubtedly require you to obtain any permits and licenses necessary to operate your franchised business. Ask your attorney for help in reviewing and negotiating any local or federal environmental requirements before signing the lease.

Signage Requirements and Contingencies

Your signage is crucial to you and your franchisor, so be sure that the landlord approves it before you sign your lease. Typically, a drawing of the signage, including specifications that apply to it, should be reviewed by the landlord as part of the lease finalization process. To get approval in writing, have the landlord initial a copy of the plans.

Some signs and some building modifications may need special permission from government authorities. In a number of municipalities, for example, an exterior (walk-up) window requires a variance or is not permitted at all. Therefore, your lease should provide that it does not become effective until you receive the required approvals or variances, or allows you to terminate the lease if such approvals or variances are not obtained by an outside date.

A good location is crucial to the success of your franchised business. If you proceed carefully and work tirelessly until that location is found, your chances of success will be greatly enhanced.

Looking for Mr. Good Buy: A Personal History of Franchise Selection

Charlene Gross

Although every franchisee has a different story to tell, those stories follow a basic outline: Would-be franchisee feels compelled to own a business and conducts a search that is colored by the compulsion; individual determines that a franchise is the best course of action; individual purchases franchise. But the devil is in the details, and the details make the story. This is a tale of hindsight—no pun intended.

Born to Own

My husband and I had talked about owning our own business for many years. Coming from a long line of employees, we had no idea how to implement such a vision. Growing children, frequent moves, and our own timidity made opening a business seem unlikely until the sun, the moon, and the stars realigned themselves. My husband retired from the military, our children were nearly finished with college, and we began to think that we really could take the financial and emotional risk required to start our own business.

But I didn't just jump into a business. First, I reflected on whether I was ready to be a sole proprietor. Could I work long hours for little initial reward? Was I willing to do very commonplace chores like running the vacuum cleaner after hours? Was there anything I was willing to think about 24 hours a day? Could my previous experience in computing help build the business I would start? Was there any business in which I could make a difference? I used these questions as a yardstick of my interest during months spent reading about different business opportunities.

One Enchanted Evening

For a long time, no business description inspired me. My future changed one Sunday when I was reading the classified ads in the newspaper. As I was discarding such ventures as cleaning services, donut shops, and restaurants, I saw an ad for my perfect business: a franchise that offered computer training to children. My first reaction: "Here's a business that takes advantage of my years in computing." My second: "Too bad it's a franchise."

All I knew about franchises was that there were a lot of them and people made very little money from them. Years earlier, a college instructor had compared buying a franchise with being mugged. He offered to help us lose the same money in less time by meeting us at midnight on a dark street corner (sans gun) and relieving us of the money we would have spent on a franchise.

But this business was too exciting to ignore. I tore out the ad and called the company. They sent me information about their company and the costs of ownership. The material indicated there was a plan for success and name recognition. Even though the prospect of working with children and technology measured favorably on my yardstick, cost was a big obstacle. I would have to cash in family stocks, land assets, and house equity to make it work. With regret, I decided that was too much of a risk. I never sent in the franchise application, but I did stuff the ad in my wallet. From time to time I would take it out, look at it, and wonder what would happen if I had had the guts to follow through.

Doing More Homework

I began to read more about businesses and their success rates. My reading indicated that franchisor excesses of the 1960s and 1970s had ended. In fact, government studies had shown that franchises were more successful than independent start-ups. Since I had already fallen in love with a particular franchise, that was good news to me. Other articles suggested that the structure and name recognition of franchised businesses gave beginners a better shot at creating a thriving business in a relatively short time.

About nine months later, the local paper ran an ad announcing the opening of a franchise unit from the system whose ad I carried in my wallet. Realizing that someone had actually done what I had only thought about, I took out a piece of paper and did the numbers on how many children I would need to teach at what rate to make a profit. The results weren't good. I tore out the ad, added it to my wallet, and decided to wait.

Another nine months passed. During a particularly rough day on my job, I decided I'd rather be someone who tried and failed than someone who only wished she had tried. I called the local franchise to get phone numbers for head-quarters. The owner answered. Coincidentally, he said, I had called on the very day he had decided to sell his business. It would be cheaper to buy an existing business, he said, and he had already built up a clientele. The locale wasn't as close to my home as the company would have liked, but he felt sure that it would be a good deal to start out with an established territory.

This development was totally unexpected. I was hoping it was a sign that this was the right thing to do, even though it would mean using up most of the money we had accrued in our 25-year marriage. Personal financing was the only option I understood because I knew no investors and had heard that Small Business Administration loans were very hard to get. It would also mean giving up an $80,000 job. Even though I didn't expect to make the same money, I understood from the owner that he cleared about $3,000 a month. Having my own business and giving kids a head start in technology seemed like a good trade for a lesser salary.

All's Fair in Love and Franchises

Lest you think I decided to buy this business in one day, let me say that I did research its prospects. I went to the International Franchise Show to talk with representatives of the company, who explained its links with Microsoft and Disney. Joint shows in various cities with Microsoft and coupons for the company in Disney software seemed to indicate that this company had the stamp of approval from these organizations. That was impressive as those two companies are among the biggest and the best in the world.

We discussed whether it would be better to buy a used or a new territory and whether multiple territories were a good idea. The franchise representatives made no earnings claims, but I had already read in an article that franchise systems could not make earnings claims without divulging all of their finances. I did ask if it was reasonable for a person making $80,000 to chuck the position to go into their franchise. I don't remember the exact words, but I came away feeling that I could at least make a profit.

By this time, I had decided that I wanted to own and operate this business. The favorable articles in the press on franchising had swayed my originally negative view. The company representatives had answered all of my questions. I had a concrete example of how the business would look in the existing franchise unit that was for sale. It seemed easier and safer to try a franchise than to rely on the value of any of my own ideas.

Coming Down to the Wire

At this point, I thought my choices were clear: take the leap with this franchise system or continue my corporate job. I was amazed at the encouragement I received from coworkers to go for it. It seems that the dream my husband and I had shared was one shared by the multitudes. When I tested out the viability of the franchise concept itself, I got the unanimous response that it was a "cool" idea that couldn't miss.

I paid another visit to the franchise to review its finances. On the drive there, I prayed that there would be a sign if this was a bad idea. The owner's business bank transactions indicated that he had consistently put money in the business account without drawing any salary. He said that he had started working part-time at another job after three months and thought that the extra work had diverted his attention and earnings away from the franchise. I was dismayed and remembered my request for a sign. I decided that the financial status was only a sign that things would be hard and I needed to be persistent.

Meanwhile, I talked with the regional director to see if the lack of profit was the franchise owner's fault or a general condition of other franchisees. The regional director said that others were making a comfortable living and that this owner had just not invested the time this business deserved. Because my intention was to work full-time at the business and because I had the confidence that I could move this business I already loved on a forward path, I accepted these explanations. I decided to buy not only the existing franchise but also two more territories closer to my home. My thought was that the existing franchise would support the opening of a second location, and the second would support the third.

Moving Forward on All Fronts

Now came the most exciting and happiest time in my life. I concentrated on three things: completing the purchase of the existing and new territories, planning the disposition of the assets we would use to pay for the businesses, and wrapping up loose ends on my job. Everything about the future looked positive, and friends and family were praising me for taking control of my life. One coworker did mention that some franchisors make most of their money on the franchise fees at the time of sale rather than from franchisee profits. I was sure that my franchisor was not among that dastardly bunch.

The franchise agreements and assorted papers arrived. I read the franchise agreement carefully and noted several places where the terms sounded a little scary. However, I had by now talked with several people at franchisor headquarters and felt that the company didn't really mean the phrases the way they sounded. My thinking was that if the government allowed these franchises to be sold so openly, the conditions of the agreement must not be as they seemed. I signed the contracts and returned them, committing myself to a ten-year relationship with the company.

Selling off assets was an eye-opener. I never thought we had that much cash available to us. To purchase three territories, we sold a rental house, two parcels of land, and stocks from two companies, raising around $100,000. Knowing that undercapitalization is often the reason for business failure, I wanted to have more assets than the franchisor estimated were necessary.

The week after I left my job, I started my training, which I paid for. In my absence and through the summer, the previous owner stayed on to manage the summer programs. The week after the training, I attended the required convention, again at my expense. I was amazed to meet several disgruntled franchisees, but I felt they didn't represent what could be accomplished. Because the franchisor had explained that some of the older franchisees couldn't get used to the changes being made for the good of the system, these complaints sounded like sour grapes to me.

At the fancy dinner on the last night of the convention, the president and founder of the franchise came forward to the podium to give his speech. He started out with a little joke. "You know how to make a small fortune in _____?" he laughingly asked. "Invest a large one."

Lessons Learned

Now that I have owned the franchise for three years, I can look at this story from the perspective of an experienced business owner. I tell people I have the equivalent of a very expensive MBA. People laugh, and I do too—sort of. In recounting this story, I know that I thought I was making a good-faith effort to select a business I could eat, sleep, and drink for 24 hours a day. That effort, however, had very little to do with solid business practices. Now I know that the following points would have enhanced the process I used:

Examine the dream before financing it. None of the discussions my husband and I had about owning a business ever included a business reason for having such a dream. It was all about satisfaction, fulfillment, creating a good environment, and making good decisions. We never talked of ourselves as an existing corporation that was planning on taking on a new line of business—a view that might have been more productive and realistic.

Risk means risk. Without losers, how would the winners know they had won? I expected a cosmic referee to give me success credits for taking the leap into business ownership—but that referee doesn't exist, and taking a risk means you can lose. Confidence is good, but a realistic appraisal of how it might feel to lose it all is essential.

Do real research. I looked at articles in business magazines and a few books. I talked with a few people. I did not get an attorney. I had only a short conversation with an accountant. I relied on the franchisor to tell me all. I could have gone to the library and read about the franchise industry or small business. I could have surfed the Internet for information. I could have studied more than one franchise and met with franchisees of various systems to understand their views and problems. In short, I should have done—and you should do—as much preparation for this kind of decision as you would for any other life commitment.

Consider the source. Franchising is an industry and like most industries has several factions with differing points of view. Each of these factions gets articles published in national magazines. When reading information about earnings, success or failure rates, the attitudes of franchisees or franchisors, or any other material related to business success, check the source of any statistics. Then go further and read what others say about the reliability of the sources and reports.

Do a business plan before falling in love. Writing a business plan is an onerous but necessary task. If you cannot put on paper what the business is about, how it will be financed, and how it will grow, you don't know enough to be in love with the business. There are numerous sources for getting business plan templates, including the Small Business Administration's Web site and various software packages.

Know now how you will expand later. Even though your first year will be spent getting the business off the ground, you need to know what you are going to do *next* year. No business succeeds by being the same thing year after year. You must plan to branch out, have new alliances, and gain new avenues for delivery. Think in evolutionary terms, or plan for extinction.

Love the bottom line as much as the business. A recent article about a failed business mentioned that if you aren't fascinated by the bottom line, then you don't belong in business. I had very little interest in the bottom line. It was only an indicator of progress, not the goal. My goals were to contribute, to show I could create a positive working environment, and to make people feel comfortable with the all-important technology of the modern world. I now think that the business could be about anything; but without that interest in the bottom line, success will at best be a fluke.

Never underestimate a contract. A franchise agreement is a contract designed to cover every possible circumstance that may arise in the conduct of business. Always assume that every word of the contract is intentional, because it is. All clauses will be fully enforced. Don't be misled by reassurances to the contrary. Whether the contract is for credit, for an employer, or for a franchise, the clauses always mean what they say. When you sign the contract, you are agreeing to everything in it.

Talk with as many people who are against your plan as those who are for it.
I sought out the people who would agree with my plan. I regarded lack of approval as lack of faith in my ability. It is better to listen and answer the folks who don't agree with you than to waste time with those who do agree with you. After all, you already know what the agreeable ones think!

Acquiring Your Franchise

You've selected a franchise that meets your criteria in an industry that interests you. Now it's time to sign a lease and a franchise agreement and figure out how to finance the deal. Suddenly you're swimming in paperwork and hearing a whole new vocabulary of financial and legal terms. Help!

It's essential to surround yourself with good advisers during the franchise acquisition stage. This is not a time to be penny wise and pound foolish. You need professional help to understand the fine print on real estate, franchise, and financing documents. *Never* enter into any contract lightly, thinking that the fine print doesn't matter. Its contents do matter. When a dispute arises between you and a landlord, franchisor, or banker, the first place all parties look for resolution is the contract. It spells out what you agreed to as a sane person at that moment in time before you launched your franchise. Whatever you agreed to in a contract will probably be enforced by the courts—for the 10 or 20 years left in your contract.

The professionals you hire to see you through this phase can help keep your eyes on the big picture even when you're swamped with preopening details. They will remind you that favorable lease terms are more important than carpets or window treatments. They will also help you take time to understand and negotiate documents and assist you in developing a comprehensive, well-thought-out business plan and financial projections. But there's one job that only you can do: making sure you feel comfortable with every aspect of the deal. Don't be afraid to walk away from an unfair lease or an unfair franchise agreement. If you suspect something is a bad deal or it just feels wrong, don't go through with it. If it doesn't feel right in the beginning, it will never feel right.

CHAPTER 8

Understanding the Franchise Documents

L. Seth Stadfeld and Keith J. Kanouse

The Federal Trade Commission (FTC) franchise rule requires a franchisor to give a disclosure document, or uniform franchise offering circular (UFOC), to a prospective franchisee on or before the first personal meeting and at least ten business days before the prospective franchisee can give the franchisor any money or sign any agreements. Because most franchisors use the UFOC format, which requires the disclosure of 23 items of information, our references here will be the UFOC.

The purpose of this disclosure document is to give you all the material information about the franchise offering *before* you buy so you can make an intelligent investment decision by understanding your economic commitments and can develop a business plan.

Like the franchise agreement, the UFOC is a legal document that is difficult but essential to read. Study it carefully, preferably with the help of a lawyer who is an expert in franchise law. Hidden in pages is the truth about the franchise system you are considering buying: its stability, its future plans, its obligations to you, and how much you will have to invest in order to purchase and start a location.

This chapter will help you read the UFOC by briefly summarizing the information each item contains and commenting on its significance. In many cases, you will find additional questions and issues for you to consider that may not have been fully discussed in the offering circular. These questions and issues are part of your due diligence investigation and should be directed to other franchisees, former franchisees, and the franchisor.

Federal Trade Commission Cover Sheet

What it tells you. The Federal Trade Commission cover sheet distinctively and conspicuously shows the name of the franchisor, the date of issuance of the disclosure statement, and a statement from the FTC. The statement reminds you that the FTC has *not* checked to see whether the information provided in the document is accurate and that the federal government has *not* approved or certified the franchise offering in any way. Remember, *no franchise offer has been approved by the government!*

What to consider. Check the effective date of the UFOC. If it is several months old, ask for any material changes, including new litigation, current financial statements, and terminated franchisees that may have occurred since the effective date.

State Registration Page

What it tells you. Used only in franchise registration states, the state cover page includes a sample of the primary business trademark, logotype, trade name, or commercial label or symbol under which the franchisee will conduct business, a brief description of the franchise business, and the franchisor's name, type of business organization, and the principal business address and telephone number. It also discloses the total amount that the franchisee will have to invest in order to purchase the business as well as several risk factors, such as the laws or mediation process that will govern any dispute and the venue where that dispute will be decided.

What to consider.
- Check to make sure the franchisor owns its trademark.
- Study the risk factors carefully and discuss their consequences with your attorney.
- Call the FTC or your state agency to see if there is any other information (or complaints) it has about the franchisor. Remember, registration in a state does not mean that the state has approved the quality of the franchise offering. That's for you to determine.

Twenty-three
Items of the UFOC

Item 1: The Franchisor and Its Predecessors and Affiliates

What it tells you. Item 1 reveals basic facts about the franchisor, including where it does business, what kind of product or service it plans to offer, and whether the franchisor and its personnel have any prior business experience in its field. The item must also disclose the names and business experience of any predecessors and affiliates of the franchisor. Most important, it will tell you whether this company has previously offered franchise opportunities under its own or another name.

What to consider.
- Has the company changed its name often? If so, why?
- If there are special industry laws, what are their effect and the cost of compliance? For example, do you need to have a special license to own and operate the franchise business? What does it take in terms of education, experience, tests, time, and money to obtain the license?
- How experienced is the franchisor in the business it is franchising? One of the things you are paying for when you purchase a franchise is the franchisor's "experience curve."
- What market share does the franchise system have in its industry segment?
- What is the franchisor's marketing position and market niche?
- Does the franchisor own and operate company units? Make sure these units are not unsuccessful units that have been reacquired by the company as partial settlement of existing or threatened litigation by the franchisees. Make sure that the franchisor does not cannibalize your sales by operating units in your trade area.
- What happened to any predecessor businesses?
- If the franchisor is new and you are one of the first franchisees, be aware that you may be a "guinea pig." Although it may be a ground-floor opportunity (the "next McDonalds"), you run the risk that it will never get off the ground.
- What are the franchisor's future marketing plans, particularly in your state and locality? Does the franchisor sell, or plan to sell, its products through other channels of distribution—for example, in a supermarket next to your location? (See item 12.)
- Does the franchisor operate another line of business that could compete with yours? You may negotiate an exclusive territory for your Taco Bell restaurant, but the franchisor may open a Pizza Hut right next door.
- What is the franchisor's five-year business plan? Is the franchisor considering selling the entire franchise system to someone else?

Item 2: Business Experience

What it tells you. Here, the franchisor must disclose the principal occupations, employers, and whereabouts for the last five years of all officers, board members, executives, management personnel, and franchise brokers.

What to consider.
- How experienced are the franchisor's personnel in franchising?
- Do they have significant experience in the particular industry? You are buying the ability to jump on the franchisor's learning curve. Make sure it is sufficient!
- Does the franchisor have enough staff to adequately service and support you, or is this organization primarily focused on franchise sales? How far away is the franchisor from your unit? If far away, does it have a nearby regional office?
- Is the entire system dependent on its founder? What if the founder retires, becomes disabled, dies, or goes to a competitor?
- You may want to ask for the principals' résumé to determine their business activity more than five years ago.
- You may want to independently check out the franchisor and its principals (for example, a Dun & Bradstreet report).

Item 3: Litigation

What it tells you. This section tells you whether the franchisor, its predecessors, the persons listed in item 2, and affiliates offering franchises under the franchisor's principal trademark are involved in pending or past litigation or have been subject to injunctions or restrictive orders.

What to consider. If the franchisor is large and mature, don't be surprised if litigation is disclosed. The kind and frequency of litigation will tell you whether there is cause for concern.

- What is the nature of the claims? Is there a pattern to the litigation? Several claims filed about one subject could indicate abuses within the system. Be concerned if there are a number of claims by franchisees alleging fraud and misrepresentation or a lack of service and support. But if the franchisor is suing franchisees for deviating from system standards, you can be assured that the franchisor is actively policing the system to maintain uniformity and quality control.
- Talk to existing or former franchisees that are or have been in litigation with the franchisor. Their side of the story may be different from the one told in the court documents.
- If the principals have been involved in numerous kinds of litigation, consider this a red flag requiring further investigation.

- Ask for information about all kinds of litigation, not just what has to be disclosed.

Item 4: Bankruptcy

What it tells you. In item 4 the franchisor must disclose bankruptcy matters involving itself, its affiliates, its predecessors, and its officers or general partners that occurred within ten years of the date of the offering circular. Directors and other executives do not have to disclose bankruptcy matters involving them. If a bankruptcy matter that is required to be disclosed exists (not every kind of bankruptcy needs to be revealed), the franchisor must disclose the name of the person or company that was the debtor under the U.S. Bankruptcy Code, the date of the action, and the material facts.

What to consider. Even if bankruptcy is no longer the "kiss of death" it once may have been, it still may adversely affect the franchisor's ability to borrow funds necessary for continued growth or viability.

- Find out whether the bankruptcy is relevant to the business operation of the franchise system.
- Determine whether the bankruptcy was triggered by a character issue or market forces. Avoid companies whose character seems flawed, but give a second look to otherwise sound franchisors that may have grown too fast, lacked cash, or entered the wrong market before correcting their mistakes and fine-tuning their operation.

Item 5: Initial Franchise Fee

What it tells you. This item tells how much you will have to pay on signing an agreement and the conditions under which the initial franchise fee is refundable. It tells you whether payment is due in a lump sum or in installments and discloses the installment payment terms. Installment payment terms also are discussed in item 10. If the initial franchise fee is not uniform, this item tells you the formula for, or the range of, initial franchise fees paid in the fiscal year before the application date and the factors that determined the amount.

What to consider.
- Use information about a nonuniform initial franchise fee as your "foot in the door" to negotiate the amount and timing of the payment.
- Compare the size of the initial franchise fee with what you get in return.
- What are the initial franchise fees of the franchisor's competitors?

- If the fee is nonrefundable on signing the franchise agreement (and most are), negotiate circumstances where it is refundable.
- Are there other up-front fees such as those for software and site location? Make sure you compare apples to apples as you examine different franchise systems and their initial franchise fees.

Item 6: Other Fees

What it tells you. This item tells you the amount and payment schedule of royalties, lease negotiations, construction, remodeling, additional training, advertising, group advertising, additional assistance, audits, accounting, inventory, and transfer and renewal fees. The franchisor must tell how these fees are calculated, under what circumstances they are refundable, and when they can be increased. The franchisor must disclose whether company units are members of any advertising cooperative and, if so, the voting power of the company units in the cooperative. If the company units have controlling power, the franchisor is required to disclose a range for the fee.

What to consider.
- If you pay no royalty, are you obligated to purchase items from the franchisor or its affiliates? There may be a disguised royalty in the form of a markup in the wholesale price to you. Make sure this markup is reasonable.
- If you must pay a royalty on items you purchase from the franchisor or its affiliates, make sure that the franchisor is not double-dipping.
- Compare the royalty fee with the value of what you are getting in return. Compare it with fees charged by the franchisor's competitors.
- Remember that a flat royalty fee gives the franchisor little incentive for providing services.
- What are your total obligations for local advertising, contributions to an advertising cooperative, and contributions to a regional or national advertising fund? If you are obligated to contribute to a tenant advertising fund, are these payments credited against your advertising obligations under the franchise agreement?
- What benefits ("bang for the buck") are you going to get for your advertising dollars?
- If the franchisor has not established advertising programs, how does the system plan to generate brand name recognition and more sales?

Item 7: Initial Investment

What it tells you. Item 7 helps you prepare your business plan by providing a ballpark range of what it takes to operate a typical system store. It requires the franchisor to disclose the cost of property; equipment, fixtures, and other fixed assets; construction, remodeling, leasehold improvements, and decorating costs; inventory; security deposits, utility deposits, business licenses, and other prepaid expenses; and additional funds required by the franchisee before operations begin and during the initial phase of the franchise. These expenditures are listed in a table showing preopening expenses first.

Pay attention to the "working capital" category in this table. Historically, franchisors underestimate the amount of working capital needed for the first several months. In many cases the "additional funds" item indicates how much additional money or working capital you will need to put into the business to cover your expenses until you reach the break-even point.

What to consider. These numbers are estimates, not exact numbers.

- Have your accountant review this item and item 19 if an earnings claim is made to assist in developing your own business plan.
- What will your future capital requirements be as the result of changes in technology, repairs and maintenance, renovation, and so on? Create reserve accounts in your financial forecast.
- Double-check the "working capital" figure as franchisors have a tendency to underestimate the amount of working capital a franchisee needs.

Item 8: Restrictions on Sources of Products and Services

What it tells you. This items tells you whether franchisees are obligated to purchase or lease products and services from the franchisor or its designee or from suppliers approved by the franchisor or under the franchisor's specifications. Basically, it tells you who supplies the products and where suppliers are located, how much you have to purchase from these sources, whether you can get new vendors approved, and who carries the warranty on products that are resold.

What to consider.
- Are you obligated to buy all of your goods from the franchisor or an affiliate?
- Does the franchisor have a reasonable policy for approving new vendors?
- Where are the vendors located? Can you pay the transportation costs and still make a profit? Watch out for distant vendors and expensive shipping procedures.
- Is there a purchasing cooperative that offers discounts on purchases?
- Make sure the franchisor's product specifications are really for uniformity and for quality control purposes and not a "ruse" to force you to deal only with the franchisor or its affiliates.
- What product warranties do you receive? What are your warranty obligations to your customers for defective products?

Item 9: Franchisee's Obligations

What it tells you. In this item, your obligations as a franchisee are listed in a table and cross-referenced to the section of the franchise agreement and UFOC item where they are discussed. A long list of obligations is discussed, including selecting, acquiring, leasing, preparing, and opening your site; training; fees; standards and policies; territorial development and sales quotas; advertising; noncompete clauses; and dispute resolution.

What to consider. Because most of the franchise agreement relates to the franchisee's obligations to the franchisor, don't just rely on the table. Read the franchise agreement carefully, discuss it with your attorney, and renegotiate troublesome provisions. Chapter 9 covers the provisions that deal with your obligation in detail.

Item 10: Financing

What it tells you. This item discloses the terms and conditions of each financing arrangement that the franchisor, its agent, or affiliate(s) offers directly or indirectly to the franchisee. The terms of each financing arrangement may be summarized in a table with additional information provided in footnotes.

Here you will find useful information about lenders, interest, repayment periods, security interests, and personal guarantees that may be required and your potential liabilities on default, including any accelerated obligation to pay the entire amount due, court costs, and attorney fees.

Item 22 will contain specimen copies of these financing documents, including the loan agreement, promissory note, security agreement, UCC-1 financing statement, guarantee, lease, and so forth.

What to consider.
- If the franchisor offers financing, compare its interest rate and costs with rates and costs offered by other lenders.
- If the franchisor does not provide financing, ask existing franchisees where they got financing.
- Compare your financing arrangement with arrangements made for other franchisees. Are they relatively equal and fair? If a franchisor appears to be financing fees for others but is not willing to finance yours, explore the personal relationship between the franchisor and those franchisees. Are they relatives?

Item 11: Franchisor's Obligations

What it tells you. This section discloses the franchisor's obligations to the franchisee, such as assistance in locating, leasing, and preparing a site; hiring and training employees; and offering products or services. It also gives the nitty-gritty of the franchisor's advertising and training program, tells whether you are required to purchase an electronic register or computer system, and discloses the table of contents of the system's operating manual. For each item, the pertinent section of the franchise agreement is cited.

Scrutinize this section carefully. It spells out everything the franchisor plans to do to add value to your business. For a promise to be honored, it needs to be described here.

What to consider. Remember, if the franchisor says it "will" do something, that is a contractual promise. If the franchisor say it "may" do something, that is not a contractual promise.

- Analyze whether the franchisor's advertising strategy benefits you.
- Does the franchisor use advertising funds to sell more franchises? As a profit center?
- Even if the table of contents of the manual is disclosed, it is best for you to give it a glance to determine its thoroughness and completeness while you are visiting the franchisor's headquarters. The franchisor will probably want you to sign a confidentiality agreement.
- If the franchisor provides field representatives, how often do they visit? What do they do to help you? What happens if they find something wrong?
- Does the franchisor hold, or plan to hold sometime in the future, an annual national or regional convention? Are you required to attend? What are your time requirements and costs?
- Does the franchisor provide a newsletter or other regular type of communication to its franchisees?
- What type of research and development does the franchisor undertake to remain a leader in the industry?
- Is the training program comprehensive enough for you to be adequately trained to operate the business?
- What ongoing training is provided at the time you open the franchise and thereafter?
- Budget your costs, disclosed in item 7 to attend training.
- What will the franchisor do to help you find the right location for your business?
- How sophisticated is the franchisor's demographic analysis? Has the franchisor developed a customer profile for its business? Does it use modern lifestyle analysis? Will it find where your best customers are located?
- Are the franchisor's ongoing services part of your royalty payments or are there additional charges?

Item 12: Territory

What it tells you. This section tells you about and describes your territory. It discloses whether the franchisor has now, or may later, establish another franchisee, company unit, or other channel of distribution using the franchisor's trademark or selling or leasing similar products or services under a different trademark in your territory. It will also disclose what it takes to maintain territorial exclusivity and under what circumstances a territory may be changed.

What to consider.
- How is a territory determined: By population? Geography? Zip code? Find out.
- If there is no exclusive territory granted (a "location only" franchise), the franchisor may be able to open another unit close to you —even down the block.
- Try not to allow the franchisor to terminate or reduce your territory.
- Pay close attention to any alternative methods of distribution such as grocery stores, gas stations, or college campus cafeterias. These are increasingly popular with franchisors and increasingly detrimental to franchisees.

Item 13: Trademarks

What it tells you. This item tells you whether the franchisor owns its trademark and has a federally registered trademark that is incontestable by others. It discloses the principal trademarks to be licensed to the franchisee and notes any agreements that significantly limit use or license of the trademark.

What to consider. One of the cornerstones of a sound franchise system is a well-recognized and incontestable trademark. To become incontestable a trademark must be filed in the Principal Register of the U.S. Patent and Trademark Office and used continuously for at least five years.

- Is the franchisor's trademark federally registered and incontestable?
- If the franchisor does not own the trademark, ask for a copy of the license agreement between the franchisor and the true trademark owner that gives the franchisor rights to the trademark to make sure you can continue to use the trademark if the franchisor loses its rights to it.

Item 14: Patents, Copyrights, and Proprietary Information

What it tells you. This item tells whether the franchisor owns rights in patents or copyrights that are material to the franchise and whether the franchisor can and intends to renew the copyrights. If the franchisor claims proprietary rights in confidential information or trade secrets, the franchisor must disclose their general subject matter and the terms and conditions for use by the franchisee.

What to consider.
- If you are considering becoming part of a product franchise, is the product patentable? Does the franchisor have patent rights to the product?
- If what you are going to sell is a copyrighted work, does the franchisor own the copyright?

Item 15: Obligation to Participate in the Actual Operation of the Franchise Business

What it tells you. This item clarifies whether you are obligated to participate personally in the direct operation of the franchise business or whether the franchisor just recommends participation.

What to consider. In general, franchising is not a passive investment vehicle. The strongest systems require you to run your franchise yourself. A requirement to do so can be construed as a sign of the franchisor's strength.

- If you are planning to be a passive investor in the franchise, make sure the franchise agreement allows you to have a manager to run the business. If that's the case, be prepared to have lower revenue and profit than if you ran the business yourself.
- If you are going to be the owner/operator, what happens if you become disabled or die?

Item 16: Restrictions on What the Franchisee May Sell

What it tells you. This item describes your product line. The franchisor must disclose restrictions or conditions that it imposes on the goods or services that the franchisee may sell or that limit the customers to whom the franchisee may sell goods or services.

What to consider.
- Do you have some flexibility to sell products or services other than the franchisor's that reflect local market conditions—what your customers want?
- Are the sales restrictions reasonable?
- Make sure your market research indicates that the locale you are considering is suitable for the product line you will be permitted to sell.

Item 17: Renewal, Termination, Transfer and Dispute Resolution

What it tells you. This item clarifies your rights to terminate, renew, or transfer your franchise and resolve any disputes with the franchisor. It covers a number of very specific areas that are summarized in a table that references the section of the agreement that covers each subject.

What to consider. Honeymoons do end. Disputes do arise. It is critical to understand your right to renew, terminate, or transfer the franchise agreement and resolve disputes.

- Note how and where disputes will be resolved. In your state? At franchisor headquarters? Will disputes be subject to arbitration and mediation or resolved by judge and jury?
- Don't just rely on the table in the UFOC. Read the franchise agreement thoroughly and discuss the issues with your attorney. Chapter 9 covers the agreement provisions in great detail.

Item 18: Public Figures

What it tells you. This item discloses the role of public figures in marketing campaigns for the franchisor. It tells how these celebrities are compensated, the extent to which they are involved in the actual management or control of the franchisor, and the total investment of the public figure in the franchisor.

What to consider. An endorsement by a celebrity doesn't necessarily guarantee the success of a franchise system and enhance its products.

- Is the celebrity paid for the endorsement or is he or she involved and really believe in the product or service sold by the franchise system?
- What is the financial arrangement with the celebrity?
- How will the withdrawal of the celebrity or negative publicity about the celebrity affect your business?

Item 19: Earnings Claims

What it tells you. You're buying a franchise to make money —to earn a living for yourself and your family. Consequently, you want to know how much money you can reasonably expect to make. Unfortunately, UFOC guidelines don't require the franchisor to provide an earnings claim.

An earnings claim made in connection with an offer of a franchise must be included in full in this item and must have a reasonable basis at the time it is made. If no earnings claim is made, this item must contain the negative disclosure. An earnings claim must include a description of its factual basis and the material assumptions underlying its preparation and presentation.

What to consider.

- Most franchisors (86 percent) do not make an earnings claim. If such is the case in the UFOC you are reading, you'll need to do additional homework, including analyzing industry statistics and talking to existing franchisees.
- Even if an earnings claim is made, don't blindly assume that you'll achieve the same numbers. These are just estimates. Prepare your own financial projection for your business.
- If item 19 states no earnings claim is made but the franchisor or its broker orally or in a separate writing (the "cocktail napkin") makes an earnings claim, get the oral statement in writing or have the broker sign and date the cocktail napkin so it can be an exhibit attached to the franchise agreement.
- If an earnings claim is made, is the basis of the claim historical figures or unsubstantiated projections? Were all units included? Are the assumptions reasonable? What do the disclaimers say? Did an independent certified public accountant prepare the earnings claim? If so, was the earnings claim prepared in accordance with the American Institute of Certified Public Accountants Standards for Financial Forecasts or Projections?

Item 20: List of Outlets

What it tells you. This item lists the total number of franchise outlets and supplies the names, addresses, and telephone numbers of at least 100 franchisees and their outlets. It also tells how many outlets have, in the last three years, been transferred to new owners, canceled, terminated, or reacquired by the franchisor, or have otherwise ceased to do business in the system. Names and the last known home address and telephone number of these franchisees are supplied.

What to consider. Here is the starting point for your research!

- Call and meet with as many existing franchisees as possible to see how satisfied and profitable they are.
- Is the number of franchisees the franchisor expects to sell in the next 12 months realistic? Can it sell these and still have the resources to adequately service and support you and the other existing franchisees?
- Have there been a lot of franchisee casualties such as terminations, cancellations, nonrenewals? If yes, why?
- Does the franchisor pay existing franchisees a referral fee? Although not improper, it may cloud a franchisee's recommendation. This should be disclosed in item 2.

Item 21: Financial Statements

What it tells you. This item includes audited financial statements of the franchisor's business, including balance sheets for the last two fiscal year-ends before the application date as well as statements of stockholders' equity and of cash flows for each of the franchisor's last three fiscal years. You may also find financial statements of the franchisor's affiliated company or companies, any corporation in which it owns a direct or beneficial controlling financial interest, and any sub-franchisor-related entity.

What to consider: Financial documents are complex and hard to read. Review this section with a qualified accountant to answer the following questions.

- What is the franchisor's net worth? The FTC franchise rule does not require a franchisor to have a certain minimum net worth, but a negative net worth is a bad sign. If it is negative or small, will the franchisor be able to continue to operate? Consider an escrow of the initial franchise fee.
- Look at the accountant's notes contained at the end of the financial statements very carefully. They may say something important that is not otherwise mentioned in the UFOC.
- Does a parent company guarantee the franchisor's obligations?
- Does the use of an unaudited opening balance sheet by a start-up franchisor or unaudited year-end financial statements by the franchisor violate UFOC guidelines?
- Has the franchisor set up a shell corporation to sell franchises but moved the bulk of its assets into other corporations? This may make it difficult for you to ascertain the franchisor's real financial strength or weakness.
- High receivables from franchisees may indicate that the franchisor is financing the franchise fee for many outlets. See if you can get the same deal.
- If no earnings claims are included in this document, use the gross royalty figure included in this item to roughly estimate earnings using the formula explained in Chapter 4.

Item 22: Contracts

What it tells you. Here, the franchisor must attach a copy of all agreements that you will need to sign, including the franchise agreement and any leases, options, purchase agreements, and financing documents that may be significant.

What to consider. Chapter 9 discusses the provisions in the franchise agreement in great depth.

Item 23: Receipt

The last page of the offering circular is a detachable document acknowledging receipt of the offering circular by the prospective franchisee. There should be two copies of the receipt: one for retention by the franchisee and one for the franchisor's files to prove compliance with the delivery and timing requirements of the FTC. Go ahead and sign it and return a copy to the franchisor. It is not a contract and the franchisor is required to have it for its compliance files.

CHAPTER 9

Negotiating the Franchise Agreement

Harris Chernow, L. Seth Stadfeld, and Keith J. Kanouse

Leveling the Playing Field

By the very nature of the franchisor-franchisee relationship, franchise agreements are, on their face, unfair from the franchisee's perspective. That's because the franchise agreement captures in black and white the policies, systems, and controls that the franchisor has developed to create and ensure a uniform system. And a successful, uniform system is the primary benefit the franchisor offers the prospective franchisee.

But "uniform" doesn't have to mean unfair. Even though the franchisor will always have the upper hand in the relationship, there is no reason for any franchisee to sign an agreement that asks everything of the franchisee and nothing of the franchisor.

Even a negotiated contract is an unbalanced agreement. Recently, one of this book's authors negotiated a franchise contract that contained 17 pages of codicils and attachments. Even those 17 pages were not sufficient to make it a truly balanced agreement—but it certainly helped level the playing field for the franchisee.

Why don't more franchisees insist on negotiating important points in the agreement? One reason is that many franchisees simply don't know that they *can* negotiate certain provisions—or even why they should. They don't understand why certain provisions are unfair and what the consequences of those provisions may be in years to come.

Supply and demand is another reason why negotiations, until recently, have been uncommon. Well-established franchises like McDonald's or Dunkin Donuts are in a position to dictate agreements that suit them. If one prospective franchisee doesn't want to sign an unnegotiated contract, another may be ready to. Newer franchises or start-ups may be more willing to negotiate with prospective franchisees. They need units up and running.

Another reason negotiations have been uncommon is that many would-be franchisees neglect to have their agreement reviewed by an attorney with expertise in franchising who could alert the prospective franchisee to unfair or problematic provisions and assist in negotiating alternatives with the franchisor.

Let this chapter be the beginning of your education. It lists in alphabetical order, provisions that may appear in the agreement. Study them closely. Even if you are not able to negotiate them as we recommend, at a minimum you should understand the ramifications of each provision. Signing a five-year or ten-year franchise contract is an enormous obligation. You should know what's in the "fine print" before you sign it!

With your franchise lawyer, carefully study the franchise agreement in conjunction with the UFOC. Together these two documents identify the ins and outs of the franchise system and will lead to the red flags that need to be further investigated and discussed with the franchisor. Then, when you understand the provisions of the agreement and know which ones you want to change, you will be ready, with your attorney, to negotiate.

Don't rush this process. After all, by law you are not even allowed to sign the agreement for ten days after you receive it. It will take time for your lawyer to review the contract thoroughly and translate its contents into language you can understand, and it will take time for negotiation by the franchisor and your attorney. Your attorney also needs time to draft an addendum to the franchise agreement reflecting the negotiated provisions and time for your final review. Remember, when it's signed, the agreement becomes a 10-year, 15-year, or even 20-year legal and binding contract that is irrevocable except for certain contingencies it may contain.

If you are not successful in deleting or changing provisions, take heart. A negotiated franchise agreement is the exception rather than the rule, and an unnegotiated agreement is not necessarily a bad one. But if you are not comfortable with what the system is asking from you, walk, and look for another franchise opportunity.

Is reading the agreement time consuming, laborious, and dull? Yes. Is it essential? Absolutely. By understanding the most common provisions and what each means to you, you and your franchise attorney can negotiate a better, fairer contract.

Potential Items for Negotiation

Acceleration of Royalties

Many franchise agreements provide that the franchisor may accelerate and make immediately due and payable the total royalties that would have been paid for the remaining term of the franchise agreement if the franchisee defaults and prematurely terminates its agreement. Acceleration can be costly. If this provision exists, insist on its deletion. If you can't eliminate it entirely, reduce it to a specified period of time such as three years, and apply a present-value discount factor (for example, 8 percent) because a dollar payable a year from now is worth less than a dollar prepaid today. Likewise, delete any clause permitting liquidated damages on premature termination. (See "Liquidated Damages.")

Advertising Obligations

The franchisor will probably require you to spend a percentage of your gross revenues on local advertising, which you will place directly in your local market using marketing materials developed by the franchisor. In a single advertising market (called an ADI, an area of dominant influence) where two or more franchised units are located, an advertising cooperative may be created to economize on the cost of advertising. The franchise agreement will usually allow payment to a cooperative to be credited against your local advertising obligations. You may also be required to contribute to a franchisor-controlled regional or national marketing fund used to purchase regional or national advertising, such as television commercials and ads in national publications. Don't let franchisor-owned units get a free ride. Make sure they, too, contribute to all advertising funds. Item 11 of the UFOC will tell you whether they do.

If the regional or national marketing fund is administered by the franchisor, make sure all funds are considered trust funds used solely for advertising products or services offered by the system and are not used for promoting the sale of additional franchises or any other purposes. The franchisor may charge a reasonable administrative fee if in fact it administers the fund and provides services. You should receive an audited accounting of the fund on an annual basis. Have the franchisor be a fiduciary; a fiduciary has greater obligations to care for your money and use it properly.

Arbitration and Mediation

Because going to court ties up tremendous amounts of time and money, many franchise systems are implementing such alternative dispute resolution mechanisms as mediation and arbitration. Several private, independent organizations specialize in providing these services to franchisors and franchisees, including the Center for Public Resources - National Franchise Mediation Program, Endispute, Franchise Arbitration & Mediation, Inc., and the American Arbitration Association.

If your franchise agreement provides for mediation and arbitration of disputes, make sure it takes place in your county rather than at the franchisor's home office (see "Venue"), that one of these specialized organizations is used, and that the nonprevailing or losing party pays the attorney fees and costs of the prevailing or winning party (see "Attorney Fees"). However, arbitration is not perfect. In many disputes a franchisee is better off having the issue decided by a jury of his or her peers. Discuss this issue with your attorney.

Attorney Fees

If a provision for attorney fees is included, make sure it applies to the prevailing party and is not just for the benefit of the franchisor. Otherwise, in the event of a dispute you may have to pay your own attorney fees even if you win.

Audit by Franchisor

Where a royalty is paid on gross revenues, most franchise agreements give the franchisor the right to audit the franchisee's books and records, and if revenues have been underreported, they make the franchisee bear the cost of the audit. To prevent harassment, limit the frequency of those audits; to avoid being unduly penalized, limit damages to situations in which the underreported amount is significant (2 to 5 percent of gross revenues) and intentionally underreported. You don't want to be responsible for the franchisor's audit costs if you have made an honest mistake.

Choice of Law

A choice-of-law provision clarifies which state's laws govern the rights and obligations of the parties under the agreement. Most agreements provide that the law of the state where the franchisor's headquarters is located will govern. If you live in a state having no franchise laws and the franchisor is headquartered in a state having franchise laws, then this provision is probably satisfactory, provided the franchise agreement does not specifically exclude these franchise laws. If you live in a state having franchise laws and the franchisor is headquartered in a state having no franchise laws, then it probably is better to have your state's laws govern. However, this provision is hard to renegotiate because of the franchisor's desire for uniformity of the laws applying to its many franchise relationships.

Consent or Approval of the Franchisor

The franchise agreement contains numerous provisions in which the franchisor's consent or approval is required. Provide in the "General" or "Miscellaneous" article of the franchise agreement or in an addendum that "whenever the consent or approval of the franchisor is required, the consent or approval will not be unreasonably withheld or delayed (more than 30 days). "

Contingencies

If purchasing the franchise depends upon your ability to obtain financing, lease a suitable location, or complete training, put these conditions in the addendum and provide that if any contingency does not occur, you get all of your money back. Otherwise, you may forfeit everything you have paid. If the franchisor agrees to give a portion of the money back but keep the rest to compensate it for its services, make sure the amount it keeps is reasonable. Consider putting the money in escrow pending the satisfaction of the contingency so that you don't end up having to chase the franchisor to get your money back if the contingencies are not satisfied or waived and you elect to rescind the franchise agreement. (See "Escrow of Funds.")

Covenants Not to Compete

A covenant not to compete is a promise by you to the franchisor that you will not operate a business similar to the franchise business. The covenant applies while you are a franchisee (that is, "in-term") and for a period of time (usually two years) after the franchise agreement expires or is terminated (that is, "postterm"). If you already have, or are contemplating having, a competing business while you are a franchisee or you are, or plan to be, a multiconcept franchisee, carve out these businesses as exceptions to the covenant.

If you are already in a similar business (for example, you are an independent who is joining the system or part of another system that is being converted to a new one), negotiate to eliminate the postterm covenant altogether or to provide that it does not apply if (1) the franchise agreement expires and is not renewed, (2) the franchise agreement is transferred to a franchisor-approved buyer, or (3) the franchise agreement terminates from a default by the franchisor. One state, California, refuses to enforce any postterm covenant not to compete.

Customer Lists

The agreement may provide that a copy of your customer list must be given to, and is the property of, the franchisor. Try to change this or at least provide that the franchisor can't use your customer list to compete against you by, say, sending a direct mail piece to your customers that urges them to order from the franchisor.

Customer Restrictions

Does the franchise agreement limit the type or class of customers (for example, residential and not commercial; retail and not wholesale) with whom you can do business? Item 16 of the UFOC will disclose this. If there are restrictions, what are their business justifications? Are they reasonable? If you think they are unreasonable—renegotiate.

Death, Disability, or Incompetency

What happens to your business if you die or become disabled or incompetent? Do you have time to transfer the business to your family or sell the business? Is there insurance between you and the franchisor whereby the franchisor is the beneficiary and is obligated to buy your franchise with the insurance proceeds? This needs to be addressed.

Default by Franchisor

Most franchise agreements set forth innumerable ways the franchisee can default without addressing a single way that the franchisor might default or breach the agreement. It certainly is not unreasonable to request a provision that requires the franchisor a 30-day grace period after written notice to cure (correct) a default. Also, try to provide that if the franchisor fails to cure a default, you have the option to terminate the franchise agreement and, in addition to a claim for damages, you can continue to operate the franchise unit under the franchisor's trade name without further payments or other obligations to the franchisor.

Default by You

Your default events normally fall into three categories. First, there are events that cause automatic termination of the franchise agreement without notice or right to cure if they occur. Make sure insolvency is not such an event. Otherwise, the franchisor may be able to terminate your franchise agreement just before you file for bankruptcy relief and you would lose flexibility if you are trying to do a Chapter 11 reorganization. Although it seems remote, you may someday need to reorganize under Chapter 11, terminate your franchise agreement, and not be subject to a postterm covenant not to compete. If you enter bankruptcy proceedings, U.S. bankruptcy laws will supersede the franchise claim and the franchise will not be able to declare you in default.

The second category of default by you includes events that cause termination of the franchise agreement on notice by the franchisor if they occur but with no right to cure. Limit these events to truly egregious actions on your part, such as conviction of a felony or a willful breach of confidentiality or a noncompete covenant by you, not by some low-level employee.

The third category includes events that cause your termination if they occur but only after written notice from the franchisor and your failing to cure them in a timely manner. Make sure the events are reasonable and that you have at least 10 days to cure a monetary default and at least 30 days, after written notice from the franchisor specifically describing its nature, to cure a nonmonetary default.

Entire Agreement

Most franchise agreements have a provision in the "Miscellaneous" or "General" article stating that the document represents the entire agreement between the franchisor and the franchisee. Legally referred to as an "integration" or "merger" provision, it makes unenforceable and nonbinding any oral representations, promises, or understandings by the franchisor or its representatives (including franchise brokers), such as unauthorized earnings claims that are not specifically included in the franchise agreement or in an addendum in writing. This is why it is critical to include in the agreement or addendum any promises by the franchisor or its agents that are important to you and are reasons why you have decided to purchase the franchise. Make sure everything is in black and white.

Escrow of Funds

You may pay the franchisor tens of thousands of dollars on signing the franchise agreement several months before you open the business. Negotiate to have your funds held in escrow until the franchisor completes its preopening obligations, particularly if the franchise is new or doesn't have a strong financial statement. Some franchise registration states may issue an impound order requiring undercapitalized franchisors to escrow franchisee funds for all sales in, or to residents of, their state until the franchisee opens for business as a condition of state approval of the franchise registration. Regardless of the size and nature of the franchisor, it would be a prudent act to have your up-front payments placed in escrow.

Exclusive Territory

Oversaturation—having more outlets in a market than the market can handle—is a major problem in franchising today. In addition, many major brand names and franchise systems are opening outlets on college campuses, airports, highway facilities, hospitals, and in other nontraditional locations. Unfortunately, when these outlets are within existing franchisees' trade areas, sales decline as customers are "cannibalized"—diverted to the new nontraditional locations that are usually owned by the franchisor. That is why it is so important to negotiate an exclusive territory.

Do you get an exclusive territory within which the franchisor or another franchisee can't operate—for example, within a three-mile radius or 30,000 households? Does your exclusive territory depend on your achieving a certain sales level? Can the franchisor unilaterally reduce your territory? Try to get an exclusive territory that is reasonable for your trade area. Don't accept a "location only" (no exclusive territory) provision. If you do, the franchisor may, if it expressly reserves the right, open a company outlet or franchised outlet across the street or next to you that will cannibalize your sales.

Try to eliminate encroachment caused by the franchisor's reserving certain rights to operate directly within your exclusive territory through sales to supermarkets, catalog sales, and national accounts without your consent or participation. Try to develop a "win-win" scenario by participating in the alternate distribution method. The issue of territorial exclusion should be disclosed in item 12 of the offering circular.

Force Majeure

Force majeure is a French term meaning superior or irresistible force and usually refers to acts beyond the control of the parties, such as riots or earthquakes, floods, and other acts of God. If a force majeure provision does not appear in the agreement, suggest that it be added to protect the interests of both parties. If the provision is solely in favor of the franchisor, insist that it be made mutual so you also benefit. You never know when a fire, flood, earthquake, hurricane, riot, bombing, or other disaster will occur!

Franchisor's Right of Access

Most franchise agreements give the franchisor and its representatives the right to enter your premises at any time, without prior notice, for inspections and to show the business to prospective franchisees. This can become disruptive to you and your business. Limit the franchisor's right of access during normal business hours and on reasonable notice (except for emergencies) so as not to disrupt your operations. Don't allow your unit to become the franchisor's training facility or showcase unit without reasonable compensation to you.

General Release

Most franchise agreements provide as a condition to the franchisor's agreeing to a sale, transfer of the franchise, or renewal of the franchise that you release the franchisor from all claims you may have, known or unknown, against it. What if you have a valid claim and/or are in litigation with the franchisor at the time of renewal? Try to eliminate this provision or have it state that the franchisor has to grant you a general release and further provide that the release will not include known claims and pending or threatened litigation. In several states this type of release is not enforceable. Check with your state or a franchise attorney.

Gross Revenues

Read the definition of gross revenues carefully. You want to place revenues from other activities not associated with the franchisor's trade name outside the definition so you don't pay royalties on them. Make sure that "phantom income" is excluded from the definition of gross revenues—for example, sales tax collections, shipping and handling charges, customer credit and refunds, revenues from employee meals, and the like.

Guaranty of Franchisee's Obligations

Most franchisors want you and your spouse to individually sign the franchise agreement. They may allow your corporation to sign the franchise agreement provided you and your spouse make a personal guarantee. The franchisor wants you and your spouse to be personally obligated for unpaid royalties, unpaid product purchases, indemnity obligations, and other obligations as well as personally bound to the confidentiality and noncompetition covenants in the franchise agreement.

Try to make your corporation the franchisee and to avoid giving your personal guarantee. Offer to sign, with your spouse, confidentiality and noncompete agreements. If a personal guarantee is required, try to limit it to the first year or two of the franchise agreement. Don't have your spouse sign the guarantee with you; doing so will expose most of your joint personal assets.

Your ability to renegotiate this provision may depend on the financial strength of your corporation. It's a long shot, but you might try saying you'll guarantee the franchise agreement if the principals of the franchisor guarantee the franchisor's obligations. That should be good for a laugh!

Indemnification

Indemnification means a promise by one party to reimburse another party for a loss through payment, replacement, or repair. Generally, this language is drafted in a completely one-sided fashion. Guess in whose favor? The franchisee fully indemnifies the franchisor for all liability of any form or fashion. Renegotiate this provision so that the franchisor must indemnify you and your agents, employees, and contractors from any action or inaction on the part of the franchisor, its agents, employees, or contractors based on negligence or a willful act that results in a claim, suit, demand, or judgment for liability. If the franchisor or its affiliates sell products or services to you, it needs to provide a warranty covering these products or services. (See "Product Warranties.")

Initial Franchise Fee

Most franchisors charge an initial franchise fee to cover legal and accounting expenses as well as costs involved in creating and marketing the franchise, training you, and helping you become operational. The reasonableness of the initial franchise fee depends on the value of the benefits you are receiving in return. If you are short on capital, try to negotiate installment payments or defer a significant portion until you become operational. (See "Escrow of Funds.")

Insurance

Consult an insurance agent that specializes in franchisee insurance about the insurance provisions contained in the agreement. After reviewing how much and what kind of insurance is required, the agent can determine whether the requested insurance is reasonable and necessary for your business and how much it will cost. Some franchise agreements, for example, require. business interruption insurance, which is expensive and may not be obtainable for a start-up. Your agent must also deliver a certificate of insurance to the franchisor naming the franchisor as an additional insured and/or loss payee (depending on the type of insurance) and provide 10 to 30 days' prior written notice of a change or cancellation of the policy.

If the franchisor or an affiliate sells you products or services, make sure that it maintains adequate product liability insurance or errors and omission insurance.

Late Charges

Most franchise agreements allow franchisors to impose a late charge if you are late in paying your royalty, advertising contribution, or other fee. Try to include a five-day to ten-day grace period before a late charge is imposed. Try to negotiate an elimination of a percentage charge (for example, 5 percent) or a fixed fee (for example, $1,000), which can be excessive, in favor of an interest charge.

Limitation of Claims

To prevent old and stale claims from being litigated, the law imposes statutes of limitations—limits on the period of time in which a claim may be asserted. Generally, the period ranges from one to five years from the event, depending on the nature of the claim. Look for, and try to eliminate, any provision that shortens the time you can bring a claim against the franchisor and vice versa. Such a provision hurts you more than the franchisor because you may not know you have a claim against the franchisor until you have a problem and consult a franchise attorney. The franchisor's claim is usually for unpaid royalties of which the franchisor is immediately aware.

Liquidated Damages

A liquidated damages provision provides for the payment of specified damages for certain wrongdoings without requiring either party to prove its actual damages. Let's say, for example, you sell unauthorized products or services. Your agreement may specify that the franchisor is to receive $500—even though it lost only $150 in royalties because of your sales. If this provision is in the franchise agreement, make sure it is reasonable. Some states (for example, New York) may not enforce it.

Location of Your Unit

Is your unit at a fixed location such as a store or is it mobile, such as a cart? If mobile, can you go anywhere? If fixed, can you relocate if you lose your lease through no fault of your own or if the building is destroyed or taken by eminent domain or condemnation? Must you operate only at this location? What about home delivery? Can you market outside your trade area by direct mail, catalog, toll-free number, and so on? (See "Sales restrictions.")

Minimum Performance Requirement

Some franchise agreements condition the grant of the franchise or the exclusive territory on your achieving a certain level of sales. It would be best not to have a minimum performance requirement in the agreement. If it stays in, make sure the requirement is fair and achievable through reasonable, not superhuman, effort. The penalty for not achieving a reasonable performance requirement should be the reduction or loss of exclusivity, not the loss of the franchise.

Minimum Royalties, Advertising Contribution, or Other Payments

The franchise agreement may require you to agree to minimum royalties, advertising contributions, or purchases. The problem here is that sometimes this arrangement can cost you when sales are low. Say, for example, the agreement sets your minimum royalty at $500 per month—but if you multiplied a slow month's sales by the actual royalty rate, you would only pay $420. Here's another example. Carvel franchisees must purchase at least 10,000 gallons of ice cream mix a year from Carvel. However, the average franchisee uses only about 6,000 gallons each year. The minimum royalty becomes 167 percent of what the royalty should be. Some "minimum!" See if you can put a maximum amount on those fees or purchases, delay them until you are fully operational, or eliminate them altogether.

Name, Home Address, and Telephone Number

Under the new UFOC guidelines, a franchisor is required to include the name, home address, and telephone number of all franchisees who left the system within the previous fiscal year or who have not communicated with the franchisor within the ten-week period before the effective date of the UFOC. The franchise agreement probably now addresses these issues and requires you to agree to it. While you are a franchisee and for over a year after you cease to be one, you can expect phone calls. Remember how much you appreciated being able to talk to existing and former franchisees when you were a prospective franchisee. You can return the favor by talking to these prospective franchisees provided they are courteous and appreciative of your time.

National Accounts

If the franchise system sells its products or services to national accounts, the franchisor probably has reserved the right to deal with these national accounts directly, even where a branch of the national account is located within the exclusive territory of the franchisee. There are legitimate reasons for this; the national account wants uniform pricing (see "Pricing") and a single sales or service contact. You should, however, have the franchisor grant you the right to service national accounts whose branches are located within your exclusive territory on terms mutually agreeable to you and the franchisor.

Obligations of the Franchisee

Understand fully your obligations under the franchise agreement and any other agreement you are required to sign, such as a sublease, guarantee, software license agreement, telephone power of attorney, and the like. Know what is required of you *before* your unit opens, *after* your unit opens, and *after* the franchise agreement expires or terminates. A table briefly describing your obligations is set forth in item 9 of the UFOC. Read the specific provisions of the franchise agreement very carefully to fully understand your obligations.

Obligations of the Franchisor

One or more sections of the franchise agreement set forth what the franchisor will do for you. Be careful to note whether the franchisor "shall" or "will" do something versus "may" do something. If the franchisor "shall" or "will," the franchisor must perform the obligation or default under the franchise agreement. If the franchisor "may" do something, the franchisor's obligation is discretionary; if the franchisor does not perform that obligation, you probably cannot legally complain. Surprisingly, many franchise agreements provide few ongoing services that the franchisor is legally required to provide to you. Item 11 of the UFOC sets forth in tabular form a description of the franchisor's contractual obligations to you.

Option to Purchase by Franchisor

Some franchise agreements grant the franchisor the option of purchasing the franchisee's business on termination or expiration of, and sometimes at any time during, the term. This may not be in your best interest as the franchisor would only be interested in buying your franchise if it is very successful. If the franchisor insists on an option, limit it to when the franchise agreement expires or terminates as the result of your default. The price should be fair market value on an ongoing business basis and not some lesser formula such as book value.

Payment System

Many franchise agreements require the franchisor and franchisee to establish an automatic payment system through a financial institution so the franchisor can access the franchisee's bank accounts for royalties, advertising contributions, and other payments using special checks or electronic funds transfer. Many franchisees find this intrusive and negotiate it out of the agreement. There are practical ways around it. For example, some franchisees "sweep" their operating accounts by maintaining only minimal balances in the account that is accessible by the franchisor and transferring funds into a savings account to which the franchisor does not have access.

Posttermination Obligations

At the expiration or termination of the franchise agreement, you may have a number of obligations to the franchisor:

- The franchisor may have the option (not just a right of first refusal) to purchase your franchise business. If so, make sure it is at fair market value rather than book value so you get a higher and fairer price. (See "Option to Purchase by Franchisor".)
- The option to purchase may be limited to items bearing the franchisor's proprietary marks, such as inventory, paper goods, equipment, signage, and so on. Require the franchisor to purchase these items because you probably can't resell or use them, whereas the franchisor can. Make sure the purchase price is at cost or fair market value, whichever is greater.
- If you sublease the premises from the franchisor, the sublease may provide that the expiration or termination of the franchise agreement constitutes a default under the lease. Even if you lease from an unrelated third party, your agreement may require you and your landlord to agree to allow the franchisor to take over the lease and the premises if you default under the agreement. You then can be evicted from the premises. Try to negotiate the right to stay and operate a dissimilar business under a different name if you desire.
- If you stay at the premises, the franchise agreement will likely require you to "deidentify" the premises—that is, make changes in signage, color, layout, and the like so that the public doesn't know it was once part of a franchise chain. Know, before executing the franchise agreement, what the franchisor expects of you in this regard and the likely cost.
- You may be required to sign a telephone power of attorney that allows the franchisor to control the telephone number and listing. You will have to get a new number, which may not be listed in the telephone book for several months. If you remain at the premises, try to retain the right to the same telephone number.

Many of these posttermination obligations are penal in nature. They may be appropriate if you default, but are they if you decide not to renew and want to operate independently? They certainly do not appear to be appropriate if you terminate the franchise agreement because of the franchisor's default! (See "Default by Franchisor" and "Default by You.") Try to negotiate that these provisions apply only on termination resulting from your default.

Pricing

Under federal antitrust laws it is illegal for the franchisor to dictate the prices at which franchisees sell products and services. The franchisor can only recommend or offer a manufacturer's suggested retail price (MSRP), which is why commercials include disclosures like "at participating dealers only" or "prices may vary." A provision in the franchise agreement that dictates prices is probably illegal and shows the drafter didn't know the law.

Product Warranties

Make sure the franchise agreement provides for a product warranty on all products manufactured by the franchisor or its affiliates, a "pass-through" of all warranties from third-party manufacturers, and maintenance of adequate product liability insurance.

Purchases from Franchisor; "Most Favored Nation" Clause

If you are obligated to buy all or any portion of equipment, inventory, or other products or services from the franchisor or an affiliate, you are locked in. It's like dealing with the utility company without a public service commission to hold it in check. Although the franchisor is certainly entitled to make a reasonable profit on the sale of these items, you will want to determine how the wholesale price is arrived at to prevent price gouging. What is the pricing formula? On what basis can the franchisor increase prices? Clarify these pricing issues. Also negotiate a provision whereby you receive the most favorable pricing terms available to any customer for these items (a "most favored nation" clause).

Release of Prior Claims

In the "Miscellaneous" or "General Provisions" section, many agreements contain a "Release of Prior Claims" provision whereby, on signing the franchise agreement, you release the franchisor from any prior claims you may have against the franchisor including the franchisor's violation of franchise laws. In some states this provision is unenforceable. It is best to delete it.

Relocation Rights

Condemnation, casualty, and loss of lease are just a few of the factors beyond your control that may take away your right to operate the franchise business on your premises. Make sure the franchise agreement provides that if one of these events occurs, you have a reasonable period of time to relocate the franchise business without forfeiting your franchise. Will minimum royalties abate (stop) during this period? Does the franchisor charge a relocation fee? Ask about the franchisor's relocation policies. Get them in writing and renegotiate them if they appear unreasonable from your perspective.

Renewal, or Option, Fee

A renewal, or option, fee is a fee charged by the franchisor in connection with the renewal of the franchise. It can range from zero to the tens of thousands of dollars that constitute another initial franchise fee. Because the franchisor incurs few out-of-pocket costs when renewing your franchise, negotiate to eliminate any fee or make the fee reasonable—not a profit center for the franchisor!

Renovation of the Premises; Modification of the System

Your franchise agreement may require you to renovate, update, or modernize your premises in the future. Clarify how often you are required to do this—every five years, for example, or on renewal. Include a limit on capital expenditures so you can budget for renovation by setting aside earnings in a reserve account. Also, negotiate a dollar cap on expenditures to conform to such system changes as a change in system color or menu. Make sure system changes are thoroughly tested and implemented in all franchisee- and franchisor-owned units—not just yours.

Reporting Requirements; Confidentiality

If you pay royalties as a percentage of gross revenues, the agreement may require you to supply the franchisor with copies of your sales records and sales tax returns. You will also be required to supply quarterly financial statements (balance sheet, profit and loss statement, and statement of cash flows) as well as year-end financial statements prepared by an independent certified public accountant. Make sure you have at least 45 days from the end of each quarter and 90 days from the end of each year to supply these statements.

It is also important to make sure that the year-end financials are compilation statements (preferable) or review-level statements (next most preferable) but definitely not audited financial statements. Audited financial statements cost several thousand dollars more than compilations and should only be necessary if you are caught underreporting.

Make sure that the franchise agreement provides for the franchisor to keep your financial records confidential except for compiling an earnings claim for use in the UFOC.

Right of First Refusal by Franchisor

Most franchise agreements give the franchisor the right of first refusal to purchase the franchisee's business, if the franchisee receives an offer from a third party, on the same terms and conditions as contained in the third-party offer. Make sure that the franchisor's time to exercise the right of first refusal is no more than 30 days (preferably 10). If it's longer, your third-party prospective buyer may cool off and walk away while the franchisor is mulling it over.

Right of First Refusal by Franchisee

You may want the right of first refusal to purchase an additional franchise in a nearby territory. If you do, negotiate it in the franchise agreement in a separate agreement. Make sure you have sufficient time to exercise your right when the opportunity materializes.

Right of Setoff

If you owe the franchisor a dollar and you think the franchisor owes you 50¢, you might want to setoff that debt by paying 50¢ instead of a dollar. Unfortunately, setoff provisions are very difficult to get. Franchisors fiercely protect their right to collect all royalties and payments due. Most franchise agreements specifically provide that your obligations to pay royalties and other payments are independent of any obligation of the franchisor to you. In addition, the courts uniformly hold that unless the franchise agreement provides to the contrary, a franchisee cannot accept the benefits of the franchisor's trademark by continuing to operate under the trademark without paying royalties, even when the franchisee may have valid claims against the franchisor.

Therefore, you should try to negotiate for the optional ability to perform the obligations of the franchisor under the franchise agreement on the franchisor's failure or refusal to perform and to set off any sums expended against the royalties or other monetary obligations under the agreement. In many instances this will be your only remedy if the franchisor fails to perform. The franchisor should be afforded reasonable notice and an opportunity to cure—to correct the problem—before you exercise this right.

Sales Restrictions

Are there restrictions on the types of customers you can deal with or the types of products you can sell? Can you sell outside your location by offering home delivery? Can you solicit business outside your exclusive territory using a toll-free number, advertisement, or catalog sales? Find out the answers to these questions and negotiate to lift or lessen any of these restrictions.

Security Interest

Are you required to give the franchisor a security deposit or a letter of credit, or grant the franchisor a security interest or collateral? If you must grant a security interest, try to limit it to the products purchased. If you must grant a security interest in your business assets, negotiate to have the franchisor agree to subordinate its security interest to

- your landlord's lien,
- the security interest of a reputable institutional lender for a loan to you for working capital purposes,
- the security interest of an approved equipment vendor for any equipment you purchase or lease and use in the operation of the franchise business, or
- the security interest of a supplier of approved products sold at the franchise business.

Securities Offerings

Although many single-unit franchise agreements don't address this issue, some agreements and most area-development agreements prohibit or severely restrict a franchisee from raising capital through a private or public securities offering. If you have a capital-intensive franchise or are an area developer, you may want to reserve the right to raise capital through the sale of securities. Your franchisor has a legitimate business interest in reviewing the offering materials before public dissemination to make sure they fully and accurately describe the relationship between you and the franchisor so that the franchisor will not have any liability arising from your securities offering. It is fair to let the franchisor charge you a reasonable offering fee in order to cover attorney fees and other costs.

Term and Renewal Rights

The initial term of the franchise agreement should be long enough for you to reasonably amortize your investment. A minimum of ten years is preferable. The agreement normally gives you a limited renewal right, meaning at some point in 15 to 25 years the agreement terminates. What happens then?

You are buying a franchise as a long-term investment to sell and retire or pass down to your children. Negotiate unlimited ("evergreen") rights to renew, whereby the franchise agreement is automatically renewed at your option provided you are not in default under the franchise agreement and that other reasonable conditions are met. Examples of reasonable conditions that the franchisor may require include the payment of a minimal renewal fee (see "Renewal, or Option, Fee") and execution of the franchisor's then-current form of franchise agreement. The franchise agreement that is current at the time of your renewal may be substantially different from the one you initially signed. If you must sign the new version, make sure it doesn't change the basic terms of your agreement, such as royalties, territory, and noncompetition clauses. Avoid executing a general release (see "General Release").

"Time Is of the Essence" Clause

A "time of the essence" provision makes all time periods specified in the franchise agreement for performance practically fixed in stone. Because you may be in material default under the agreement if you don't satisfy these time periods, try to eliminate such a provision.

Trademarks

One of the cornerstones of a franchise system is a well-recognized trade name. The right to operate under the franchisor's trade name is one reason you are willing to pay an initial franchise fee and ongoing royalties. Have the franchisor warrant its ownership of the trademarks in the franchise agreement. In addition, make sure that the franchisor really does own the name and has obtained, or is in the process of obtaining, a U.S. registered trademark. (Item 13 of the UFOC discusses the franchisor's rights to the trademarks licensed to the franchisee.)

If you are sued for trademark infringement by a third party for using the franchisor's trade name according to the franchise agreement, make sure the franchisor indemnifies you and holds you harmless for any damages sustained by any third party, including court costs and attorney fees. Include a provision that the franchisor will reimburse you for your costs in new signage, stationery, business cards, paper goods, and the like if the franchisor changes its trade name. Also, add a provision that the franchisor will do nothing to dilute the value of the trademarks, such as selling inferior products, using inferior ingredients, or selling frozen items instead of fresh (if the latter was the system's market position).

In many franchise systems an affiliate of the franchisor actually owns the trademarks, the manuals, and the system, and licenses them to the franchisor. The franchisor is given the right to sublicense and loan these items to the franchisee under a license agreement between the affiliate and the franchisor. This should be disclosed in items 1 and 13 of the UFOC. What happens to your right to use these items if the franchisor defaults under the license agreement with the affiliate? Is the affiliate obligated to assume the franchisor's obligations to you? Can you continue to use these items?

Transfer by the Franchisor

Your agreement may allow the franchisor to transfer the franchise agreement to anyone it chooses without your consent. You may try to provide that the transferee (new franchisor) must have sufficient business experience, aptitude, and financial resources to perform the franchisor's obligations under the franchise agreement.

Transfer by You

The franchise agreement probably provides that the franchise is granted to you and that you cannot transfer the franchise agreement (or a majority interest of the voting stock of a corporate franchisee) unless several conditions are met. Those conditions include the following:

- *A waiver of the franchisor's right of first refusal.* Make sure the franchisor's right of first refusal requires the franchisor to make up its mind to buy or not to buy your franchised unit within 10 to 30 days from receipt of the offer from the proposed buyer of your franchised unit. If it is longer than 30 days, your proposed buyer may get cold feet. (See "Right of First Refusal by Franchisor.")
- *The buyer's assumption of the existing franchise agreement or execution of the franchisor's latest version of the franchise agreement.* Try to negotiate for an assumption of the existing franchise agreement rather than execution of a new franchise agreement.
- *The payment of a transfer fee.* Make sure the fee is reasonable and merely covers the franchisor's administrative costs and the costs of training the buyer. It shouldn't be a windfall for the franchisor. (See "Transfer Fee.")
- *The execution and delivery by you of a general release to the franchisor whereby you release the franchisor from any claims you may have against it.* Ask that the franchisor give you a general release as well or, better yet, eliminate the provision entirely. (See "General Release.")

Transfer Fee

Your franchisor charges a fee when you transfer your franchise to a third party. This transfer fee is intended to reimburse franchisor for the legal costs as well as for investigating, approving, and training the transferee. Make sure the fee is reasonable in light of the obligations and services performed by the franchisor (the average is around $5,000) and is not an additional profit center for the franchisor. Negotiate to provide that the fee does not apply when the transfer is by you to your corporation, by you to a trained and qualified family member, or to another franchisee in the system.

Venue

Venue means the place (district, county, etc.) where a lawsuit or a mediation or arbitration proceeding will be held. Generally, the franchise agreement provides that venue will be in the county where the franchisor's headquarters is located and not the county where your business is located. If it is hundreds or thousands of miles away from you, prosecuting or defending a claim will be costly and difficult! Although a few states will not enforce these provisions (for example, California, Connecticut, Illinois, Massachusetts, and Michigan), most states will. Try to change jurisdiction and venue to the state where you are located.

Waiver of Punitive Damage Claims

Some franchise agreements now limit the ability of the parties to sue each other for punitive damages. Because most punitive damage awards are against the franchisor and in favor of the franchisee, it's no wonder this provision is cropping up in franchise agreements. Negotiate its deletion.

Waiver of Trial by Jury

When you agree to the waiver of a trial by jury provision, you give up the right to have a jury of your peers decide issues of fact. Instead, the judge decides. If you agree to binding arbitration, the arbitrator will decide. (See "Arbitration and Mediation.") Years ago, an old-time Florida attorney said, "The only thing I allow my clients to wave is the American flag." This is good advice!

CHAPTER 10

Negotiating a Lease

Harris Chernow, Keith J. Kanouse, Richard Rosen

Negotiating a fair lease for your location is just as important as negotiating a fair agreement with your franchisor because a poorly negotiated lease can cripple one's chances for success.

For starters, your lease dictates what may be your largest monthly fixed cost: rent along with such additional factors as utilities, taxes, common area maintenance charges, and certain hidden costs. A lease that costs too much may destroy you financially. But your lease protects your investment in your location. If you have a ten-year contract with your franchisor but a five-year lease with your landlord, what will happen when your lease runs out? The terms of your lease need to match the terms of your agreement.

Other factors are just as important. You want to be able to renew your lease on favorable terms. You will want to be able to sublet the premises if the ownership of your company changes or if you need to move. If your business grows quickly, you may want the right to take over adjoining space when it becomes available. And you certainly want to be sure that your ability to run your business is protected should your landlord go bust.

No two leases are alike. A lease from a single-unit building may be 3 pages long; a lease from a large shopping mall may run as long as 50 pages. A very small and unsophisticated landlord may not even want to sign a lease, but you should insist on one. When a lease has been negotiated properly, it protects your interests as well as the landlord's.

But no matter how long the lease, you should never sign one without examining it carefully—because a lease is *never* standard or innocuous. It was drafted by the landlord's attorney to protect the landlord. You'll need to negotiate many provisions with the landlord (or at the very least *understand* the legal and financial terms and consequences), including some that the landlord considers boilerplate (i.e., standardized) but that need to be renegotiated to make the landlord-tenant relationship more equitable.

Before you begin negotiating, ask the landlord to show you his or her owner's title insurance policy and copies of existing mortgages, restrictions, easements, and the like. This will verify that you are dealing with the proper owner and also determine what restrictions and rights exist on the property that may affect your ability to operate the franchised business and what rights the landlord's mortgagee has that may be adverse to your interest.

Items for Consideration in Lease Negotiations

Negotiating a lease can be difficult. Chances are your landlord has more leverage than you do—first, because you're probably a novice when it comes to commercial real estate, and, second, because the landlord knows you are interested in the site and will ask you for certain concessions before leasing to you.

Following are several ways you can increase your bargaining power:

- Familiarize yourself with the contents of a typical lease so you can discuss each article knowledgeably. Reviewing this chapter will help.
- Hire an experienced franchise lawyer to review your lease—preferably the same lawyer who helped you negotiate your franchise agreement. Let the lawyer explain its contents, recommend changes, and represent you in discussions about proposed changes with the landlord or attorney. The lawyer may negotiate provisions by telephone, by mail, or in meetings with you and the landlord. Any method that works is fine. Just make sure you let your lawyer do the job he or she was hired to do—review *and* negotiate your lease. Don't pinch pennies by trying to negotiate the lease yourself or you may someday find yourself spending hundreds or even thousands of dollars trying to free yourself from a bad lease.
- When it's time to bargain, leave your emotions at home. Don't let your enthusiasm for the site lure you into agreeing to unfair lease terms. The economic factors of a lease can ruin a beautiful franchise business!
- Be prepared to be patient. Negotiating a lease takes time. Don't rush or worry about what will happen if negotiations fall apart. If you have carefully negotiated your franchise agreement, you should have an "out clause" that permits you to cancel the agreement if you don't obtain a lease.

Leases are not identical, but you should be aware of commonly included provisions described in the following sections.

Abandonment of Premises

Most leases provide that if you abandon (i.e., vacate) all or a portion of the premises, you are in default of the lease even if you continue to pay rent. Try to eliminate this clause and retain the right to "go dark" provided you continue to pay the rent.

Acceleration of Rent

Most leases contain language allowing the landlord to accelerate or collect the total rent due for the remaining lease period when the tenant defaults or prematurely terminates the lease. Do your best to have this clause eliminated. Tell the landlord unequivocally that you do not sign leases containing acceleration language as acceleration could prove to be costly to you. If you are in a good bargaining position, this approach may work. At a minimum, change the acceleration language to limit your liability to either a present valuation of the total rent (for example, a present value discount of 8 percent) or the difference between the total rent due and the value of the rent that the landlord could anticipate receiving from a successor tenant. In addition, have the landlord agree to mitigate (minimize) damages by making a best effort or, at a minimum, a reasonable effort to relet the premises at comparable rent. Then, if you face a $40,000 rent bill because you have moved out in the first year of a five-year lease, your bill may be lowered or dropped if the landlord finds a tenant to take your place.

Although some states require landlords to mitigate damages without express language, you should insist upon incorporating this protective language. If a lease contains a liquidated damages clause (that is, a fixed dollar amount if you default), insist upon its deletion unless it is small.

Alterations and Improvements

Try to reserve the right to make nonstructural alterations or improvements to the premises subject to the landlord's reasonable requirements and approval. The landlord may require builder's risk insurance, a qualified contractor, building permits, and a waiver of any mechanic's lien; the landlord may also ask you not to change the general character of the premises.

Assignment and Subletting

Most leases prohibit a tenant from assigning the lease or subletting the premises. Sometimes this is an absolute prohibition; other times, the landlord's consent is required. Note that a transfer of controlling interest in a corporate tenant (for example, a transfer of 50 percent or more of the voting stock) may be considered an assignment.

Make sure you have the right to assign or sublease with the landlord's consent and that consent can't be unreasonably delayed more than 30 days or withheld altogether. Specify reasonable conditions for assignment or subletting that are fair to the landlord and with which you and your transferee can comply. Try to provide that on assignment you are released from any further obligations under the lease.

Otherwise, you end up being a guarantor of the assignee's obligations under the lease. In addition, negotiate a provision that the assignee may use the premises for any lawful purpose provided the use doesn't conflict with any exclusive use previously granted by the landlord to any other existing tenant in the building.

Attorney Fees

Most standard leases require you to pay the landlord's attorney fees and costs if the landlord sues you. This one-sided provision isn't fair and should be made reciprocal. Therefore, you should insist upon a prevailing party attorney fees provision whereby the successful party (either you or the landlord) in any suit concerning the lease or its interpretation would be entitled to the payment of its attorney fees and costs by the losing party. Alternatively, provide that each side pays its own attorney fees no matter what.

Audit by Landlord

Some leases give the landlord the right to audit the books and records of the tenant, most frequently when the tenant's rent is a percentage of the tenant's gross sales, called "percentage rent." If you won't pay percentage rent, this provision is unnecessary, intrusive, and should be deleted. If the landlord retains the right to audit, make sure the lease provides that the expense is the landlord's unless the audit reveals at least a 2 percent deficiency. You don't want to have to pay for an audit if your 1 percent discrepancy is the result of a simple error, but you may need to if the landlord uncovers a larger discrepancy that may indicate an intent to deceive. Also provide that the results of the audit remain confidential except in connection with financing, the sale of a shopping center, tax proceedings, and other legal requirements.

Broker

If neither you nor the landlord has retained a broker, state so in the lease. If you and/or the landlord used a broker, provide that the landlord pays the brokerage commission.

Commencement Date

The commencement date is the date on which you begin to pay rent. Examine the commencement date clause closely. Because the premises may not be ready for occupancy when you sign the lease—the building or shopping center is under construction or the existing tenant hasn't vacated on time—make sure to reserve the right to terminate the lease, get your deposit back, and go elsewhere if the landlord fails to deliver the premises to you by a certain date (called the "drop-dead" date). Furthermore, you should provide that whether or not you are in possession of the premises, rent will not begin until a certain anchor tenant opens for business or until a certain percentage of the building or shopping center is occupied by tenants. Try to negotiate a delay in paying rent for 60 to 90 days while any tenant improvements are being made.

Condemnation

It may seem unlikely that a governmental unit would seize a substantial portion of a building or shopping center, but new highways or wider roads have a way of eliminating condemnation as merely an academic exercise. You should ensure that you retain your rights to all damages that may be awarded a tenant in the event that your premises, building, or shopping center is condemned. Even though you may end up negotiating whether you or the landlord retains the award for the value of the leasehold in the event of a short-term lease, you should *not* negotiate damages for relocation, loss of business, or other costs that you may have a right to recover from the condemning authority. For the possiblity of a partial taking, have a provision in which the landlord and its lender agree to use the condemnation proceeds to reconfigure the center and premises if feasible.

Condition of the Premises

Because most leases provide for the tenant to accept the premises "as is," make sure you thoroughly inspect the premises first. You may want to hire a building inspector and give the landlord an inspection report or "punch list" of items that need repair before you take occupancy. If equipment is included, it should be in good working order at the time you take possession. Have the landlord warrant that the premises comply with all applicable building codes, including the Americans with Disabilities Act.

Contingencies

Once you sign the lease you become obligated to the landlord—unless your lease contains contingencies or "out clauses" that describe conditions under which you may cancel the lease. For example, if you require financing to build out or improve the interior of the premises or to otherwise operate the business, you need to negotiate a financing contingency providing that if you cannot obtain your necessary financing, you can terminate the lease and get back any money you previously paid the landlord. If the property is presently not zoned for your intended use, you need to provide that if you are unable to obtain rezoning or a variance, or if you cannot obtain a building permit, you can terminate the lease and get back any money you paid the landlord.

Cost-of-Living Adjustment

Many leases provide for rent increases based on increases in the Consumer Price Index (CPI), which the U.S. Department of Labor uses to measure inflation. Try to negotiate a period of time (three to five years) before the first increase as well as a ceiling or cap on the increase—but be prepared to give the landlord a floor on a decrease to protect its income in case the CPI suddenly plummets.

Covenant of Quiet Enjoyment

Under a covenant of quiet enjoyment, the landlord promises you that your rights under the lease will not be disturbed by claims against your landlord. In effect, it promises that as long as you live up to the terms of your agreement, you are entitled to occupy your space no matter what. Such a provision is essential to prevent your lease from being canceled or affected by a mechanic's lien or foreclosure action against your landlord.

Damage by Fire or Other Casualty

If your premises or a substantial portion of your building or shopping center is damaged by fire or other casualty, the landlord should agree to a proportionate abatement (i.e., cessation) of rent and common area maintenance (CAM) charges. The abatement should continue until the premises or common areas have been rebuilt or repaired and you are operational again. Some language should be included requiring the landlord and its lender to use any insurance proceeds to repair or rebuild the premises or the common areas unless 50 percent or more has been damaged or destroyed. Review the landlord's mortgage to make sure the lender cannot apply insurance proceeds against the loan instead of giving it to the landlord to rebuild the building.

Because you may lose employees and customers while you are closed, retain the right to cancel the lease if the rebuilding is not completed within a realistic time frame (such as six months) and your business is adversely affected. Alternatively, the landlord should be limited in its right to cancel the lease. Landlords often retain the right to terminate the lease if a casualty occurs during the last three years of the lease. Limit this right to the final year of the lease term.

Default by Landlord or Tenant

A default is a breach of the lease by one of the parties. Many leases don't address the possibility of default under the lease by the landlord—because the lease was drafted by the landlord's attorney! You need to add a provision covering the possiblity of the landlord's default in order to have some recourse if the landlord fails to provide utilities, signage, lighting, maintenance, and other services.

A lease almost always contains a laundry list of ways the tenant can default under the lease. To protect yourself, insist on a 10-day grace period before the late payment of rent and other charges are deemed a default. All other obligations should have a minimum 30-day period before a failure to perform is considered to be a default under the lease provided you are given written notice detailing the nature of the default and what steps should be taken to correct it. The period should be longer if the nature of the default is such that it cannot be reasonably cured within 30 days provided you start and diligently work to correct it within the 30-day period.

With respect to bankruptcy or insolvency proceedings, the time frame for dismissing, discontinuing, or vacating the proceeding should be at least 90 days. In any event, the landlord may be limited by the federal Bankruptcy Code and by the actions of a bankruptcy court in pursuing its rights under the lease.

Description and Size of the Premises

Make certain that the lease contains a clear and unambiguous description of the premises to be leased (i.e., demised premises in legal language). The size of the premises should at least equal the net leasable square feet exclusive of common areas required by, and compatible with, the franchisor's basic floor plan.

Entire Agreement

Most leases have a clause near their end, usually in the "Miscellaneous" or "General" section, which states that the lease represents the entire agreement between the landlord and the tenant. Legally referred to as an "integration" or "merger provision," it clarifies that any oral representations, promises, or understandings by the landlord or its leasing representatives not specifically included in writing in the lease are not enforceable or binding on the landlord. Thus, it is critical that any promises by the landlord or agents that are important to you and are reasons why you have decided to enter in the lease *must* be included in the lease or its addendum. To be binding, everything must be in black and white.

Estoppel Certificate

An estoppel certificate is a letter from a tenant or a landlord to a third party confirming certain details about the lease, such as its term, rent, prepaid rent, security deposit, the existence of any default, and so on. Once you send an estoppel letter, you are estopped, or prevented, from saying the information you put in the letter was wrong. Lenders and prospective purchasers of the property may require estoppel letters from the landlord's tenants before they lend money or buy the property. Someone assuming a tenant's interest in a lease as part of a franchise purchase may require an estoppel letter from the landlord.

Make the obligation to give an estoppel letter mutual. In other words, on a reasonable request you'll give one to the landlord and the landlord will give one to you. Don't agree to appoint the landlord as your attorney-in-fact for executing estoppel certificates or other confirmatory documentation. As your attorney-in-fact, your landlord can act without your knowledge and draft an estoppel certificate that is inaccurate and against your best interests.

Exclusivity

Whenever you lease space in a multistore property or from a landlord who owns several nearby buildings, you can and should negotiate exclusivity for the sale of your products and/or services. You don't want a competitor next door or in the same center. Most landlords will agree to an exclusivity provision that is specific and reasonable. Try to negotiate a radius for exclusivity if the same landlord owns other buildings or strip centers in close proximity to your premises. Although it is more difficult to convince a major mall developer to grant exclusivity, it may be possible to limit the number and location of competitors within the mall to protect the integrity and viability of your franchise business.

Expansion Rights for Additional Space

Consider negotiating an option for adjacent space or a right of first refusal for the space to give you flexibility in expanding next door. While you may not be able to get an option, a right of first refusal is not uncommon. In this event, when the landlord finds a prospective tenant for the space, you will have a short period of time (for example, 10 to 30 days) to elect to take over the space. If you fail to elect at that time, the landlord is free to lease the space to the third party.

Force Majeure

Force majeure, as noted in Chapter 9, means a superior or irresistible force and usually refers to acts beyond the control of the parties, such as riots or earthquakes, floods, and other acts of God. If a force majeure provision does not appear in the lease, suggest that it be added to protect the interests of both parties. If the provision is solely in favor of the landlord, insist that it be made mutual so you also benefit.

Free Rent

Try to negotiate a period of free rent, particularly if there is a period when your business is under construction and not open for business (see "Commencement Date above").

Guaranty of Tenant's Obligations

Try to have your corporation be the tenant and avoid giving your personal guarantee on the lease. The landlord has probably limited its own liability (see "Nonrecourse against Landlord" below); you want to limit your own as well. It may not be possible to avoid signing the personal guarantee and becoming individually responsible for the lease. If a personal guarantee is required, try to limit it to the first year or two of the lease. Don't let your spouse sign the guarantee with you; doing so will expose most of your joint personal assets.

Hazardous Substances and Waste

Under federal and state environmental laws you may be held liable for hazardous substances, including hazardous wastes present *before* you take occupancy. Consider asking an environmental inspection firm to conduct an environmental audit so you know what you are getting into. You should insist upon indemnification by the landlord for any existing hazardous condition at the time of delivery of the premises or for any hazardous substances that might be brought into or onto the premises during the term of the lease by the landlord, its agents, employees, or contractors. You may be required to make similar representations and indemnification to the landlord while you are in possession of the premises.

Holdover Rent

A holdover is a situation in which the tenant continues to occupy the premises after a lease has expired without signing a new lease. If the lease contains a provision setting the rent during any holdover period, the holdover rent should be limited to 150 percent of the base rent only, as opposed to 200 percent or even 300 percent that some leases provide.

Hours of Operation

Make sure that the building or shopping center is open when you are open—particularly the common areas, stairways, and elevators important for your traffic. Ask the landlord to state the hours of operation in the lease. Make sure your hours of operation under the lease are consistent with your franchise agreement. Make sure the parking areas remain lighted at least until you close (see "Parking" below).

Indemnification

Indemnification, as explained in Chapter 9, means a promise by one party to reimburse another party for a loss through payment, replacement, or repair. Most leases are completely one-sided, requiring the tenant to fully indemnify the landlord for all liability of any form or fashion. Renegotiate this provision so that the landlord must indemnify you and your agents, employees, and contractors from any action or inaction on the part of the landlord, its agents, employees, or contractors based on negligence or a willful act that results in a claim, suit, demand, or judgment for liability, including hazardous waste.

Ingress and Egress

Look at the site plan of the building or shopping center. Can your customers get to your business easily? Where are the curb cuts? Do you have or need an easement over another portion of the property or someone else's property to get to the main highway? If so, get the landlord's assurances in writing, backed up by appropriate documentation.

Insurance by Landlord and Tenant

If the landlord is to carry property and casualty insurance, make sure the lease provides that the landlord maintains adequate amounts. Ask to see copies of its insurance policies to make sure they are in force.

A provision will also require *you* to maintain certain insurance throughout the term of the lease for your and the landlord's benefit. Ask your insurance agent to review the insurance provisions first and tell you whether the coverage is reasonable and how much it is likely to cost. In all likelihood your insurance agent will be required to give the landlord a certificate of insurance as well as a copy of the policy.

It may be in your interest and the landlord's to insert a provision regarding waiver of subrogation whereby either party's insurer may not file suit against the other party in an attempt to recover losses caused through the negligence of a party. Also check the terms of the landlord's mortgage to see whether it allows insurance proceeds to be applied to the loan rather than to rebuilding the property at the option of the lender. If so, try to get it changed. As for bonding during the construction period, most landlords will delete this unnecessary expense from the body of the lease.

Landlord's Consent or Approval

Many provisions in the lease require the landlord's consent or approval. You don't want the landlord to be able to act arbitrarily. Require that in all cases the landlord's consent or approval will not be unreasonably withheld or delayed. Thirty days is a reasonable time for any decision to be made! Also, where the approval of a governmental body is required—for example, for signage—add a short, separate paragraph at the end of the lease that provides the landlord automatically approves whatever the governing body approves.

Landlord's Contractor

If the lease requires you to use the landlord's contractor, then include a requirement that the contractor charge reasonable fees customary for the locality. It would be better to have several approved contractors so you can get competitive bids.

Landlord's Lien

Try to include a provision that the landlord will not be granted any security interest in, or lien on, your leasehold improvements and equipment. Many state laws grant the landlord a statutory lien on a tenant's personal property located in the premises as security for the tenant's obligations. At a minimum, the landlord must agree to subordinate its security interest or lien in such improvements and equipment to the entity or entities that have provided, or will provide, you with financing. Certain landlords try to insist that such subordination be limited to the initial financing of the business, but this sharply limits your ability to obtain subsequent financing to refurbish or expand business operations. Check your franchise agreement to see if you have granted your franchisor a security interest. You need to sort out the conflicting desires of your landlord, your franchisor, and your lender to be in the position of top priority.

Landlord's Maintenance Obligations

Obtain a general obligation of the landlord to keep the common areas of the building or shopping center up to a specified standard, such as "first class," or "in a good and sightly condition consistent with commercial retail developments of like nature." Include exterior painting, landscaping, parking areas, and walkways. You'll pay for the upkeep of these areas, so you should have a voice in this important matter.

Landlord's Right of Access

Most leases give the landlord the right to enter the premises at any time without prior notice to repair, inspect, or show the space to prospective tenants or buyers. Limit the landlord's right of access during normal business hours and only on reasonable notice (except for emergencies) so that you and your business are not unduly disrupted. If the landlord maintains an easement for pipes, cables, wires, and the like, respect its need to access such equipment. Don't modify your premises in a way that makes it hard to repair equipment that may be above the ceiling.

Seek to limit the landlord's right to display For Rent signs at the premises during the final three to six months of the lease term. This practice—particularly in strip malls and on-street locations—can adversely affect your business during the final months of occupancy.

Late Charges

Most leases allow landlords to impose a late charge on tenants that pay their rent late. Try to include a five-day to ten-day grace period before a late charge is imposed. Try to eliminate a percentage charge (for example, 5 percent of the outstanding amount) or a fixed fee (for example, $100 a day), which can be excessive, in favor of an interest charge, which is typically benchmarked to current bank or credit card rates on a per annum basis.

Leasehold Improvements

Leasehold improvements refer to the construction of the interior of the premises, including walls, shelving, flooring, partitions, and so on. Closely scrutinize provisions covering your obligations and the landlord's obligations with respect to leasehold improvements. Secure a signed, detailed work letter that specifies which work you will do and which work the landlord will do, and refer to the letter in the attachment to your lease. Include a date after which, if landlord improvements are incomplete, you have the right to terminate the lease or impose certain penalties such as a per diem charge against the landlord.

In an overbuilt real estate market, you may have more leverage. If the landlord has 20 vacant storefronts, you may be able to require it to contribute toward your costs or to obtain a loan for the improvements on your behalf.

Any "as is" provision within the lease whereby you are deemed to accept the condition of the premises at occupancy should be subject to the completion and correction of your "punch list" (see "Condition of the Premises"). Try not to pay rent until the leasehold improvements are completed. Also make sure the landlord agrees to review and approve your plans and specifications promptly and not unreasonably withhold or delay its consent. Be certain to incorporate language stating that delays in the landlord's construction and delivery of possession automatically extend the period of time within which you must complete your leasehold improvements.

Leasehold Title Insurance Policy

In addition to a landlord's warranty of title and covenant of quiet enjoyment (see above), you may want to consider obtaining a leasehold title insurance policy ensuring your interest under the lease, and perhaps requiring the landlord to supply the policy at its expense. If the lease is for a long period of time and for a significant rental amount, you want to be sure that the landlord is owner of the property and no encumbrances or liens exist that may affect your tenancy.

Maintenance and Repair

Specify who has what obligations for maintenance and repair. Try to make the landlord responsible for the structural elements and common areas (see "Landlord's Maintenance Obligations").

Minimum Rent

Verify the square footage and percentage of building figures before you sign. Landlords and their staffs often make errors.

"Most Favored Tenant" Clause

A "most favored tenant" clause is a provision whereby the landlord agrees that you will pay lower rent (usually on a square foot, yearly basis) if another tenant in the building is charged a lower rent, thus allowing you to benefit if rents fall after you sign the lease. You must be in a superior bargaining position with the landlord to obtain this difficult-to-get provision.

Nonrecourse against Landlord

Many newer leases include a provision that the tenant's recourse against the landlord (that is, a claim for damages against the landlord) is limited to the landlord's equity in the building or shopping center and the landlord is not personally liable for its obligations. If the building or shopping center is mortgaged and the landlord has little or no equity in it, you'll be out of luck. Try your best to eliminate a nonrecourse provision or at least exclude the landlord's willful acts or negligence from the provision. You should also cite such a provision in trying to negotiate the elimination of any personal guarantee of the tenant's obligation (described above).

Notices

If receipted hand delivery constitutes notice to the tenant, then receipted hand delivery should constitute notice to the landlord. In addition, the notice provision should also include receipted overnight delivery as an acceptable means of delivering notice. If you are a franchisee, your franchise agreement may provide that a dual and contemporaneous notice from the landlord should be sent to both the franchisor and you at the premises.

Option to Purchase

If you want the right to purchase the building at a specified price at, or for, some specified time, negotiate an option to purchase the property in a separate legal contract. An option to buy will typically not appear in a lease for a strip mall or shopping center.

Option to Renew

Make sure your right to renew is on the same terms contained in the lease except perhaps for a reasonable change in rent. In other words, you want to occupy the same premises and enjoy the same privileges, but you will pay $12 a square foot (for example) instead of $10.

Other Landlord Covenants

Covenants, or promises, are scattered throughout the lease. Some of the promises you should obtain from the landlord include a covenant that your use under all zoning and other governmental regulations applicable to the premises is permitted, and a covenant of title to the property on which the premises are located. Ask your attorney to identify areas in which a covenant might be a good idea.

Parking

What are the parking arrangements for your employees and customers? The parking rights of other tenants? Do you have exclusive parking spaces? Are there covered or underground parking spaces? Is there a monthly fee associated with any exclusive parking spaces? Is the parking area adequately lighted, and when do the lights operate? What about handicapped parking? These are important issues; button them down in writing.

Percentage Rent

Percentage rent is rent or additional rent that is based on a percentage of your gross sales. Verify the percentage rent and breakpoint figures. Make sure that the language detailing when percentage rent is paid is clear. Some leases contain language that could be construed to require payment of percentage rent from the first dollar earned rather than from sales above the breakpoint figure. Make sure you and the landlord agree on the definition of "gross sales." If percentage rent is collected, be certain that the definition of gross sales is limited to sales made from the premises and does not include sales from other locations. If no percentage rent is collected, then gross sales need not be reported to the landlord.

If the lease contains language requiring an audit or preparation and certification of an annual financial statement by an independent certified public accountant, require instead that you certify the accuracy of the statement and thus save accounting fees. If reports of your gross sales are to be submitted to the landlord, then add a provision by which the landlord agrees to maintain your sales figures in confidence except in connection with financing, the sale of the shopping center, tax proceedings, and other legal requirements. Landlords can be quite free about sharing their tenants' confidential sales figures.

Plans and Specifications

Require the landlord to agree to review your plans and specifications promptly and not withhold or delay their approval unreasonably. It is also advisable to include an acknowledgment by the landlord that you are part of a national franchise system and that its design and trade dress, including signage and colors, are in accordance with a prescribed design program.

Radius Restriction

If you are an area developer or otherwise have a right to open additional franchises in the area, radius restriction language prohibiting a tenant from operating another unit within a defined radius of the shopping center can be unduly limiting. Unfortunately, this issue is among the most difficult to negotiate. Landlords may insist on outlandish limitations of five miles or more, particularly if percentage rent is involved. In areas experiencing tremendous population growth, a radius restriction of a mile or more can prohibit rapid growth in concentrated areas. A restaurant in a regional mall food court may not be in competition with a freestanding unit in another location owned by the same landlord! Try to agree on distances that take into account the long-term potential for, and your obligation to open, additional franchise sites.

The penalty for a violation of the radius restriction may include injunctive relief and the payment of percentage rent on all sales made at a secondary location operated in violation of the restriction. In other words, even though your landlord does not own the premises where your new outlet is located, it may be due a percentage of all sales made there.

Real Estate Taxes

A tenant should only pay taxes for the portion it leases of the total leasable square footage of the shopping center or building. Make sure the total leasable square footage figure includes the landlord's unleased spaces. Unless they are taxed separately, anchor stores or stores with greater bargaining power should not have their square footage deducted from the equation. Be certain that the base year and month for determining tax escalation coincides with commencement of the lease if taxes are paid on increases assessed after the commencement date.

Reports and Records

If your lease doesn't provide for percentage rent, then any provision requiring you to give the landlord financial reports and records should be deleted as unnecessary. If the landlord insists on your financial reports and records, make sure the lease provides that the landlord will keep this information confidential.

Right of First Refusal

If you can't negotiate an option to purchase, the landlord may agree to a right of first refusal—the right to match an offer made by a third party when that offer is made. However, you won't know what the price is or when the offer will be made until it is made, and you will only have 10 to 30 days to make up your mind. If you don't exercise it, the right is gone. The right of first refusal can be in the lease or in a separate legal contract.

Right of Setoff against Rent

Most leases specifically provide that the tenant's obligations to pay rent is independent of any obligation of the landlord. Although it will be difficult, try to negotiate for the right to perform the landlord's repair and maintenance obligations if it fails or refuses to do them and the right to set off any sums you expend against rent or other monetary obligations under the lease. In many instances this will be your only sufficient remedy in the event the landlord fails to perform. The landlord should be offered reasonable notice and an opportunity to remedy the problem before you are able to exercise the right.

Rules and Regulations

Review closely the rules and regulations of the building or shopping center before you sign the lease. If these rules have yet to be adopted but are referenced within the lease, insist on seeing them or even helping draft them. Insist that all rules and regulations be reasonable, nondiscriminatory, and uniformly enforced and applied against all tenants and the landlord.

Sales Tax

Determine if sales tax is due on the rent and who pays (usually the tenant). For instance, Florida charges a 6 percent sales tax on commercial rents.

Security Deposit and Prepaid Rent

Many landlords want two months' base rent paid in advance plus a security deposit usually equal to one month's base rent. Do not pay more. The landlord's lender probably prohibits any more than this in the mortgage documents. Try to negotiate the elimination of a security deposit or the extra months' rent. Alternatively, have the security deposit placed in a separate interest-bearing account for your benefit and/or have the security deposit returned in a year after faithful performance on your part.

Services and Utilities

Verify what utilities are available and if they are sufficient for your particular needs. Do hookups need to be provided and, if so, who pays for them? If utility impact fees are assessed, how much are they and who pays them? Who pays for utilities, janitorial services, and pest control?

Become familiar with your electrical service needs. Negotiate for increased service to the premises at the landlord's expense, and always require the landlord to bring all utilities into the premises. Landlords often require the tenant to bring (and pay for the privilege of bringing) mechanical services to the premises. The costs for bringing services to the premises from the landlord's main mechanical room can be substantial and can add unnecessarily to the cost for leasehold improvements.

Try to install separate electric and water meters instead of paying utilities per square foot, a method utilized by many landlords. Make sure that payment for electrical service is not based on the landlord's perceived estimate of your use. In essence, the landlord calculates the tenant's use based on 24 hours a day, 7 days a week of the tenant's installed heating, ventilating, and air-conditioning (HVAC) and equipment, figured on 100 percent capacity. The net result of such a provision is that your electric charges can be significantly higher than your actual usage.

The HVAC language must also be scrutinized in conjunction with your architect. Regional malls generally provide access to a universal HVAC system but may limit the amount of service. Food court tenants with ovens, grills, and refrigeration equipment that generate heat should negotiate an increase in the level of service the landlord provides. In strip mall centers that require you to install your own HVAC equipment or additional HVAC equipment, negotiate for access to the roof and the ability to make cuts in the roof without the landlord's consent.

Signage

Make sure that your franchisor's standard signage and graphics requirements are permitted under the lease. Have the landlord agree that it will approve your signage if it is approved by the appropriate local government authority. Make sure you are included on any centerwide pylon signage or directory signs.

Subordination, Nondisturbance, and Attornment

In all likelihood the landlord borrowed money to construct the building or shopping center and has granted one or more mortgages to lenders as security for the loan. The landlord's lease probably provides that your interest under the lease is subordinate and inferior to the interest of any mortgagees under any mortgages that exist now or may be placed on the property later.

Having a covenant of quiet enjoyment is not enough to protect you if your landlord defaults on its mortgage. As a condition to agreeing to this provision, demand a nondisturbance agreement whereby the landlord's mortgagees will recognize your rights under the lease and not disturb you in the event of foreclosure of the building or center so long as you are not in default under the terms of the lease. Otherwise, if the landlord fails to pay its lender and the lender forecloses, the lender can include you in the foreclosure suit and you can be evicted from the premises or be subject to a higher rent or other more onerous terms even though you were never in default under the lease!

Surrender of the Premises; Removal of Trade Fixtures

Agree in advance which fixtures, furnishings, machinery, equipment, and other personal property are yours and which are your landlord's. Be certain that the provision covering surrender of the premises enables you to remove without recourse all trade fixtures and other property you own. Don't agree that you have to restore the premises to their original condition. Generally, the landlord will require a provision that a tenant agrees to repair any damage caused by the removal of the trade fixtures. At the expiration or termination of the lease (other than as the result of your default), you must be allowed two or three days to remove your equipment, fixtures, and inventory following receipt of a written notice from the landlord of the expiration or termination.

Tangible Commercial Property Taxes

Check to see whether your state imposes an annual *ad valorem* tax on property used in business, a tax similar to a real estate tax. If it does, find out how much the tax will be. Does the lease provide for the landlord or the tenant to pay the tax? Usually, this is a tenant obligation, so you need to include this expense in your budget.

Term

The initial term of the lease must match the term provided in the franchise agreement. A shorter initial term with liberal renewal provisions will satisfy this requirement.

Triparty Agreement between You, the Landlord, and Your Franchisor

Because the franchisor has an interest in keeping the leased location if you default under your lease, the franchise agreement may contain a provision to the effect that a default under the lease constitutes a default under your franchise agreement (a "cross-default" provision). Normally, the franchise agreement stipulates that the following provisions be included in your lease or in an agreement signed by you, the landlord, and the franchisor:

- The franchisor's right to receive notices of your default under the lease
- The franchisor's right (but not the obligation) to correct any default
- The franchisor's right to assign the lease to another franchisee
- The franchisor's right to protect its interest under the franchise agreement, including entry to the premises and removal of signage
- The franchisor's right to consent to any material modification to the lease
- The obligation of the landlord to make available to the franchisor sales reports or other data that you make available to the landlord

Use and Operation

Leases will vary markedly in the obligations they place on a tenant's use and operations. Be certain that the lease does not limit nonselling space unreasonably. Because you may require significant space for office use and storage of inventory, you should not be limited by specific percentages. If your business is a restaurant, delete any language limiting the release of food odors, particularly if the restaurant is located outside the confines of a food court. If such a clause is included, adjacent tenants can make life difficult for a food-service tenant that must necessarily emit food odors in the course of its operation. In addition, be familiar with your floor-load needs. If they are unusually high, be certain to require the landlord to specify that the load-bearing capacity of the floor is sufficient for your needs or to make the necessary improvements if possible.

Use of Common Areas

The landlord should be restricted in its right to change freely the access to and through the common areas, the addition or removal of structures within the common areas, and the access to, and use of, the parking areas if any such changes will affect the access or visibility of your premises. These changes might include a relocation of access to the shopping center that could eliminate the flow of traffic passing your premises, the construction of kiosks or fountains and the like that could eliminate, or substantially block, the visibility of your premises and signage, and the elimination of proximate parking, which could be a major deterrent for customer traffic, particularly in strip mall locations. Most landlords will grant some language limiting their ability to affect access to, or visibility of, your premises.

Use of the Premises

The use clause should be drafted as broadly as possible. A broad "permitted uses" provision permits greater marketability if subletting or reassignment becomes necessary.

Use of Trade Name

The landlord may try to restrict you to using the trade name authorized in the franchise agreement. What if the franchisor changes the trade name? What if you leave the franchise system and operate independently under a different name? Make sure the lease does not restrict your use of a particular trade name.

Waiver of Trial by Jury

Many leases contain a waiver of your right to have a jury decide issues of fact in the event of a trial. Although some landlord-tenant actions are decided by a judge in a summary eviction proceeding (for example rent payment deficiencies or nonpayment of rent with no counterclaim), you should not agree to a jury waiver provision.

Visibility

Visibility from the street can be crucial to the success of certain businesses. If the lease allows the landlord to alter the common areas, including the parking lot, make sure that the landlord cannot construct improvements that may affect your visibility without your consent.

Zoning; Restrictive Covenants

Don't just rely on the landlord's or its agent's representation that the zoning for the building allows your type of operation. You, your contractor, or other advisor should check directly with the city or county zoning department to make sure your use of the premises is within the property's current zoning classification. Review any restrictive covenants that may affect your usage. If the property is not properly zoned, you'll need to obtain rezoning or a variance from the municipality and/or county before you take occupancy.

Lease Provisions for Shopping Centers and Strip Malls

Anchor Stores

An anchor store is a large department store, supermarket, or other retailer that draws consumers to a shopping center or mall. In a brand-new mall or shopping center, a delay in the opening of anchor stores may adversely affect your business initially. If this is a possibility, negotiate a substantially reduced base rent and eliminate the payment of any percentage rent. Try to negotiate paying only a straight percentage rent for the period from your opening until the opening of the anchor store or stores.

If your premises are located in an older center that has experienced a loss of tenants, a reduced rent should be negotiated if one or more anchors close or if a significant percentage of nonanchor tenants go out of business and their premises remain unleased. Fewer operating stores inevitably means fewer customers for you.

It's a good idea to delete a provision for increasing the base rent if additional anchor stores open during the lease term. New anchor stores built onto outlying sections of a shopping center rarely generate increased foot traffic for the smaller tenant, so no rationale exists for increasing your base rent.

Merchant's Association and Advertising

Some leases require you to join a merchant's association composed of all the tenants in a shopping center that engage in collective advertising activities. Before signing, determine your probable contributions to the merchant's association and weigh them against benefits you may derive. If the association is inactive, you may wish to resist having to join unless you're placed on the governing board of the association. You might also wish to strike the membership clause from the lease.

The larger the mall, the more a tenant will be required to contribute to the merchant's fund, seasonal advertising circulars, and print advertising. New or newly renovated shopping centers often impose an initial grand opening advertising charge. These advertising contributions can be unreasonably expensive, particularly if your store is 1,000 square feet or less. If you must make a minimum contribution, tie it to the actual size of the premises. Try to negotiate a cap on annual increases for the merchant's fund and other advertising contributions, and consider negotiating a set-off against such required sums for your individual advertising using that uses the center's name.

If the franchisor requires you to contribute to its regional or national franchise advertising program, have the landlord remove any obligation to expend monies on local advertising or to participate in seasonal advertising circulars. Generally, the landlord will acknowledge that the advertising contributions to the franchisor fulfill the landlord-directed obligations on the part of the tenant to advertise. Alternatively, make sure any payments to the merchant's association are credited against your local advertising requirements under your franchise agreement.

Operating or Common Area Maintenance (CAM) Costs

In some regional mall locations, tenant contributions to operating costs or common area maintenance (CAM) may cost more than the base rent! Tenants located in food courts are assessed additional maintenance fees. Try to negotiate a cap on these contributions either by basing the figure as a percentage of your gross revenues or by establishing a base figure for the first year of the lease and limiting increases to a set percent of the Consumer Price Index (CPI). If the CPI is used, then remember the days of double-digit inflation and cap the CPI increase.

Scrutinize the description of items that comprise CAM fees. Require that the landlord delete those items that are capital expenditures, not expenses, such as replacement (or new construction) of roofs, buildings, parking lots and common areas, major equipment, and mechanical systems. These costs should be amortized over their useful life, not expensed in a single year. Try to negotiate the elimination of a contribution for any significant common area refurbishment or major capital improvement during the final year of the lease term, as you will derive little benefit from these capital costs.

Negotiate a reasonable cap on administrative or management fees, particularly if the management company is affiliated with the landlord. Make sure the management fee is reasonable and is not coupled with an administrative fee, which is just more rent in disguise.

Your proportionate share of total operating costs should be based on the proportion of your premises to the *total* leasable areas in the entire building or center, not just areas actually leased. The landlord, not you, should be responsible for the operating costs of unleased premises. You should also determine whether the center is fully built. If it isn't, consider some type of provision that will limit operating cost increases in the event of additional building out of the center.

All tenants should receive an annual statement showing how CAM fees are computed and how tenant contributions are disbursed. You should also have the right to review the landlord's books and records covering the shopping center to determine the accuracy of the operating costs.

Relocation

Shopping center leases frequently include a provision giving the landlord the right to relocate a tenant to another area within the center. Because this may drastically affect pedestrian traffic, visibility from the highway, and proximity to undesirable tenants, you should steadfastly refuse to have such a provision in the lease even if the landlord promises compensation for unamortized leasehold improvements, moving and design expenses, and comparable rent. If the new location is not as strategically placed or desirable, your sales will suffer in the long run.

Provisions That Relate to a Sublease from the Franchisor

In some franchise systems—McDonald's, Subway, and Carvel are good examples—the franchised sites are controlled by the franchisor. The franchisor either owns the land and leases the premises to you or is the tenant and subleases the premises to you. These arrangements allow the franchise to operate a company-owned outlet or install another franchisee if you default under the lease or franchise agreement and must be terminated as a franchise and/or tenant.

If you will be subleasing from the franchisor, review the lease between the landlord and the franchisor-tenant. This way you'll know exactly what the franchisor's and the landlord's obligations are.

Shell Corporation as Lessor or Sublessor

To limit its liability, a franchisor that owns real estate will often set up a subsidiary or affiliate corporation with few assets to be the lessor or sublessor. Thus, if you as tenant have any claims against the lessor or sublessor, there may be no assets from which to collect on a judgment. Furthermore, the lease or sublease may include a provision barring recourse against the landlord—the nonrecourse provision described earlier.

Administration Fee

Your sublease may include a rent surcharge that compensates the franchisor for its liability under the lease and for its administrative expenses. Try to eliminate this fee; all it does is increase your rent.

Consent of the Landlord

Obtain the written consent of the landlord to the franchisor's subleasing the premises to you.

Notices from the Landlord

Make sure your sublease includes a provision requiring the franchisor to give you copies of all notices it receives from the landlord. Better yet, have the landlord include copy you for all notices sent to the franchisor as tenant.

Pass-Through of the Landlord's Benefits

Have the franchisor pass through all landlord credits, free rent, building allowances, and the like to you, and particularly if you are the initial operating tenant in the premises.

Right to Correct (Cure) the Sublessor's Defaults

In addition to having the landlord give you notice of the franchisor's default, negotiate the right to cure the default and become the primary tenant under the lease. Otherwise, if the franchisor-tenant defaults under its lease and the landlord terminates the lease, your sublease may be automatically extinguished. This is a nondisturbance agreement from the landlord similar to a nondisturbance from the landlord's lender.

CHAPTER 11

Selecting the Best Entity to Own and Operate Your Franchise Business

Keith J. Kanouse

Because you buy and operate a franchise business to earn money—not to lose your investment and expose your personal assets—it is most important to determine the type of business entity that will own and operate your franchise *before* you purchase or open it. The business entity you select will affect a number of issues, including liability, taxes, transferability of interest, ease of financing and capitalization, and the relationship between managers and owners. Selecting the proper business entity will not guarantee the success of your business, but selecting the wrong business entity may contribute to its failure.

Most business owners operate their business under one of the following entities:

- Sole proprietorship
- General partnership
- Limited partnership (a form of general partnership that limits liability and exposure)
- Joint venture
- C corporation (if family has no other income)
- S corporation (if family has income from other sources)

Other forms not as commonly used are:

- Limited liability company
- Registered limited liability partnership

Unfortunately, there is no perfect entity for operating a business. Each has its advantages, disadvantages, and unique qualifications. Each possible type of entity must be explored to determine which makes sense for your particular business situation.

The Business Entity Comparison Chart in Figure 11.1 compares each type of business entity. Business entities are creatures of state law, not federal law. Even though most states have adopted some version of the Uniform Laws approved by the Commissioners on Uniform State Laws regulating business entities (for example, the Uniform Partnership Act, the Uniform Limited Partnership Act, and the Model Business Corporation Act), the Uniform Laws vary from state to state.

Sort out your options with an experienced business attorney and a certified public accountant knowledgeable in tax matters. To determine which business form is best for you, you'll have to consider a number of issues that arise as you form, operate, and dispose of your business. Your tax adviser will help you understand federal and state tax consequences of forming, operating, and disposing of a business entity.

The Ins and Outs of Partnerships

Partnerships are very common in franchising because family members, friends, and other prospective partners are a good source of capital. They can become a source of frustration, however, if the terms of the partnership are not carefully pinned down in advance, which is why two related or unrelated individuals considering a partnership should work with an attorney to draw up a partnership agreement that is signed and witnessed.

Start by hammering out the ground rules of your partnership, keeping in mind points discussed below. When you see eye-to-eye, take your notes to your attorney. If you don't agree on the following issues, think twice about entering into a partnership. If you can't agree now, how will you resolve issues when the going gets rough?

- Make sure each partner understands that the franchise will probably not generate enough income in the first five years to pay back the investment. It's very difficult to take money from a business during its first years. If one partner wants out, the other can't just write a check. The business probably can't afford it, and the bank probably won't allow it because equity is subordinated money that must remain in the business until the bank is paid off. The terms of most bank loans insist that the equity remain in the business. A lump-sum payment won't be possible, so the exiting partner will have to settle for a payment plan.
- Never set up a 50-50 partnership. One of you should have a 51 percent or greater interest, the other a 49 percent or less interest. As franchise owners, you'll need to make decisions quickly. Unless someone has the final vote when partners are deadlocked, you may find your business stifled by your inability to agree. Determine what rights your percentage entitles you to.

FIGURE 11.1 Business Entity Comparison Chart

Issue	Sole Proprietorship	General Partnership	Limited Partnership
Number of owners	Only one	Unlimited (at least two)	Unlimited, must have at least one general partner and one limited partner
Liability	Unlimited personal liability	Joint and several unlimited personal liability	Limited liability only if limited partners do not participate in management; unlimited liability for general partner
Federal income tax	Taxed at individual level	No tax at partnership level	No tax at limited partnership level
Management	By sole proprietor	By all partners	By general partners only to prevent limited partners from losing limited liability
Transferability of interest	Unrestricted—sale or transfer of business assets	Determined by partnership agreement	Determined by limited partnership agreement
Duration	As long as proprietor lives and operates	Indefinite, but may have to terminate earlier on occurrence of certain events (death, bankruptcy) to qualify as partnership for tax purposes	Indefinite, but may have to terminate earlier on occurrence of certain events (death, bankruptcy of a general partner) to qualify as partnership for tax purposes

Issue	Joint Venture	"C" Corporation	"S" Corporation
Number of owners	Unlimited (at least two)	Unlimited	Up to 75 individuals; no corporate, trust (with certain exceptions), or nonresident alien shareholders
Liability	Joint and several unlimited personal liability	Limited liability for shareholders even with shareholder participation in management	Limited liability for shareholders even with shareholder participation in management

FIGURE 11.1 Business Entity Comparison Chart *(Continued)*

Issue	Joint Venture	"C" Corporation	"S" Corporation
Federal income tax	No tax at partnership level	Taxed on both corporate and shareholder level (double taxation)	Generally not taxed at the corporate level
Management	By joint venturers	By board of directors or shareholders	By board of directors or shareholders
Transferability of interests	Determined by joint venture agreement	No restriction but subject to securities law and shareholders' agreement	No restriction but subject to securities law and shareholders' agreement
Duration	Indefinite, but may have to terminate earlier on occurrence of certain events (death, bankruptcy) to qualify as partnership for tax purposes	Perpetual	Perpetual

Issue	Limited Liability Company	Registered Limited Liability Partnership
Number of Owners	Unlimited (but at least two in certain states)	Unlimited (but at least two)
Liability	Limited liability for members even with their management participation	No personal liability of partners for debts of the partnership or the malfeasance or malpractice of other partners
Federal income taxes	Not taxed at the company level; taxed as a partnership (no entity level of taxation)	Not taxed at the partnership level
Management	By member or a manager	By all partners
Transferability of interest	By statute other members must consent or no right to participate in management	Determined by limited liability partnership agreement
Duration	Maximum of 30 years, but may have to terminate earlier on occurrence of certain events in order to qualify as partnership for tax purposes	Indefinite, but may have to terminate earlier on occurrence of certain events (death, bankruptcy) to qualify as partnership for tax purposes

FIGURE 11.2 Influences on Your Choice Business Entity

Formation Phase	Operation Phase	Disposition Phase
Number of participants (stockholders, partners, members)	Management and control	Continuity of life (e.g., the right to pass your business on to your heirs)
Types of participants (individuals, foreigners, trusts, partnerships, corporations)	Personal liability of the participants for the debts of the business	Conveyance and restrictions on conveyance (e.g., selling your business to someone else)
Nature of assets and type of business	Anticipated credit and additional capital needs	Potential estate tax and probate problems for the owners
Special legal requirements or restrictions	Tax consequences of the operation	Tax consequences on the disposition of the business
Ease and cost of formation and operation		
Capital requirements (equity and debt)		
Personal liability of the participants for the debts of the business		
Centralization of management		
Tax consequences on formation		
Securities law issues (e.g., passive investors)		

- Specify how much time each partner is expected to devote to the business and which areas each will be responsible for. Will one handle customer relations and operations, the other accounting and sales? List all the duties that will be required to run the business, and divide them between you. Spelling out duties up front will prevent you from getting in each other's way in the months and years to come.
- Discuss additional financial responsibilities. If the business is losing money, how much additional money is each partner expected to contribute? Losing money is a very real possibility during the first two years.
- What happens if one partner wants out? How will the value of the business be determined when it is time to dissolve the partnership? Trying to buy out a partner in the early years of a business is dangerous. Devise a payment plan that will satisfy both partners. Set a target payback date and an

interest rate. Will payments begin immediately or a year from now? Will they be a fixed monthly figure or a percentage of positive cash flow? Will the interest rate be prime or one point below? Set interest below the market rate to avoid overburdening your business.

- Think about succession, too. What happens if one partner dies and a relative inherits the business; or one partner divorces and loses the business to his or her spouse in the settlement? What happens if one partner becomes incapacitated?

Once you have hammered out all these issues with your prospective partner, take your notes to an attorney who can draft a formal partnership agreement.

Forming and Maintaining Your Business Entity

Once you select your entity, be sure to comply with *all* the formalities required by your form of business. If you decide to incorporate, it's not enough to file such documents as the articles of incorporation. You must also complete bylaws, prepare minutes, have minutes signed by the necessary shareholders and directors, issue stock, complete the stock transfer log, pay any applicable stamp taxes, and adopt appropriate resolutions. If you fail to take these steps, it will be easier for a plaintiff's attorney to "pierce the corporate veil"—that is, you would not be treating your business entity as a separate "person" so it would be easier for a plaintiff's attorney to hold you personally liable for claims against your business.

Compliance with formalities applies to all types of business entities, not just corporations. Comply with all of the legal formalities applicable to the particular business entity, including the following:

- Keep your corporate records current and have your attorney and accountant review them at least annually.
- File all necessary federal and state tax returns (including information returns when the entity does not pay taxes) on or before their respective due dates.
- Sign all contracts as an officer or other authorized representative of the business and not just in your own name. For example:

John Jones, Inc. By:_____
                              John Jones, President

Don't sign or guarantee any business obligation personally.

Transferring a Franchise Agreement to an Entity

Sometimes people buy a franchise personally and decide, after signing the franchise agreement, to incorporate. The franchisor will usually allow you to transfer the franchise agreement to a corporation or other entity provided you remain personally obligated as franchisee to the franchisor for the entity's obligations. The reason the franchisor will agree to this transfer is that it will want you to have the benefit of limited liability and other benefits of a corporation or another entity in your dealings with such third parties as your employees, vendors, customers, and the general public.

The franchise agreement may specify a number of conditions imposed by the franchisor for its consent to the transfer from you to your entity that may include the following:

- You must be the sole, majority, or controlling shareholder or owner of the corporation or other entity.
- The entity must be newly formed and its activities confined exclusively to acting as a franchisee.
- The entity cannot use the franchisor's trade name as part of the entity's name but may use the franchisor's trade name as part of the entity's fictitious assumed name or trade name.
- The entity must specifically assume your obligations under the franchise agreement.
- You must remain personally liable under the franchise agreement. The franchisor may require you to sign a guarantee.
- All stock certificates or other evidence of ownership interests must contain a legend putting third parties (prospective buyers) on notice of the restrictions on transfer contained in the franchise agreement.

You'll probably find it difficult to get the franchisor to agree to an assignment from yourself to your business entity releasing you from personal liability under the franchise agreement. Try to compromise by agreeing to remain personally obligated for the confidentiality and noncompetition covenants but not for the monetary obligations of the assignee entity as franchisee.

Fictitious Name, Trade Name, or Assumed Name Registration

You eat at Joe's Restaurant. Who is Joe? If you wanted to contact the person or entity who owns Joe's Restaurant, how would you go about it? Most states require some sort of central registration of a business name so people can find out who owns the business.

If you own and operate a business as a sole proprietor and you use your full name as the name of your business (for example, Joe Smith's Restaurant), you probably don't have to do anything. If you own and operate your business as a business entity (other than a general partnership in a state where there is no registration of the partnership agreement) and use the complete entity name as the business name, the entity's name is registered as part of the organization process.

If, however, you own and operate your business as a general partnership or under a name different from your full name or the complete legal name of your entity, then you probably need to comply with your state's fictitious name, trade name, or assumed name statute. This may entail giving some sort of notice to the general public by way of a legal advertisement and/or registering with the county where the principal place of business is located or with the secretary of your state.

Most franchise agreements don't allow you to use the franchisor's trade name as part of your corporate or other entity's name (for example, Blockbuster Video of Any Town, U.S.A., Inc.). Instead, you have to comply with your state's fictitious, trade name, or assumed name statute to do business under the franchisor's trade name (for example, John Jones d/b/a Blockbuster Video or ABC Inc. d/b/a Blockbuster Video).

Ask your attorney about your state's fictitious name, trade name, or assumed name statute, whether you are subject to the statute, and what needs to be done in order to comply with it.

CHAPTER 12

Where the Money Is and How to Get It

Ann Dugan

Many ways of financing a franchise business are available. This chapter is designed to guide you through the maze of options and help you identify the sources that best meet your needs.

Financial assistance is available from many sources in both the public and private sector. The public sector includes sources provided by federal, state, and local governments. The private sector includes banks, nonbank lenders, and financial institutions as well as businesses and associations that are set up solely to lend money. Your franchisor may have a lending arrangement with a preferred provider who will quickly approve your loan, although not often at the lowest cost.

Always comparison shop before you commit. Fee structures are different for each financing sector and may include origination fees, yearly maintenance fees, account monitoring fees, and early payoff penalties and fees as well as many others. These fees are in addition to the most obvious cost of borrowing: the interest rate. Make sure that you understand the *total* cost of borrowing before you sign on the dotted line.

To avoid being pressured into accepting the fastest, most costly deal, start your analysis of potential financing sources early in your franchise investigation. And remember, your business plan—discussed in Chapter 13—is your admission ticket to the lending process.

Debt Financing versus Equity Financing

There are two ways to finance a business: with debt or with equity. In debt financing, which includes equipment loans, mortgages, leases, and bonds, the owner borrows someone else's money and agrees to pay back the principal with interest. Many times the lender will require the debt to be secured by one or more assets for which the financing is obtained. For example, if you borrow money to buy equipment, your lender will secure that equipment. If you default on the loan, the lender will seize and sell your equipment to cover the loss. Often, lenders also require you to secure a loan with your personal assets: the equity in your home, jewelry, an art collection, stocks and bonds, and other assets.

The main advantage of debt financing is that you retain complete ownership of your franchise business and need not share profits or decisions with partners. The biggest disadvantage is the potential for overleveraging. When a business is overleveraged, it has too little equity and has debt payments that are too high for the business to support.

In equity financing, you sell a portion of your ownership in the franchise business to someone who shares control of the business—an operating partner, a silent partner, or a venture capitalist. Like a marriage, an equity partnership can be a blessing and a curse. On the positive side, a partner can bring complementary skills to the table. A partnership in which one person is strong in finance, accounting, and operations and the other is strong in sales and marketing is likely to be strong. A good partnership can also move the business forward because tasks can be divided between two people instead of burdening only one.

On the downside, a partner will second-guess you. Even a so-called silent partner may feel he or she has the right to know what is going on in the business. A partnership also means that you share the profits of the business, thus lengthening the period before you obtain your income objectives or realize a return on your investment. In addition, the potential for conflict over the business's direction is high.

For advice on structuring a partnership, see Chapter 11.

What Do Lenders Look For?

Lenders have long used formulas or "tools" to ensure that they cover all of the fundamental elements of credit. You can greatly facilitate the lending process by structuring your information to answer questions in four important areas: people, purpose, payment, and protection.

1. *People.* Are you a person of unquestioned integrity, willing to repay under difficult circumstances? How have you handled credit in the past? Do you have a good track record? Prepare explanations for any problems, and bring them to the attention of the lender early. Lenders hate surprises. Some black marks on your credit history can be overcome but not if you have lied about them or they come as a surprise.
2. *Purpose.* Does the purpose of your loan conform to sound business practices? Does the concept of this franchise and the details of your market as

provided by the business plan make sense? Does the purpose of the loan conform to the risk that the lender is willing to take and the rewards that the lender expects for taking that risk?

3. *Payment.* Is the primary source of repayment adequate to repay the loan? Are the assumptions used in the cash flow projections reasonable? Is the market for the product/service offered by the franchise sufficient and clearly understood for the term of the loan?

4. *Protection.* If the business cannot meet the terms of the loan, is the secondary source of repayment adequate? What other collateral do you have to offer the lender as security? Can the lender secure this additional collateral for the term of the loan?

If your business plan adequately deals with the issues surrounding these four areas, then you should be successful in obtaining the money you need. A strong business plan also will help you negotiate low fees and a favorable interest rate. On the other hand, if your answers indicate weaknesses, it becomes critically important for your business plan to stress your strengths and downplay any weaknesses.

How Much Do You Need?

How much money do you need to start your business? It depends on many factors, including whether you are purchasing a service, retail, or distributor franchise, your location, the current economic and credit market conditions, your inventory, and industry credit policies. Although you will identify these factors as you develop your business plan and financial projections, keep in mind that there are three basic types of costs/expenses you will have to cover: start-up costs, operating costs, and personal living requirements.

Start-Up Costs

Start-up costs begin to be incurred long before you open your doors and receive that first customer dollar. They can include, but are by no means limited to, the initial franchise fee, legal and accounting fees, the real estate purchase and construction, signage and equipment, opening inventory and supplies, and franchisor training. Start-up costs are usually financed through personal savings and capital as well as money borrowed in a term loan that is paid back monthly but amortized over a 5-year to 8-year period. Commercial real estate mortgages are typically for a 15-year to 20-year period.

Operating Costs

Very few franchises open and immediately achieve breakeven—the point at which all of your monthly operating expenses are met by your sales. Until you reach breakeven, you need working capital to operate. How much you need depends upon your sales, the terms of credit that you provide your customers, the amount of inventory that you must carry, and the terms your suppliers extend to you.

Debt retirement is a significant monthly operating cost. The more money you are initially able to put into the franchise and the longer you have to repay your loan, the less you must repay each month. Working capital is usually borrowed in the form of a line of credit that you use only when you need assistance in meeting operating obligations as you build your sales volume to breakeven and eventual profitability.

Personal Living Requirements

Your financial projections as well as your working capital requirements need to include the minimum monthly salary you need to take out of the business. Many potential franchisees overlook this area to their regret. Remember, an owner of any business is the last paid. In the early years of your franchise you may not be able to pay yourself the kind of salary you need to maintain your lifestyle. You can prepare for this situation in two ways. First, start to downsize your personal living requirements before you open for business, or at least evaluate what you can cut quickly should the business not provide your salary requirements. Second, have at least six months of household operating costs in savings.

Applying for a Loan

Applying for a business loan is not the same as applying for a mortgage or a consumer loan. Business lending is a different arena and should be approached in a businesslike manner to secure adequate financing at favorable rates.

Once you have identified the sources to approach for financing, you'll need to prepare for a 30-minute meeting with each prospective lender. Plan to make a brief presentation that covers your plans and summarizes the material in your loan proposal. Your written loan proposal package that you leave with the lender should be well organized and presented in a neat, professional manner. Use a folder or three-ring binder and include a table of contents. Make sure that brochures, fliers, or other exhibits are secured, not loose. Papers that spill all over the place are a no-no. In the package, include

- your business plan;
- the franchise agreement;

- three years of revenue and expense projections (the first year should show monthly projections; the subsequent two years, quarterly projections);
- a personal financial statement and the last three years of your tax returns; and
- any other supporting documents that may persuade your lender.

Lenders may require additional information once they have reviewed your application. Only after all documents are prepared and a complete loan proposal submitted will the lender begin the formal evaluation process. Depending on the size of the loan you requested, the evaluation process could take anywhere from a few days to several months. Start the process early, meet deadlines and requests for additional information in a timely manner, and be prepared to shop around for the best deal.

A well-organized loan application process will accomplish several goals. First, it requires you to research and critically analyze the potential for success of the franchise you're considering, and to present your findings and financial projections to lenders. Second, a good presentation of the business concept and your management capabilities will build your lender's respect and confidence in you. It will show that you pay attention to detail, plan ahead, and communicate well with the franchisor and other important stakeholders.

Numerous agencies are available to assist you in developing your business plan and loan proposal. Your franchisor is also a valuable partner in collecting and building on the information that you need, but unless its corporate headquarters is located nearby, you'll need local assistance with items such as locational analysis, marketing plans, and financing sources.

Small Business Development Centers (SBDCs), operating in a partnership arrangement with the Small Business Administration (SBA), are an excellent source of assistance. These centers are located at colleges and universities throughout the country and for the most part their services are provided at no charge. Call 703-448-6124 to find the SBDC office in your area.

What Type of Financial Information Will Franchisors Provide?

Potential franchisees as well as financiers are often frustrated by the lack of financial information at the operating level that is provided by franchisors. Federal law in this area is very clear. It says simply that a franchisor is under no obligation to provide financial information, but if it does, it must provide it in writing.

Claims about earnings have created controversy through the years and still remain a double-edged sword for franchisors. Franchisors may want to provide information about earnings, but if a particular franchise doesn't meet the claims, it may be sued for misleading franchisees. Conversely, potential franchisees need to be able to forecast results to estimate the business's potential as well as provide forecasts for financing sources.

As a compromise, many franchisors now include gross sales numbers in their disclosure circulars. To protect the privacy of their franchisees, figures are provided in the aggregate or are based on the length of time a franchise has been open. This method seems to satisfy the interests of both franchisor and franchisee. The franchisor protects existing franchisees and is not forced to provide figures that may come back to haunt it; the franchisee has a starting point from which to develop financial projections.

Sources of Financing

The Federal Government

The Small Business Administration (SBA) is the primary advocate of small business within the federal government. Although it provides many services to the small business community, the SBA is best known for its small business loan guarantees.

Through its loan guarantee programs, the SBA provides financing access to small businesses that cannot obtain financing on reasonable terms through normal lending channels—particularly true of start-ups, businesses with insufficient collateral, or businesses that need longer than customary repayment terms. Rather than rejecting these types of loan requests, the lender can ask the SBA to guarantee up to 80 percent of the loan amount, thus reducing the lender's risk of nonpayment and providing the potential business owner with needed capital. Participation in an SBA-guaranteed loan program adds another partner to the transaction, so be prepared for a delay in processing time.

SBA funds are accessed through an approved lender, not directly from the SBA. The SBA can guarantee small business loans made by banks, credit unions, economic development organizations, and other nonbank lenders. Not all lenders, however, have experience in making SBA-guaranteed loans, and some may be unwilling to use the agency because of the extra paperwork required.

Terms and conditions of SBA loans change from time to time, so it is important to understand the current program status early in the process. In addition, the SBA has started to pay careful attention to very restrictive clauses in franchise contracts. In some cases the SBA has declined to participate because of its belief that such contracts unfairly restrain the ability of potential franchisees to be successful. Again, ask early in the process if the franchise under your consideration has had any problems getting SBA-guaranteed loans.

The following federal programs are accessed most often by potential franchisees:

- *7(a) loans*, comprising the most common SBA loan program, guarantee loans up to $750,000 made through approved participants. Personal guarantees are required by the borrowers and personal assets may be required as security.

- *LowDoc* is a general purpose loan guarantee program designed for quick processing of loans of $100,000 or less. It uses a one-page application and focuses on the strength of the applicant's character and credit.
- *FASTRAC* is a general purpose loan guarantee program now in its pilot stage that offers faster processing than other loan programs because the preferred lender does the credit check and approves the loan as a preferred lender under guidelines established by the SBA.
- *Microloans* are offered directly through approved local economic development agencies and top out at $25,000; they have higher interest rates than SBA programs and lending sources.
- *504 loans* are made through local certified economic development agencies. Financing is asset based and tied to job creation. Agencies are limited to 40 percent of the total project but in no case more than $1 million.
- *Prequalification programs* for minorities and women, also in the pilot stage, use local private sector agencies as intermediaries to assist minority and female-owned businesses to prepare their loan applications, review their personal and business credit, conduct a credit analysis, and submit a prequalified application to the SBA. If the SBA approves the prequalification, it issues a letter to the potential borrower containing the SBA's commitment to issue a loan guarantee. The borrower can then take the letter to a commercial lender to apply for an SBA-guaranteed loan of up to $250,000.

State Government

State loan programs that assist in the creation and development of businesses vary from state to state. In general, these programs have limited dollars available, favor manufacturing, and are usually tied to job creation as a requirement for receiving the loan. Check with your local SBDC as well as your state department of commerce for more information.

Local Government

Because the pool of funds available is usually small, local government is often overlooked as a source of financing. However, it can be a way to finance facade improvements, utility enhancements, and landscaping. Check with the authorities in the areas you are considering for information.

Commercial and Private Sector Sources

Commercial banks. Ask the bank that handles your personal accounts about business loans and services and how much they cost. Nor should savings and loan associations and credit unions be overlooked. Two national banks that are now very aggressive in the franchise marketplace are Bank of America (800-733-9858) and Wells Fargo (800-35-WELLS).

Nonbank lenders. One of the best sources for SBA loans are nonbank lenders. They are for-profit private sector companies regulated by the SBA but not by state regulations. Nonbank lenders are located throughout the country and are a major source of franchise loans. Ask your franchisor whether it has a relationship with one of these. Nine of the most active nonbank lenders in the franchising arena are:

AT&T Small Business Lending Corp.
44 Whippany Rd.
Morristown, NJ 07962
800-221-7252
Fax 973-397-4086
Areas of interest: Nationwide
LowDoc loans 800-707-0609

Allied Lending Group
1666 K St. NW, 9th Floor
Washington, DC 20006
202-331-1112
Fax 202-659-2053
Areas of interest: Nationwide

Business Loan Center
645 Madison Ave., 18th Floor
New York, NY 10022
212-751-5626 Fax 212-751-9345
Areas of interest: Nationwide except
   California, Oregon, and Alaska

Emergent Business Capital
7 North Laurens St., Suite 604
PO Box 17256
Greenville, SC 29601
864-232-6197
Areas of interest: Southern and
   southwestern states

G.E. Financial
635 Maryville Centre Dr., Suite 120
St. Louis, MO 63141
800-447-2025
Areas of interest: Nationwide

Heller First Capital Corp.
650 California St., 23rd Floor
San Francisco, CA 94108-2604
415-274-5700
Fax 415-274-5744
Areas of interest: West of the
   Mississippi River

Independence Funding, Inc.
3010 LBJ Freeway, Suite 920
Dallas, TX 75234
972-247-1776
Areas of interest: Local

The Money Store Investment Co.
3301 C Street, Suite 301
Sacramento, CA 95816
916-446-5000
Areas of interest: Nationwide

PMC Capital, Inc.
17290 Preston Road, 3rd Floor
Dallas, TX 75252
800-486-3223
Areas of interest: Nationwide

Friends and Relatives

Family and friends are a common source of funds—especially for the 20 to 40 percent of your own money that you need as a down payment for financing (e.g., equity). As Chapter 2 noted, make sure friends and relatives understand your plans and the risks, and don't expect to be paid back during the early years of your business. In most cases, you won't be able to pledge any assets to them as the bank or other debt providers will want to have first place on the collateral.

Equity Investors

Raising equity is a difficult process. Venture capitalists and "angel" investors most often work with the creators of franchise systems, not individual owners. At the franchisee level, equity investors are interested in area development franchise contracts as well as firmly established franchise systems with strong trademarks and brand identification.

Telephone Directory of Miscellaneous Financing Sources

SBA Answer Desk	800-827-5722
American Venture Capital Exchange	503-221-9981
National Association of Investment Companies	202-289-4336
National Association of Women Business Owners	312-322-0990
Small Business Investment Companies Directory (SBIC)	202-205-6510
Small Business Advancement National Center	501-450-5377

Online Directory of Miscellaneous Funding Sources

SBA Online	(www.sba.gov/financing)
Entrepreneurial Edge	(www.edgeonline.com)
Loan Authority	(www.insiderreports.com/business-loan.html)
Finance Hub	(www.financehub.com/vc)
USADATA	(www.usadata.com)
Lending Rates	(www.freeyellow.com)
Venture Capital Marketplace	(www.v-capital.com.au)
Small Business Securities Issues	(www.sec.gov)
Area development (site and faciilty planning)	(www.area-development.com)

CHAPTER 13

The Franchise Business Plan

Ann Dugan

The franchise business plan is an extremely important, but often neglected, document. Too often prospective franchisees believe that all the planning that is necessary has been completed by the franchisor and that once the logistics of site selection, "buildout," and start-up are behind them, all they need do is open the door and welcome their customers. This is simply not true! Yes, your franchisor has planned for the growth of its franchise system. But you must deal with the operational, market, and human factors that are unique to your market location. The franchisor's plans and operating manuals may help, but you still need to develop a business plan for the location and market in which you will operate.

A business plan has many uses. First, it forces you to take a critical look at the aspects of the business you are entering and objectively evaluate their impact on your chances for success. Second, it is a key element in your ability to secure financing at favorable rates and to bring stakeholders such as landlords, employees, managers, and family members up-to-date on your business plans. And, finally, your plan will be a road map for you during the hectic opening years of your business. Don't put it in the drawer and forget about it. Compare your projections to your actual operating results, make changes as needed, and plan to update your plan at least annually.

This chapter covers "Section One" and the first half of "Section Two" of the contents shown in the box below. Income projections and cash flow projections are discussed in Chapter 14. Breakeven analysis and historical financial reports for existing franchises or conversions are not covered in this book. Consult a knowledgeable accountant for assistance in preparing these and other financial figures. No sample supporting documents are included either because those will be drawn from your own personal history.

Outline of a Franchise Business Plan

I.   Cover Sheet
  A. Name and location of corporate headquarters of franchisor
  B. Your name, address, and contact numbers
  C. Date of plan

II. Executive Summary

III. Table of Contents

IV. Section One: The Business
  A. Description of franchise
  B. Products/Services
  C. The market
  D. Location of the franchise
  E. Competition
  F. Management
  G. Personnel
  H. Contractual obligations

V.   Section Two: Financial Data
  A. Sources and application of funding
  B. Equipment list
  C. Leasehold improvements
  D. Sources of supply
  E. Additional franchise obligations
  F. Income projections (profit and loss statements)
    1. Three-year summary
    2. Detail by month for first year
    3. Detail by quarter for second and third year
    4. Notes of explanation
  G. Cash flow projections
    1. Detail by month for first year
    2. Detail by quarter for second and third year
    3. Notes of explanation
  H. Breakeven analysis (if applicable)
  I. Historical financial reports for existing franchise or conversion
    1. Balance sheets for past three years
    2. Income statements for past three years
    3. Tax returns

VI. Section Three: Supporting Documents (Franchise contract, personal résumés, personal financial statements, letters of reference, copies of leases, supplier contracts, and anything else relevant to the plan)

The Executive Summary

Offer a broad overview of the status of your business in the executive summary of your business plan. State your objectives and let readers know how you intend to use the plan. Besides serving as an operating and planning guide, will it be used to convince your franchisor that you can handle a master agreement and additional territories or used to secure financing? Address the interests of all your potential readers: private or commercial investors, landlords, leasing agents, managers, key employees, and suppliers. If you are seeking financing, state how much you'll need and how you'll use it.

Example of an executive summary. Don Quixote Enterprises, a potential franchisee of Ten Star Pizza, is wholly owned by Susan and John Wayne and is incorporated in the state of Georgia. Don Quixote Enterprises is developing this plan as a guiding tool for its franchise over the next five years. It is starting with one location in southeast Atlanta and is intent on opening at least one other location in the adjoining territory during the next five years. The company is currently seeking $75,000 of outside capital to be used as follows: leasehold improvements, $25,000; equipment, $50,000. The company is prepared to make an equity investment of $25,000 that will be used for working capital. Personal guarantees are available on any debt financing and credit position is excellent.

Section One: The Business

Description of the Franchise

This section of your plan should provide the basic information about the franchise and the franchisor.

Example. Ten Star Pizza is a federally registered franchise founded in Pittsburgh, Pennsylvania, in 1989 that is currently registered in all states requiring additional state registration. There are 40 company-owned locations and 20 franchised locations in Pennsylvania, Ohio, Maryland, and Tennessee as well as a recently opened location in southern Georgia. The franchise was founded by brothers Alvin and Martin Goldstein, who are still actively involved in the daily operations. Alvin is president and Martin is vice president of operations. Before starting the franchise, the brothers were employees of the Domino's Pizza franchise for 12 years. Starting as drivers in high school, they eventually owned five franchised locations before selling out and starting Ten Star.

The franchisees are typically husband-and-wife teams with minimal experience in the fast-food business. The franchisor employs a rigorous screening process before approving franchisees. The corporate training program before a franchise opening lasts three weeks and covers all facets of the business. In addition, an opening team consisting of current franchisees and corporate support staff are present in a new store during the first month.

The franchise fee is $7,500 and is comparable to other fast-food franchises. A national advertising fee of 3 percent of gross sales is collected along with the 7 percent royalty fee on a weekly basis. Significant penalties exist for late payment of these fees. In addition to the training program, the franchisor provides comprehensive operating manuals, a 24-hour help line and monthly store visits by certified support personnel. An active franchisee association also serves as the advertising and purchasing cooperative. All members of the franchise gather annually in the spring for a conference.

Products and Services

In this section describe your products/services. Remember, one of the strengths of being part of a franchise is a uniform offering. Play up the fixed group of products/services as well as the fact that you are not permitted to modify these lines.

Example. Ten Star Pizza is a limited-menu franchise with a small seating area and an emphasis on takeout and delivery. The product offering consists of pizza in a 10-inch and 14-inch size with a variety of toppings, tossed salads, and hoagies. Dough is made fresh every day and is used in the pizzas and the hoagies. The salads are prepackaged and purchased locally. The frequency of deliveries is based on volume. Services include customer preordering by fax, free delivery within a limited area at no minimum charge by drivers using their own cars, and catering parties and other social events as needed.

The Market

Here's where you draw on your market reseach to show off your knowledge of your primary customers and their habits. Play up the number of households and tell how you'll reach them.

Example. The primary customers for this franchise are individuals between the ages of 12 and 24. Age is the most highly defined demographic of this customer base. Income is not so important as research demonstrates that even those at lower-income levels will increase their purchases of pizza around the time of the month that welfare checks are received. All age groups enjoy pizza but the frequency of ordering seems to taper off after age 24 and for income levels above $75,000. Combining several key demographic factors, we arrive at a profile of *our* primary customers as follows:

- Two-income households
- Parents aged 20 through 24
- Up to three children

The frequency rate of customer ordering based upon data collected from existing franchisees is approximately 1.7 times per week. The southeast section of Atlanta is an attractive market to locate our franchise because of the high concentration of young families and individuals within our primary customer group. Living costs are high and necessitate two incomes. Commuting can be time consuming at the end of the day as a result of traffic patterns and thus precludes many households from shopping and preparing the evening meal. Existing fast-food outlets are doing a robust takeout and delivery trade.

The market area has 20,000 households and is larger than the normal five-mile radius because of the natural boundaries created by a river and an interstate highway as well as by Lake Hatwale. We anticipate a ten-mile radius at this point.

Advertising costs will be somewhat lower because of only one zip code in this area for our direct mail, one newspaper for print advertising, and only two radio stations. The TV stations are controlled by the Atlanta market and are cost-prohibitive unless the franchisor is involved, which is not likely as we are the first franchise in the area. Neighborhood activities revolve around youth activities, sports, and school functions.

Location of the Franchise

Draw on your research to tell why you chose this location and what is good about it. Mention traffic patterns, ingress and egress, parking, surrounding businesses, and other amenities. Make sure the details you include support your location decision.

Example. After reviewing numerous sites within the southeast Atlanta market, we decided to locate in a small strip mall on the corner of 21st and Vine. This center, called Mulberry Way, is seven years old and has recently undergone a major exterior renewal, including the parking lot. The current tenant, a bread-baking franchise, needs a larger space because of its growth. It has been there for five years and has expressed satisfaction with the landlord, other tenants, and the immediate neighborhood in general. Its utility needs are similar to ours and we do not anticipate the need to bring in additional power or water at this time.

We will have approximately 1,200 square feet that includes a walk-in cooler which we will purchase outright from the bakery. The cooler compressor is only five months old and is still under warranty. Three parking spaces will be available right in front of our door. Ample employee parking in the back. Other tenants in the center include a paint store, a small dance studio, and an auto parts store. These tenants do their primary business during the day, which will help our lunchtime trade as it tends to be more takeout than delivery. The dance studio holds classes in the evening too, which caused us concern about parking, but we have discussed our concern with the studio owner and have been assured they will not use our parking area.

Although the parking lot is narrow, there is ample room for Ten Star delivery trucks to enter and unload. Ingress and egress to the center is good from both directions and traffic volume is steady throughout the day with a slight back up occurring between 5:00 and 6:00 pm. Although not ideal, our delivery cars can exit and enter through the back of the store during this time and thus avoid any delay in deliveries.

Visibility from the road is excellent from both directions. We will be included on the large marquee sign of the center at no additional monthly charge, although we will have to pay for the initial artwork. The store is within five minutes by car of several large neighborhoods that will provide many primary customers for our delivery service. We are also on a major traffic route from the junior and senior high schools to student's homes and from the police department, which should be good for takeout.

Labor costs are reasonable in the area and part-time labor is available.

Because of its excellent location, rent at $12 a square foot is higher here than at the other sites we considered, but we believe that the sales will justify the expense. The landlord has agreed to a ten-year lease with renewal periods as follows: renewal at our option at the end of the first year, of the third year, and of the fifth year. The landlord has agreed to hold this space for a short period until we have signed the franchise agreement and obtained our bank loan for the equipment.

Competition

Who is your direct and indirect competition, and why is your product or service better? Why will customers want to come to you? Your franchisor, your lenders, your landlord, and your partners want to know!

Example. The Mulberry Center location has several direct competitors within a two-mile radius. There are two independent pizza delivery stores, a Pizza Hut with no delivery, and a Spaghetti Palace that has an extensive pizza offering but also no delivery. All of these locations are very busy in the evening and on weekends.

- **Independents.** The independents are busy during big TV events and on weekend nights, when they use about seven to ten drivers; otherwise they seem to have an average of two or three drivers. Their menus include hoagies but not salads; the menus seem to change constantly, with items being added and then taken away. The prices of the independents are comparable to ours but their food quality is very inconsistent.
- **Pizza Hut.** This is the busiest competitor in the group. The store is packed most evenings with a long waiting list on weekends. Takeout orders can take over an hour, and it is difficult to get into the parking lot to even pick them up. Pizza Hut's prices are higher than ours and its food quality is comparable.
- **Spaghetti Palace.** Pasta dishes are the mainstay of this business. It offers over 20 variations of spaghetti on any given night that are served with a small tossed salad. To round out its menu, Spaghetti Palace added pizza last year, but it is basically frozen pizza that is put on a small conveyor for

heating. The product quality of the pizza is very poor and the outlet doesn't serve hoagies.

- **Indirect Competitors.** The many indirect competitors within our market area include McDonald's, Wendy's, Burger King, Schlotzky's, Dairy Queen, and Subway as well as several small mom-and-pop coffee shops, a convenience store, and two grocery stores with fresh pizza and hoagie sections.

Consumers have many choices to satisfy their need for food in a fast, convenient manner, but our research demonstrates that the market for home delivery of pizza, salads, and hoagies is underserved.

Management

Investors and banks want to know the background and skills of the people who will be utilizing their money and paying it back. And you will need to know who will manage the five areas of business: Operations, Finance, Accounting, Personnel and Marketing.

Example. Don Quixote Enterprises is wholly owned by Susan and John Wayne. They will also serve as managers of the store and operate it on a daily basis as the franchise agreement dictates. Susan Wayne has been in the hospitality industry for over 15 years, serving in various management positions. After completing her B.A. degree at the University of Pittsburgh, she managed restaurant operations for various hotels and gradually moved into managing an entire 500-room hotel. Susan will be responsible for the daily operations of the franchise business, including oversight of personnel and marketing.

John Wayne has been the controller for an auto parts chain for eight years, and before that he worked in public accounting. John will also be involved with the daily operations of the store and will serve as backup driver when needed to save on labor costs. He will also be responsible for the business's accounting and finances.

The third member of our management team will be a shift manager who is able to close the store at night and cover for us on our occasional day off. We have not hired this person yet, although we have identified a few candidates. Should we be able to open a second location, the shift manager would be in line to become manager.

Personnel

Describe the kind of personnel you will need and how you intend to fill each position. Tell how each person will reflect the image you want your business to have.

Example. We can classify our personnel needs into two categories: inside people and outside people. Inside we need to have pizza makers, toppers, routers, and phone/counter people. Individuals can be cross-trained for these positions to cut down on personnel during slow periods. As franchisees we will have learned about all of these positions in our training school classes, which are scheduled for several weeks after we sign the franchise contract. We plan to hire four part-time people and train them in the two weeks before our grand opening. Because of some constraints on the number of young people who are available in this area, we'll be starting all insider people at $5.25 an hour. We will not offer health benefits.

Outside personnel are the delivery drivers. They will have to provide their own car and have verifiable insurance, although we will provide secondary automobile insurance. We'll provide shirts and hats for the drivers, and they will be required to wear clean navy pants or shorts. Cars must be clean and in decent shape. Drivers will be taught a delivery system, driving behavior, and a courteous manner. We intend to hire approximately 20 drivers part-time to start. We don't believe that we need this many at one time but other Ten Star franchisees have told us of their difficulties in finding good drivers who are reliable. The drivers will be part-time with several of the better ones developed into full-time drivers. Based on market conditions, we anticipate paying $4.25 an hour plus $1.00 per delivery. Drivers usually receive tips from deliveries as well.

Contractual Obligations

Here you should disclose details about your franchise agreement that a financier or other stakeholder would need to know about the franchise you are hoping to buy. Condense the important parts into a few paragraphs, but encourage lenders and others to read the entire agreement.

Example. Don Quixote Enterprises is incorporated in the state of Georgia and is wholly owned by Susan and John Wayne. Don Quixote Enterprises along with Susan and John Wayne as individuals will sign the franchise agreement with Ten Star Pizza, the franchisor. The agreement will be for a period of ten years with options to renew that are favorable to both parties.

The franchisor will provide the rights to all trade dress of the franchise system, a three-week training period at the corporate offices (travel and related costs not included), and an operating manual. Ten Star Pizza will also provide ongoing technical support by phone at our request and some advertising material that we can customize for our local use. Before opening, the franchisor will provide limited assistance on the selection of our location, but it will have final approval on the ultimate site selected.

Franchisees belong to a buying cooperative (co-op) that is under their control. All major purchases for inventory are made through the co-op. Rarely is there a better price locally but we have the right to buy locally should the case arise. The franchisee association is independent of the franchisor and is involved in resolving disputes and general strategic planning. The association has a voting seat on the board of directors of Ten Star Pizza so that the franchisee's voice is also heard.

The territory is well defined in the franchise agreement and is based on geography. We also have the right of first refusal on the two adjoining territories because we hope to expand one day. We were not required to put money down to reserve these areas, but the franchisor reserved the right to do so in the future.

Termination rights of the franchisor are very limited and our legal advisors are comfortable with these items. Our right to sell to another is based on the approval of the franchisor, but this approval cannot be withheld easily.

The contract seems to be in line with the fair franchising standards of the American Association of Franchisees and Dealers (AAFD).

Section Two: Financial Data

This section of your plan provides detail of where the money is coming from to start your business and what exactly you are going to use the money for. Notes immediately following should be used for items that need further explanation.

Sources of Funding

John and Susan Wayne	$ 25,000
Money Store, Inc.	$ 75,000
Total	$100,000

Application of Funding

Franchise fee	$ 12,000
Equipment	$ 50,000
Leasehold improvements	$ 5,000
Working capital	$ 33,000
Total	$100,000

Equipment List

Conveyor oven	$ 15,000
Slicer	$ 2,000
Mixer	$ 3,000
Cooling/Dressing stand	$ 4,000
Telephone table	$ 1,000
Cash register	$ 1,500
Stainless steel tables (8)	$ 7,000
Customer seating area	$ 5,000
Signage	$ 4,000
Misc.	$ 9,500
Total	$ 52,000

Note: The equipment listed is a mixture of used and new. We have priced these expenditures based on availability and reliabilty in the used market and, when necessary, on prices of new equipment. A list of equipment is provided in the supporting documents.

Leasehold Improvements

We have received bids from three contractors for remodeling the interior to meet franchise specifications; the price shown was the lowest reliable bid. The detailed contractor's bid that we have accepted is in the supporting documents.

Sources of Supply

The franchisee associations coop is the main supplier for our franchise. In certain circumstances we could buy locally as long as we have prior approval from the franchisor.

Additional Franchise Obligations

Royalty payments of 5 percent and national advertising payments of 2 percent are due monthly on gross sales.

Income Projections

(See Chapter 14.)

Preparing Your Income and Cash Flow Projections

Peter Rainsford and David H. Bangs, Jr.

If the first half of your business plan is descriptive, the second half is quantitive and is where you prove to yourself and lenders that your business has a future. It projects the level of sales you expect as well as expenses you are likely to incur in renting, staffing, and opening a location, and it estimates the working capital you'll need to cover deficits during your first few years.

This chapter covers two components of your plan: your projected income statement and your cash flow projection.*

Projected Income Statement

Your income statements, also called profit and loss statements, or operating statements, provide a moving picture of your franchise during a particular period of time.

Financial statements that depict a future period are called pro forma or projected financial statements. They represent what your business is expected to look like financially based on a set of assumptions about the economy, market growth, and other factors.

Income projections are forecasting and budgeting tools estimating income and anticipating expenses in the near-to-middle range future. For most businesses (and for most bankers) income projections covering one to

---

*Reprinted and adapted with permission from Peter Rainsford and David H. Bangs, Jr., *The Restaurant Planning Guide*, 2d edition, (Chicago: Upstart Publishing Company, 1996).

three years are more than adequate. In some cases, a longer-range projection may be called for, but, in general, the longer the projection, the less accurate it will be as a guide to action.

You don't need a crystal ball to make your projection. Although no set of projections will be 100 percent accurate, experience and practice tend to make the projections more precise. Even if your income projections aren't accurate, they will provide you with a rough set of benchmarks to test your progress toward short-term goals. They become the base of your budget as well as your business plan.

Nothing is sacred about income projections. If they're wildly incorrect, correct them to make a more realistic guide. When you do this is a matter of judgment. A rule of thumb is that if they are more than 20 percent off for a quarter (three months), redo them. If they are less than 20 percent off, wait for another quarter. Don't change your projections more often. In a short period, certain trends will be magnified, and these distortions will usually be evened out over the long run. Of course, if you find you have omitted a major expense item or discover a significant new source of revenue, you'll want to make immediate corrections. Use your common sense.

The reasoning behind income projection: because most expenses are predictable and income doesn't fluctuate too drastically, the future will be much like the past. In a restaurant business, for example, if food cost has historically been 38 percent of net sales, it will (barring strong evidence to the contrary) continue to be 38 percent of net sales. If you are in a start-up situation, look for financial statement information and income ratios for businesses similar to yours.

It is important to be systematic and thorough when you list your expenses. The expense that bleeds your business dry (makes it illiquid) is almost always one that was overlooked or seriously misjudged, and is therefore not planned for. Some expenses can't be foreseen, and the best way to allow for them is to be conservative in your estimates and document your assumptions.

Try to understate your expected sales and overstate expenses. It's better to exceed a conservative budget than to fall below optimistic projections. However, being too far under can also create problems—such as not having enough capital to finance growth. Basing income projections on hopes or unjustified fears is hazardous to your business's health. Be realistic; your budget is an extension of your forecasts.

Income statements and projections are standardized to facilitate comparison and analysis. They must be dated to indicate the period of time they cover and also contain notes to explain any unusual items such as windfall profits, litigation expenses and judgments, changes in depreciation schedules, and other material information. Any assumptions should be footnoted—to help remind you of how the numbers were originally justified and to provide a boost up the learning curve when you review your projections before making new ones.

Income statements should be reviewed at least once a quarter to check their validity and, if necessary, to make adjustments or make changes in your franchise's operations. As a budget tool, the actual progress of your franchise should be compared against the projections every month. You have to detect deviations as soon as possible to correct problems before they become major, and to seize opportunities while they are still fresh.

A suggested format for an income statement follows in Figure 14.1 and is based on the *Uniform System of Accounts for Restaurants*.

Remember: The purpose of financial statements and forecasts is to provide you with the maximum amount of useful information and guidance, not to dazzle a prospective investor.

Explanation of Sample Income Statement

Food Sales: Sales of food items and beverage items (e.g., coffee, tea, soft drinks) if the cost of such beverages is charged against food cost.

Beverage Sales: Sale of all beer, wine, liquor, and other alcoholic and nonalcoholic beverages whose cost is charged against beverage cost.

Cost of Sales, Food: The cost to the restaurant of the food that was available for sale to the customers. Calculated by using the formula: Beginning Inventory + Purchases - Ending Inventory = Cost of Goods Sold.

Cost of Sales, Beverages: The cost to the restaurant of the beverages that were available for sale to customers. Calculated by using the formula: Beginning Inventory + Purchases - Ending Inventory = Cost of Goods Sold.

Gross Profit: Total Sales less Total Cost of Sales.

Other Income: Income other than from food or beverage sales (e.g., banquet room rentals, gift shop items, vending machine commissions, etc.).

Total Income: Gross Profit plus Other Income.

Controllable Expenses: Operating expenses most directly influenced by the operating policy and management efficiency (see the *Uniform System of Accounts for Restaurants* for a complete explanation of the items and categories).

Occupancy Costs, Interest, Depreciation: Items that are relatively fixed based on the financing structure of the restaurant and not influenced by day-to-day management decisions (see the *Uniform System of Accounts for Restaurants* for a explanation of the items).

For the most useful projection, state your assumptions clearly. Don't put down numbers that you cannot rationally substantiate. Don't puff your gross sales projection to make the net profit positive. Give yourself conservative sales figures and pessimistic expense figures to make the success of your deal more probable. Be realistic. You want your projections to reflect the realities of your business.

Income and Cash Flow Forecasting

Franchises should make three-year projections for both planning purposes and loan proposals. The proper sequence for both income and cash flow projections is as follows:

1. A three-year summary
2. First year projected by month (If the business doesn't break even in the first year, you might want to continue the monthly projections until it does.)

FIGURE 14.1 A Sample Income Statement Format

Sales	
Food Sales	
Beverage Sales	
Total Sales	
Cost of Sales	
Food	
Beverage	
Total Cost of Sales	
Gross Profit	
Other Income	
Total Income	
Controllable Expenses	
Payroll	
Employee Benefits	
Direct Operating Expenses	
Advertising and Promotion	
Utilities	
Administration and General	
Repairs and Maintenance	
Total Controllable Expenses	
Income before Occupancy Costs	
Occupancy Costs	
Rent	
Property Taxes	

FIGURE 14.1 A Sample Income Statement Format *(Continued)*

Other Taxes
Property Insurance
Total Occupancy Costs
Income before Interest and Depreciation
Interest
Depreciation
Restaurant Profit
Other Deductions
Income Before Taxes
Taxes
Net Profit (Loss)
Source: Uniform System of Accounts for Restaurants.

 3. Years two and three by quarter

If you are already in business or are considering taking over an existing franchise, historical financial statements should be included for two immediately previous years. Tax returns help to substantiate the validity of unaudited statements.

A Note on Sales Forecasts

Sales forecasts are not easy—at least not easy if you want your forecasts to be realistic. Every franchise has its own patterns of peak versus off-peak business, times when the operation is more or less efficient. Downtime resulting from maintenance or refurbishing can seriously alter your forecast's accuracy.

One helpful technique to use involves breaking your projected sales into a three-column form to arrive at a "most likely" figure.

Begin by assuming the worst. In the column headed "Low," put down the sales you expect if everything goes wrong—poor weather, loss of market share to a new competitor, and so on. Be gloomy. Assume your employees will be loutish, lazy, and surly.

Then—this is more fun—assume everything works out the way you'd wish. In the column headed "High," put down your rosiest hopes. All your promotional efforts will succeed, markets will grow dynamically, your competition will stub their toes and slink away from the market, and your franchise will become the "in spot."

Now look to a realistic scenario, where things work out in between the high and low estimates. The figures here will, at least usually, be more accurate than a one-time estimate, as more thought has gone into their preparation. Do this for the period you need to forecast.

Sales Forecast: For (month, year) to (month, year)

Sales:	Low	Most Likely	High
Draft beer			
Bottle beer			
Liquor			
Wine			
Nonalcoholic beverages			
Food			
Total Sales:			

You can apply the same process to forecasting expenses even though most expenses are reasonably predictable once the sales forecasts have been established.

Trade figures for businesses like yours provide a reality check. Your sales level and expenses may be lower (especially for a start-up or turnaround), equal to, or higher than trade. Be ready to explain any significant deviations. Trade figures are based on the experience of going businesses in many different areas, so there may be local differences that make your numbers quite different. Experience will tend to even out your forecasts—but you have to start somewhere. An example of an income statement is shown in Figure 14.2.

Explanation for Income Statement Projections

This section will explain how the figures on the projection were calculated and detail the assumptions made.

Food Sales and Beverage Sales: The ratio of food sales to beverage sales that actually occurred in year one was projected to remain the same in years two and three. The dollar amount of food and beverage sales was forecast to increase 10 percent each year.

Cost of Sales, Food, and Beverages: The cost of food sales and the cost of beverage sales were forecast to remain at the same percentage (42.5 percent and 37.1 percent respectively) for year two as was actually obtained in year one. Although this percentage is higher than Ten Star Pizza computed in the pricing section and higher than the national average (as shown in the section on deviation analysis), the same percentage was used because of the seasonal nature of the pizza business, which makes controlling costs more difficult in the slow seasons, and because the owner wished to remain conservative in projecting income during the expansion in the second year. For the third year, the food cost percentage was projected to be lowered to 38 percent and the beverage cost percentage was projected to be lowered to 32 percent—both of which more closely resemble national averages. The reason for lowering the forecasted cost percentages in the third year was because the owners felt they would then have more time to manage costs as the business cycle should have stabilized somewhat.

Gross Profit: Total Sales less Total Cost of Sales.

Other Income: Estimated to remain fairly constant because the restaurant is small and doesn't have the room to expand offering products other than food and beverages.

Total Income: Gross Profit plus Other Income.

Controllable Expenses: All operating expenses were estimated to increase 10 percent in year two and an additional 10 percent in year three. Although these increases may seem high, Ten Star Pizza wished to remain conservative when projecting the income statement. The payroll cost is lower than the national average, but this is because the owners are working daily in the business and taking a minimal salary. The owners do not expect to take more than a minimal salary ($2,400 per month) to enable the business to accumulate capital and fund expansion. If Susan and John had to hire a full-time manager, their payroll costs would be significantly higher.

Occupancy Costs, Interest, Depreciation: Rent is not projected to increase because the landlord has agreed to a three-year lease with no increases as Ten Star Pizza is paying for all leasehold improvements. Property taxes and property insurance are both projected to increase at a rate of 10 percent each year. Interest and depreciation figures will remain constant unless the expansion is undertaken, in which case interest should increase by approximately $2,250 ($25,000 @ 9 percent interest) and depreciation will increase by approximately $4,800.

Ten Star Pizza does not expect to make much money for the first few years. This is no surprise for a business so thinly capitalized.

Information is the most valuable result of financial statements. Accurate, timely information helps you run your business.

Cash Flow Projection

The cash flow projection is the most important financial planning tool available to you. If you were limited to one financial statement (which fortunately isn't the case), the cash flow projection would be the one to choose.

For a new or growing business, the cash flow projection can make the difference between success and failure. For an ongoing business, it can make the difference between growth and stagnation.

FIGURE 14.2 Ten Star Pizza

Ten Star Pizza: Income Statement—by Month
Actual—Year One, Jan. 1 to Dec. 31, 19___

	JAN	FEB	MAR	APR	MAY	JUN	JUL	AUG	SEPT	OCT	NOV	DEC	Totals	%
Sales														
Food	7,558	7,904	11,057	14,111	25,108	34,759	46,670	44,520	22,892	15,288	7,832	4,255	241,954	78.2
Beverages	2,959	2,978	4,129	4,066	7,095	10,701	12,220	10,638	5,643	3,999	2,076	974	67,478	21.8
Total Sales	10,517	10,882	15,186	18,177	32,203	45,460	58,890	55,158	28,535	19,287	9,908	5,229	309,432	100.0
Cost of Sales														
Food	5,185	4,625	5,179	6,128	10,701	12,963	17,899	16,519	9,747	5,824	5,198	2,765	102,733	42.5
Beverage	922	1,430	1,701	1,944	2,387	3,374	4,148	3,948	2,039	1,557	712	879	25,041	37.1
Total Cost of Sales	6,107	6,055	6,880	8,072	13,088	16,337	22,047	20,467	11,786	7,381	5,910	3,644	127,774	41.3
Gross Profit	4,410	4,827	8,306	10,105	19,115	29,123	36,843	34,691	16,749	11,906	3,998	1,585	181,658	58.7
Other Income	0	0	0	0	0	0	0	828	170	56	0	0	1,054	0.3
Total Income	4,410	4,827	8,306	10,105	19,115	29,123	36,843	35,519	16,919	11,962	3,998	1,585	182,712	59.0
Controllable Expenses														
Payroll	3,153	3,128	3,923	4,047	5,023	8,406	17,761	11,804	7,633	4,313	3,247	3,012	75,450	24.4
Employee Benefits	369	982	554	853	422	2,093	1,907	1,372	665	1,056	1,062	115	11,450	3.7
Direct Operating Expenses	488	384	1,121	878	1,481	2,757	1,589	1,988	404	1,685	340	361	13,476	4.4
Advertising & Promotion	941	945	739	692	1,121	1,486	2,356	1,128	1,175	856	994	941	13,374	4.3
Utilities	535	1,212	676	1,215	443	1,355	571	1,960	607	1,486	194	411	10,665	3.4
Administrative & General	69	828	533	166	291	530	419	406	600	210	172	223	4,447	1.4
Repairs & Maintenance	99	73	554	243	1,284	1,894	1,365	884	404	1,382	166	17	8,365	2.7
Total Controllable Expenses	5,654	7,552	8,100	8,094	10,065	18,521	25,968	19,542	11,488	10,988	6,175	5,080	137,227	44.3
Income before Occupancy Costs	(1,244)	(2,725)	206	2,011	9,050	10,602	10,875	15,977	5,431	974	(2,177)	(3,495)	45,485	14.7
Occupancy Costs														
Rent	1,200	1,200	1,200	1,200	1,200	1,200	1,200	1,200	1,200	1,200	1,200	1,200	14,400	4.7
Property Taxes	374	374	374	374	374	374	374	374	374	374	374	374	4,488	1.5
Other Taxes														
Property Insurance	518	518	518	518	518	518	518	518	518	518	518	518	6,216	2.0
Total Occupancy Costs	2,092	2,092	2,092	2,092	2,092	2,092	2,092	2,092	2,092	2,092	2,092	2,092	25,104	8.1
Income before Interest and Depreciation	(3,336)	(4,817)	(1,886)	(81)	6,958	8,510	8,783	13,885	3,339	(1,118)	(4,269)	(5,587)	20,381	6.6
Interest	75	75	75	75	75	75	75	75	75	75	75	75	900	0.3
Depreciation	391	391	391	391	391	391	391	391	391	391	391	391	4,692	1.5
Restaurant Profit	(3,802)	(5,283)	(2,352)	(547)	6,492	8,044	8,317	13,419	2,873	(1,584)	(4,735)	(6,053)	14,789	4.8
Other Deductions														
Income before Income Taxes	(3,802)	(5,283)	(2,352)	(547)	6,492	8,044	8,317	13,419	2,873	(1,584)	(4,735)	(6,053)	14,789	4.8

Your cash flow analysis will

1. show you how much cash your business will need;
2. when it will be needed;
3. whether you should look for equity, debt, operating profits, or sale of fixed assets; and
4. where the cash will come from.

The cash flow projection attempts to budget the cash needs of a business and shows how cash will flow in and out of the business over a stated period of time. Cash flows into the business from sales, collection of receivables, capital injections, and the like, and it flows out through cash payments for expenses of all kinds.

This financial tool emphasizes the points in your calendar when money will be coming into and going out of your franchise. The advantage of knowing when cash outlays must be made is the ability to plan for those outlays and not be forced to resort to unexpected borrowing to meet cash needs. Illiquidity is a killer, even for profitable businesses. Lack of profits won't kill a franchise (noncash expenses such as depreciation can make your profits look negative while your cash flow is positive). Lack of cash to meet your trade and other payables will kill a franchise.

If you project your cash flow for the near to intermediate future, you can see the effect of a loan to your business far more clearly than from the income statement. You may be able to find ways to finance your operation or minimize your credit needs to keep interest expense down. Many of the advantages of studying the cash flow projection stem from timing: more options are available to you at lower costs with less panic.

Cash is generated primarily by sales, and most restaurant sales are cash; customers expect to pay cash (or use credit cards, which are instantly converted to cash). However, not all businesses have mainly cash sales. Perhaps your business is all cash—but if you offer any credit (charge accounts for individuals or companies) to your customers, you need to have a means of telling when those credit sales will turn into cash-in-hand. This is blurred in the income statement but made very clear by the cash flow. Your franchise may be subject to seasonal bills, and again a cash flow makes the liquidity problems attending such large, occasional expenses clear.

A cash flow deals only with actual cash transactions. Depreciation, a noncash expense, does not appear on a cash flow. Loan repayments (including interest), on the other hand, do because they represent a cash disbursement.

After it has been developed, use your cash flow projection as a budget. If the cash outlays for a given item increase over the amount allotted for a given month, you should find out why and take corrective action as soon as possible. If the figure is lower, you should also find out why. If the cash outlay is lower than expected, it's not necessarily a good sign. Maybe a bill wasn't paid. By reviewing the movement of your cash position, you can better control your business.

On a more positive note, the savings may tip you off to a new way of economizing. Discrepancies between expected and actual cash flows are indicators of opportunities as well as problems. If the sales figures don't match the cash flow projections, look for the cause. Maybe projections were too low. Maybe you've opened a new market or introduced a new product that can be pushed even harder.

Make sure you don't omit any ordinary cash flow item. But be sure to add any items that are peculiar to your operation.

Cash flow projections lend themselves to computerization. Spreadsheet programs such as Lotus 1-2-3™ or Excel™ (among others) are made even more valuable because you can tie in graphic displays to your hard numbers, link together several different financial statements, or play "what-if" with much greater speed and accuracy than was possible when we were limited to pencils, adding machines, 13-column accounting paper, and erasers.

Explanation of Year One Cash Flow Statement

The first year cash flow statement for Ten Star Pizza (see Figure 14.3) has been limited solely to cash flows as a result of operations in order to simplify some of the comparisons between cash flow from operations and profit or loss. The loans and investments made to Ten Star Pizza when it started in business would normally be shown as would the investment in fixed assets. When preparing initial cash flow projections for your franchise, it's a good idea for you to compute cash flows from operations first (to see if the business is going to generate enough cash to pay operating bills). Then go back and insert those items that have to do with financing the franchise and purchasing fixed assets as well as those items that indicate how debt will be repaid and dividends made to stockholders.

The first year cash flow statement is based on the assumption that all sales are in cash (credit card sales being considered the same as cash) and therefore there are no accounts receivable. If there were charge sales, then the cash receipts would be shown in the month they were actually received, not in the month that the sale was made.

The first year cash flow statement also assumes that all bills were paid immediately. If that were not the case, then cash disbursements would be shown in the month actually paid, not in the month when the expense was incurred.

A comparison of the first year income statement with the first year cash flow statement shows a profit of $14,786 and a cash flow of $19,478. The discrepancy ($4,692) is due to depreciation, which is a noncash expense and therefore is not taken into consideration on the cash flow statement.

A comparison of the two statements for the month of January shows a loss on the income statement of ($3,802) for January and a negative cash flow on the cash flow statement of ($5,804). The difference is due to the fact that expenses are allocated on the income statement to the month in which they are incurred, but they are shown on the cash flow statement in the month they are actually paid. Property taxes of $1,903 were paid in January but only $374 was allocated to the month. The same is true of the property insurance: the premium of $1,457 was paid in January but only $518 was allocated as an expense for the month. The income statement shows an interest expense of $75 for the month, but examination of the cash flow statement shows no interest payments were made until December. Finally, the income statement shows the depreciation expense of $391 in January, which, as already explained, is a noncash expense. The result of these items is that an excess of $2,002 in payments were made in January that were not allocated. The table below summarizes the results.

Examination of the overall cash flow statement reveals that although Ten Star Pizza had a positive cash flow from operations of $19,478 for the year, the cash flow started out negative and reached as high as ($11,369) during the first four months before the operating results started to show a positive cash flow. Arrangements had to be made to cover the negative cash flow in the beginning of the year, and it is assumed that John and Susan Wayne either loaned the business money from savings or arranged for a short-term loan from another source. One of the values of projected cash flow statements—as will be shown for the year two projections—is that the cash flow statement details exactly when cash loans are going to be needed because of business cycles and when such loans can be expected to be repaid.

Reconciliation of Cash Flow

Cash Disbursements:	
Property Taxes	$1,903
Property Insurance	1,457
Total Disbursements Made	$3,360
Expenses Allocated:	
Property Taxes	$374
Property Insurance	518
Interest	75
Depreciation	391
Total Expenses Allocated	1,358
Difference	$2,002
Summary	
Income (Loss) from Income Statement	($3,802)
Disbursements Made but Not Allocated	(2,002)
Cash Flow from Operations	($5,804)

A comparison of the two statements reveals other months when cash flows were different from profit or loss.

FIGURE 14.3 Ten Star Pizza

Ten Star Pizza: Cash Flow Statement—by Month
Actual—Year One, Jan. 1 to Dec. 31, 19__

	JAN	FEB	MAR	APR	MAY	JUN	JUL	AUG	SEPT	OCT	NOV	DEC	Totals
Cash Receipts													
Food Sales	7,558	7,904	11,057	14,111	25,108	34,759	46,670	44,520	22,892	15,288	7,832	4,255	241,954
Beverage Sales	2,959	2,978	4,129	4,066	7,095	10,701	12,220	10,638	5,643	3,999	2,076	974	67,478
Sales Receivables	0	0	0	0	0	0	0	0	0	0	0	0	0
Other Income	0	0	0	0	0	0	0	828	170	56	0	0	1,054
Total Cash Receipts	10,517	10,882	15,186	18,177	32,203	45,460	58,890	55,986	28,705	19,343	9,908	5,229	310,486
Cash Disbursements													
Cost of Sales, Food	5,185	4,625	5,179	6,128	10,701	12,963	17,899	16,519	9,747	5,824	5,198	2,765	102,733
Cost of Sales, Beverages	922	1,430	1,701	1,944	2,387	3,374	4,148	3,948	2,039	1,557	712	879	25,041
Controllable Expenses													0
Payroll	3,153	3,128	3,923	4,047	5,023	8,406	17,761	11,804	7,633	4,313	3,247	3,012	75,450
Employee Benefits	369	982	554	853	422	2,093	1,907	1,372	665	1,056	1,062	115	11,450
Direct Operating Expenses	488	384	1,121	878	1,481	2,757	1,589	1,988	404	1,685	340	361	13,476
Advertising & Promotion	941	945	739	692	1,121	1,486	2,356	1,128	1,175	856	994	941	13,374
Utilities	535	1,212	676	1,215	443	1,355	571	1,960	607	1,486	194	411	10,665
Administrative & General	69	828	533	166	291	530	419	406	600	210	172	223	4,447
Repairs & Maintenance	99	73	554	243	1,284	1,894	1,365	884	404	1,382	166	17	8,365
Occupancy Costs													0
Rent	1,200	1,200	1,200	1,200	1,200	1,200	1,200	1,200	1,200	1,200	1,200	1,200	14,400
Property Taxes	1,903	0	0	0	0	0	0	0	2,585	0	0	0	4,488
Other Taxes	0	0	0	0	0	0	0	0	0	0	0	0	0
Property Insurance	1,457	0	0	1,456	0	0	1,675	0	0	1,628	0	0	6,216
Interest	0	0	0	0	0	0	0	0	0	0	0	0	0
Other Deductions	0	0	0	0	0	0	0	0	0	0	0	900	900
Total Cash Disbursements:	16,321	14,807	16,180	18,822	24,353	36,058	50,890	41,209	27,059	21,197	13,285	10,824	291,005
Cash Flow from Operations													
Cash Receipts	10,517	10,882	15,186	18,177	32,203	45,460	58,890	55,986	28,705	19,343	9,908	5,229	310,486

FIGURE 14.3 Ten Star Pizza (Continued)

Ten Star Pizza: Cash Flow Statement—by Month
Actual—Year One, Jan. 1 to Dec. 31, 19___

	JAN	FEB	MAR	APR	MAY	JUN	JUL	AUG	SEPT	OCT	NOV	DEC	Totals
21,197	13,285	10,824	291,005										
Net from Operations	(5,804)	(3,925)	(994)	(645)	7,850	9,402	8,000	14,777	1,646	(1,854)	(3,377)	(5,595)	19,481
Cash on Hand													
Opening Balance	0	(5,804)	(9,729)	(10,723)	(11,368)	(3,518)	5,884	13,884	28,661	30,307	28,453	25,076	
Plus: New Loan (Debt)													
Plus: New Investment													
Plus: Sale of Fixed Assets													
Plus: Net from Operations	(5,804)	(3,925)	(994)	(645)	7,850	9,402	8,000	14,777	1,646	(1,854)	(3,377)	(5,595)	19,481
Total Cash Available	(5,804)	(9,729)	(10,723)	(11,368)	(3,518)	5,884	13,884	28,661	30,307	28,453	25,076	19,481	19,481
Less: Debt Reduction													
Less: New Fixed Assets													
Less: Dividends to Stockholders													
Less: Stock Redemption													
Less: Loans to Officers													
Total Cash Paid Out	0	0	0	0	0	0	0	0	0	0	0	0	
Cash Position—Ending Balance	(5,804)	(9,729)	(10,723)	(11,368)	(3,518)	5,884	13,884	28,661	30,307	28,453	25,076	19,481	19,481

Managing Your Franchise

Once you're up and running, it is important to institute systems to manage your business. Otherwise, your business will manage *you* and you'll be quickly worn out. Whether you are running a housecleaning franchise or controlling all of McDonald's restaurants in the Pittsburgh area, you or someone on your staff must cover five basic areas of business:

1. The financial structure of your business: how you will get and use short-term and long-term vehicles to finance assets and growth
2. Recordkeeping and accounting: how you will keep track of your business and understand how it is doing
3. Marketing: how you will use advertising, promotions, and selling to build awareness, traffic, and customer sales
4. Human resources: how you will hire, train, and retain valuable team members
5. Operations: how you will prepare and deliver your products or services to your customer

Franchisors usually do an excellent job preparing you to handle the operations at the core of their system. But you'll have to educate yourself about the other areas and determine whether you can delegate to someone else or will have to be operations manager, accountant, chief financial officer, marketing vice president, and director of human resources simultaneously. Before you open, strategize how you'll cover all these areas.

This section will help you understand what you must know about hiring, marketing, and accounting in order to manage your business. But it's up to you to find ways to add to your general management knowledge and skills. Look for low-cost seminars on business topics offered by a Small Business Development Center or a chamber of commerce. Find books and videos that cover these topics. Do everything you can to hone your skills in finance, accounting, marketing, and human resources.

When your business is well managed, you will be able to work *on* your business as you work *in* your business. Working in your business—working the counter, unloading trucks, shipping packages—is easy. Working on your business—setting goals for the future, devising strategies to meet them, thinking about how to capitalize on new business trends—can be difficult if you're swamped with those "in the business" details. Master the secrets of managing your franchise, and you can keep your eye on the big picture—all the way to reaching your goals.

CHAPTER 15

Finding and Developing Good Employees

Thomas Crimans

If signing the franchise agreement is the scariest day of your life, hiring your first employee runs a close second. Hiring employees is a vital step in making your franchise operation successful—but all too often franchisees try to delay hiring to save a few dollars. Unfortunately, this is like opening a T-shirt shop without stocking size XL. You'll save money on inventory, but you'll have a very hard time meeting customer expectations. Another common mistake is substituting yourself for an employee. This saves money, too—but the time you spend working in the business reduces the time and energy you have to manage it.

So how do you know when to hire? Your business plan should include a staffing budget. If your research and the franchisor indicate that a crew of four is needed and that training takes two weeks, you know you need to hire four people at least two weeks before opening day. Your conversations with other franchisees may also help here. What was the staffing strategy of the most successful franchisees? Learn from their experience and that of the franchisor.

Finding and hiring good employees takes several steps. First, you need to know where to find employees. Then you need to prepare questions and conduct an interview to assess their skills and aptitudes. Once they are on the job, you'll need to supervise them and correct any behavioral problems.

Some franchisors do offer some assistance in recruiting and training employees, but by and large you need to execute these steps on your own. A basic premise in franchising is that it is *your* business, not the franchisor's. Any employees are your employees. This tenet represents the position of the courts as well as of the franchisor. In a recent case, a franchisor was found not to be liable for the discriminatory actions of a franchisee. As a rule, the franchisor expects you to bring appropriate human resource skills to the table along with your business management skills. However, your franchisor may provide

- sample help-wanted ads and compensation schemes;
- employment tests for screening applicants;
- guidelines for how many employees to hire and when;
- training for managers and other employees (but you may have to pay for it);
- regional or national recruitment programs;
- insurance programs such as workers' compensation programs, bonding against theft, and occasionally health insurance.

Before you gear up to hire employees, find out which of these items your franchisor offers.

Where to Find Employees

The supply of workers varies over time. When the supply is short you must be more creative in attracting qualified prospects. Help-wanted ads, usually a good source of leads, may be less effective when many companies are competing for the same workers. Consider the following options as well:

- *State employment services.* Every state operates job placement programs in conjunction with unemployment compensation programs. List your job opening with the placement program, and its staff will prescreen applicants and even do some testing for you.
- *Temporary employment agencies.* You can always hire a temporary worker placed by a temporary agency provided you comply with its rules. Sometimes you pay no additional fee once the temporary worker has worked for a specified period of time. One great advantage of this approach is the opportunity it provides to "test drive" the employee before you hire. If the person is not working out, you simply send him or her back to the agency.
- *Seniors.* Take advantage of the growing pool of active, healthy, older people who are interested in making extra income. In many cases they have a stronger work ethic than younger employees and can bring some real talent to your new business.
- *Religious organizations.* Many large churches and synagogues provide in-house job referral systems for their members. They will be glad to make their members aware of your needs.
- *Colleges and universities.* A great source for part-time workers, colleges and universities provide job referral services to their students. All the colleges in most cities share job listings, which can make your task a little lighter.
- *Job fairs.* Sponsored by schools, local governments, and other groups, job fairs let you sell your opportunity directly to workers, although you will have to pay for booth space.

- *Your employees.* As you grow, your current staff can be a great source of additional employees. They know you and the requirements of the job, and they have a built-in desire to have coworkers who are responsible and will carry their load.

Determining Qualifications for a Position

Hiring has been described as an art. Like many artistic endeavors, however, results can be improved when hiring is approached logically and systematically. A common mistake in hiring is to focus too much on technical qualifications for the job. Managers tend to look for people with experience in the food industry for a new restaurant or folks with automotive experience in a tire franchise. In reality less than 5 percent of all employee relations problems stem from lack of technical skill.

Because most people think of a job as a collection of tasks, most job descriptions merely list tasks. To hire the best person, though, you need to think about attributes, not tasks. You need to list the qualities, abilities, and characteristics that are important to success in the position you want to fill. Good verbal communication skills, for example, are important to the success of most sales people.

Each position has a unique set of attributes, some more important than others. Attributes can be divided into three general categories:

- *Knowledge, skill, and ability* are the more obvious technical requirements of a position. Consider these carefully. If you want someone experienced and trained in sales, how much training and experience do you expect? What type of selling is important and how much training can you provide? Assigning unnecessarily high attributes or requirements may screen out good people or cause legal problems for your company.
- *Willingness* is also critical. The applicant must be willing to perform the job under the conditions that go with it: hot weather, an evening shift, a high level of rejection, and so on. A well-trained or experienced person who is unwilling to do the job or work under the conditions that go with it will not succeed. Take time to define a job with its conditions so you can accurately determine whether an applicant is willing to perform it.
- *Interpersonal skills* depend upon the context of the job. A maid must be able to build long-term trusting relationships with coworkers; a sales clerk must be able to quickly gain the trust of a customer. You need to consider exactly what kind of interpersonal skills are required for the position you want to fill.

Draw from all three categories of attributes as you create the job description for the position. To think in terms of the *whole* job, consider each of the following areas as you list desired attributes:

- Specific task-related knowledge, skills, or abilities
- Complexity of tasks
- A variety of tasks versus one or two
- Decision making/judgment
- Degree of supervision (a lot? very little?)
- Individual versus group work
- Degree of frequency in changes in job content or procedures
- Degree of interaction with others
- Type of interaction
- Written communications
- Verbal communications
- Accuracy required
- Level of detail
- Working conditions
- Hours and schedule
- Predictability of schedule
- Overtime
- Degree and type of contact with customers

Preparing Interview Questions

Once you have defined the attributes necessary for success on the job, you must determine whether the applicant possesses those attributes. Asking effective questions will help. Although no two interviews will be exactly the same, it is important to plan a line of questions that will evaluate the applicant on each attribute.

Use a mix of close-ended and open-ended questions. A close-ended question can be answered with "yes" or "no," as in "Do you work well under pressure?" Few applicants would answer no—which is why close-ended questions can be ineffective. An open-ended question like "Explain how you work under pressure" requires the responder to discuss, explain, or elaborate. Interviews are short, and you need to learn as much about the candidate as possible. Use open-ended questions to keep the applicant talking.

Develop enough questions about each attribute so you can probe the applicant until you are satisfied he or she can perform satisfactorily. The sample interview questions shown below will help you devise questions that work for you.

Open-ended Questions

Open-ended questions can be developed for almost any issue you want to explore. Try these lead-ins:

- "Explain to me how you . . . "
- "Describe a time when . . . "
- "Share with me your experience in . . . "
- "Give me an example of . . . "
- "I am interested in hearing more about . . . "
- "Tell me about . . . "
- "How did you do . . . "

The Funnel Concept

An interview should move from the general to the specific. Think of the process as a funnel. At the top, or the beginning, you use open-ended questions to fill the funnel with a lot of information. As you approach the end, or bottom, you focus that information on the attribute you want to evaluate.

That's why, later in the interview, it's appropriate to use close-ended questions to clarify and confirm your understanding. For example, "What I hear you saying is that you have been the store manager for two years, is that correct?" The questions may also be used to pin down the applicant when he or she is vague about experience. For example, "Is it true that you were the project leader?" Questions like these and those in Figure 15.1 are a guide to funnel the general discussion into a clear picture of the applicant's qualifications or attributes.

Conducting the Interview

With a pool of applicants and a handful of questions at the ready, it is now time for the interview. The questions you have developed will provide the meat of the interview, but you'll need to design a format that makes the interview as efficient and productive as possible. The sample interview shown in Figure 15.2 is a useful starting point. While an interview can be longer or shorter, proportionally each section should be about the same.

Interviews and the Law

Numerous laws affect what questions can and cannot be asked in an interview. Their collective purpose is to prevent discrimination against applicants

FIGURE 15.1 Sample Interview Questions

Attribute	Questions	What to Look For
Detail-oriented	1. What action have you taken when you noticed an error or mistake in your job area? Outside your job area? 2. Explain a job you have been responsible for that required a high degree of accuracy. How did you ensure that accuracy? 3. Give me an example of when a deadline is more important than completing every detail. Give me an example of when completing every detail is more important than meeting the deadline. 4. On a scale from 1 to 10, how would you rate yourself in terms of being detail oriented and why? 5. Describe your thoughts on being assigned tasks with detailed directions versus being given a general overview of an assignment. 6. Tell me how detail is important in your current job and give examples.	1. Does applicant respond to errors, or ignore them? Is he or she more willing to point out the errors of others than admit his or her own? Does he or she care if errors occur? 2. Does the applicant have direct experience in a detail-oriented job? 3. Can the applicant give specific examples? Does he or she demonstrate an awareness of when details are important and when there can be too much detail? 4. How does the applicant perceive himself or herself? Can the applicant give examples? 5. How would the applicant go about handling each situation? Does he or she favor one over the other and why? 6. Is the level of detail about the same as the job you are trying to fill?
Attendance and stable work history	1. Describe your reasons for leaving each place of previous employment. 2. Describe your reasons for wanting to make a job change at this time. 3. Explain why you are interested in employment with our company. What are you seeking with us that you are not getting with your current employer? 4. Describe and explain any gaps in your employment and/or school record. 5. What do you feel is a good attendance record for a year? 6. Explain a time when your job became very difficult. What did you do?	1. Are the reasons acceptable? 2. Is the applicant looking to escape his or her present position? 3. Is this reason one that would keep this person with us? 4. Are they acceptable reasons? 5. Do you agree? 6. Is the response reasonable?

FIGURE 15.2 Sample Interview Format

TIME	CONTENT	PURPOSE
3 minutes	**Introduction** Introduce yourself and conduct "small talk that is big talk" "How are you?" "How 'bout those Bulls?"	Establishes rapport Puts you and applicants at ease Gets applicants talking Lets applicants know the game plan Puts applicant on notice that they are to talk—to answer your questions Provides clear details of the process
2 minutes	**Stage Setting** Say this: "During the time we have together I want to learn all I can about you and your qualifications for the position. Let me start out by asking you some questions, then I'll answer yours. By the way, we are interviewing a lot of people so I hope you don't mind if I take notes. Feel free to do the same."	Politely postpones their questions
20 minutes	**Your questions** Ask the questions you have prepared.	Let's you gather information needed to do a thorough evaluation. (You're finished when you have all the information you need.)
10 minutes	**Applicant Questions** Listen closely showing interest and concern. Sell your organization and the position.	Lets applicants gather information needed to make a decision.
5 minutes	**Complete interview evaluation form**	Documentation is critical in the selection process and in defending possible legal challenges.

based on race, sex, color, religion, national origin, veteran status, and real or perceived disabilities. Concern about asking a "prohibited" question can prevent the interviewer from conducting a relaxed and thorough interview. But if you treat applicants with respect and follow two simple rules of thumb, you can navigate your way safely through the sea of regulations.

First, don't ask questions that would be applicable only to a particular group. "Are you pregnant?" clearly would not apply to men. Other examples are less obvious. Questions about general qualifications, such as "Do you have a high school education?" have been shown by the courts to have an adverse effect on some minority groups, who on average have a lower percentage of high school diplomas than whites.

Second, ask only job-related questions. The best way to stay out of trouble is to focus on what you really want to know anyway: whether the person is qualified to do the job and whether he or she will do it. If you are concerned that a condition such as pregnancy may cause an employee to miss work or leave soon after being hired, ask questions about the person's career plans and work habits. Questions about education and training must be job related. If you have developed questions that explore attributes required for the job, chances are good you will ask questions that are perceptive *and* legal.

There is a third rule of thumb to follow—this one stems from the Americans with Disabilities Act (ADA), which prohibits discrimination against a person considered to have a disability. The act covers persons with physiological disorders or conditions, cosmetic disfigurement, anatomical loss, and mental or psychological disorders. Further, persons who have an impairment, have a record of an impairment, or are regarded as having an impairment are also protected.

The ADA does not require you to hire an unqualified person, but it does ask you to identify whether reasonable accommodations could be made to allow a disabled person to do the job. As with any applicant, therefore, your interview should focus on the person's qualifications. If the person is not qualified, there's no reason to get into the issue of reasonable accommodation. On the other hand, a qualified person with an impairment may be the person you select for the position, so understanding the accommodation required is important. The law precludes discrimination against a qualified person who can perform *the essential functions of the job*. Employment decisions cannot be based on a marginal function.

It is important to approach a discussion of reasonable accommodation from a positive standpoint. What would be necessary to allow this person to do the job? You may have ideas; so will the applicant—ask for them. It's not necessary to resolve this issue in the interview. Employers are not required to make the most expensive reasonable accommodation. Your objective in the interview is twofold: (1) to gain a perspective on what the individual's needs are and (2) to demonstrate a willingness to work with a qualified disabled applicant to place him or her in the job without regard to the applicant's impairment.

Managing and Motivating Your Employees

Finding the right people is just the beginning. Your long-term success will depend on your ability to manage and motivate your staff. Dwight Eisenhower once said, "Leadership is the art of getting someone else to do something you want done, because he (she) wants to do it." Indeed, all the items in a leader's job description can be summarized as getting desired results from the people led. How you go about this will depend on a number of factors, including the nature of your business, the type of job, and *you*.

Let's start with you. Each of us has our own management style. On the most fundamental level, management is all about how we interact with other people. A number of psychological profile programs can evaluate your interaction style at little or no expense. Developing a profile would be a wise investment of time and money, for it will reveal your style and, more important, how it contrasts with the style of others.

The nature of your business will make a difference as well. Your business is small. You won't have a human resources staff, you probably won't be able to offer rich benefit plans, and the career paths in your organization may be limited. On the other hand, your employees get to work very closely with the CEO—you! As a result, you and your employees enjoy something that large corporations must hire consultants and design elaborate plans to get: regular, direct communication about the direction of the business and changes in the marketplace.

Likewise, employees in large companies have a hard time seeing their impact, but your employees know they are making a contribution. It's the rare person who doesn't feel the need to be needed. You can also meet your employees' needs with greater flexibility than large corporations, which have eliminated any semblance of loyalty to their employees through an epidemic of downsizing. As a small business owner, you are in a position to take care of the people who have helped you to be successful.

The type of work your business offers will also impact how you manage and motivate employees. In a fast-food restaurant or a house-cleaning service, most employees will not be in career positions. You may often be the first employment experience for many of your employees. Having complete, detailed instructions and clear, straightforward rules will be important. Managers, crew chiefs, or employees of a technical business such as automotive services or printing will have more skills and desire career opportunities. They will also expect satisfaction from their work. Offering them an environment where they can grow and develop is important. Profit sharing or some other form of sharing in the rewards of success can be appropriate. Some owners even provide employees with options for ownership in the business.

The most important part of managing your employees is to remember you are the leader. The buck stops with you. Just as the coach is a role model for players on the team, you are the role model for how things get done in your business. You set the example for how things get done and how the business operates. Results will only be as high as the *lowest* level of performance that you tolerate.

Dealing with Problem Employees

Sandy was pleased with the recruiting job she did to hire Amber as manager of the second location in Sandy's executive suites franchise. Her background in customer service looked good and she had a great background in office skills. But the first day on the job Amber came in a few minutes late; by noon she was asking Sandy for special work hours to accommodate her son's summer activities. None of this had come up during the interview. On top of everything else, Amber seemed to be trying but was having trouble handling incoming phone calls. It was clear things were not going well.

Unfortunately, Sandy's initial response was all too typical. She put off telling Amber her concerns. She tried to reassure herself that this was just coincidence and it would all work out. When a friend suggested she had made a mistake and should let the new person go, Sandy said she felt responsible; she had made a commitment to Amber and felt obliged to work things out. Fortunately, this story has a satisfactory ending. After enduring another week of Amber's poor performance, Sandy saw the light and showed Amber the door.

Dealing with problem employees is *never* on the list of things small business owners enjoy about their business. To be an entrepreneur is to be an optimist. Even though it's hard to deal with the reality that others don't share your enthusiasm, dedication, and satisfaction in a job well done, you need to confront it. Your small business cannot tolerate anyone's not living up to the requirements of the job.

Let employees know the rules of the game. Too many business owners assume that employees will follow rules of respect and fairness without having them written out. That's simply not true. Written rules not only communicate your expectations, they set the foundation for effectively applying the rules should problems occur. Basic rules should be written and posted appropriately in the workplace. Some businesses have special rules, but most have similar rules that can be divided into two categories depending on the seriousness of the offense and consequently the punishment. Offenses in the less serious category result in progressive discipline. Violation of rules in the second category can result in immediate firing.

Offenses subject to progressive discipline

- Excessive absence or tardiness
- Poor quality work
- Failure to cooperate with coworkers
- Excessive complaints from customers

> **Offenses subject to serious discipline, including immediate discharge**
>
> - Theft
> - Violent behavior toward coworkers or others
> - Violation of safety rules and procedures
> - Falsification of company records

Maintaining Standards

The first step in dealing with a potential problem is communicating with the employee orally and on paper. The next step is maintaining or enforcing workplace standards. If you do not enforce your rules, they will be worth less than the paper they are written on.

The time to deal with a problem is the moment you suspect there is one. Because most of us are not looking for trouble, we often don't see it. But chances are if a problem has caught your attention, it is serious enough to warrant further investigation. Failure to deal with one problem employee can be worse than you might imagine. Your good employees will be discouraged if you don't deal with the troublemakers. Your failure to act may encourage them to develop the same bad habits as the original offender.

Be systematic in your approach to any problem. In today's litigious world you may be called upon to defend your actions in court. Over the years the process described below has come to be accepted as appropriate for taking effective, justified discipline. Moreover, if you follow these steps your other employees are likely to see your actions as fair.

Elements of Effective Discipline

Effective discipline shares the following characteristics:

- *It comes with no surprises.* Employees know what is expected. Rules and job requirements are communicated to and understood by everyone.
- *It is timely and consistent.* Waiting weeks or months to deal with a problem is not appropriate. Consistently applying the rules is also essential.
- *It is appropriate and reasonable in relation to the offense.* Whatever disciplinary action you take must be commensurate with the offense. Does the punishment fit the crime? Except in those cases that merit immediate firing, a progression of steps from verbal warning, written warning, and suspension to discharge is appropriate.
- *It is based on facts and thorough investigation.* Everyone deserves his or her day in court. Interview the offending employee, customers, supervisors, and coworkers before a judgment is reached.

- *It is respectful of employees.* Discipline should not be done in a manner that embarrasses the individual. In other words, public floggings are out!
- *It gains employee commitment.* Whenever possible, getting the offending employee to buy into a change in behavior is the best bet for seeing improvement.
- *It is documented.* Keeping a written record in a personnel folder will serve you well should there be a legal challenge to your actions.
- *It is monitored to make sure it works.* Follow up. Did the behavior change? Has the change become the norm? Monitoring performance will ensure the desired results.

CHAPTER 16

Finding and Developing Customers

Cheryl Babcock

The market research you conducted during your franchise investigation process should have indicated a strong demand for your franchise's products. As you prepare to open your business, you will turn again to marketing—this time to begin building a strong base of customers.

As a member of a franchise system, you can expect some marketing assistance from your franchisor. Large systems will offer regional advertising cooperatives that can purchase national and regional advertising to build awareness and demand for your system's products. A handful of prominent franchises—McDonald's, Domino's Pizza, and Coca Cola are examples—may invest in spots during the Super Bowl and other major televised events. Others may underwrite space advertising in national magazines.

But while these expensive campaigns build brand identification, they do not bring customers to your door. It's your responsibility to attract customers by developing a local presence through a careful mix of space advertising, direct mail, special offers, publicity, and other promotions. Your efforts should be directed at reaching people who live within five miles of your franchise so that when a customer makes a decision to purchase locally, he or she purchases from you!

Your franchisor can't help you make local marketing decisions. It may know what works in Poughkeepsie—but what works there may not work in Scottsdale, Ventura, or Milwaukee. You need to understand what sorts of activities people in your trading radius participate in so you can reach them cost effectively.

Growing Your Business

There are several ways to build your business.

- You can sell existing products to existing customers and create growth by increasing the frequency of purchases or the size of the transactions.
- You can sell existing products to new customers by running promotions designed to attract first-time customers to your outlet.
- You can sell new products to existing customers by cooperating in test marketing activities sponsored by your franchisor.
- You can sell new products to new customers by participating in new product launches *and* stepping up promotional activities directed at people who have never visited your store.

Developing new products is the responsibility of your franchisor—but developing new customers is *your* business. New customers are the hardest to find and the most expensive to get, but you need to search for them constantly if you want your business to thrive. Selling more products to existing customers is far easier but requires creativity in packaging your product in ways that convince customers to shop more frequently or purchase more.

Advertising and promotion as part of marketing can help accomplish all of these goals.

The Marketing Plan

The first step in marketing your product or service is developing a written marketing plan. A marketing plan is a document that identifies marketing activities and responsibilities for a specific time period—often one year but shorter or longer depending on your needs. Whether they are brief or lengthy, marketing plans should contain enough information to direct your marketing efforts. Include enough detail to make it clear which marketing activities must be accomplished and how you will gauge their success.

A written marketing plan forces you to think carefully about the planning period and what needs to be done during that time. It also shows relationships among all of your business's activities.

Without a written plan, it is easy to ignore some activities, lose track of the direction of the business, or change marketing plans whenever a short-term problem occurs. Save yourself that heartache and develop a solid plan. The major parts of a marketing plan are described below.

Marketing description. The target market(s) to be served should be described in detail.

Marketing objectives. Write down your goals for the time period you've selected so you can see later whether you have been successful. Goals may relate to sales, profits, market share, customers, products, and many other factors.

Competition. Competitors and their products, customer groups, and your strengths and weaknesses should be described.

Marketing mix. Each element of the marketing mix should be described with activities related to each element, time tables developed, and responsibilities assigned. This section can be quite brief or very detailed depending on the size of the business, the number of employees, and the amount of marketing activities performed.

Budget. Develop a budget to show how funds are to be spent for major marketing activities.

Planning your marketing takes time, but it pays off. When you plan ahead, you spend less time accomplishing your objectives and you achieve better and more profitable results. You also identify and correct problems easily. Advertising and promotional activities as part of your marketing plan are critical to the long-term success of your venture. Educate yourself about effective promotional strategies, and invest adequate time in planning and developing an effective marketing program.

How Advertising Can Help a Franchise Business

The two major goals of advertising are to attract new customers and to keep existing ones. To achieve these objectives, good advertisements must do what good salespeople do: they must follow the AIDA formula. This means:

- *Attention.* The advertisement must get the attention of the desired audience.
- *Interest.* Once the attention is attained, interest must be held.
- *Desire.* In holding interest, the advertisement must create a desire for whatever is being advertised.
- *Action.* Once attention, interest and desire have been attained, the advertisement must entice the customer to act and to go to the business offering the product.

Advertising, however, is not a cure-all.

- Advertising cannot make a business succeed if that business offers a poor product or inferior service. If you conducted a diligent prepurchase investigation, this shouldn't be a problem.
- Advertising cannot lead to sales if the prospective customers it brings to the business are ignored or poorly treated. Teach your employees to recognize repeat customers and warmly welcome both new and repeat custom-

ers. Excellent customer service can be a strong incentive for a customer to return. Poor customer service will keep them away.

- Advertising cannot create customers overnight or increase sales with a single effort. It takes repetition! Research indicates that a customer must hear your business's name 17 times before the name starts to register or persuades the customer to act. And that's 17 times in just a few months—not 17 times in ten years.
- Advertising will not build confidence in the business if it is untruthful or misleading. Never, never lie.

Developing a Promotion Plan

The finest product or service is useless until it is in the customer's hands. Most people must be informed and motivated before they will buy products. Promotion can accomplish that. It is the art or science of moving the images of the franchisee's business into the prospect's mind. Promotion comes from the Latin verb *movere*, which means "to advance," "to move forward." It's an aggressive word, and you should learn to say it with a smile!

Advertising, personal selling, and sales promotion are the major ways businesses promote their products to customers. Whether a business should use them is not the question. Instead, franchisees should ask, "How much and what kind of promotion do I need?"

How much promotion depends on the depth of your pockets, but, generally speaking, a business should spend 7 to 10 percent of its first-year gross sales on local advertising. Once you've forecasted sales and set your promotional budget, you'll have to consider what kind of promotion. You could easily spend your entire budget on producing and airing a single television commercial, but that wouldn't be very effective. Instead, identify the promotional vehicles available in your target radius and find out which work best among your target customers.

Nearby franchisees may share some insights. Examining how your competitors advertise is also helpful; chances are they've learned a few things. Your chamber of commerce or Small Business Development Center may be able to tell you whether direct mail is effective, which population segments respond to coupons, and whether bus or subway advertising will make any impact whatsoever.

Your franchisor may provide some promotional materials, such as ad slicks or a jingle to use in a radio advertisement. But a jingle won't be any good unless you know which radio station your target customers listen to! That's the kind of knowledge you will develop as you become acquainted with your customers and their habits. Your promotional strategy and your target customer are interlocked. In the early months, you may need to conduct market research to plan your promotional mix.

Ask Your Customers Questions

When you're trying to figure out how and where to promote your business, ask your customers for help. Ask them the following questions:

- Is there anything you couldn't find?
- Is this your first visit to our store? (Any greeting other than "Can I help you?")
- Where are you from? (Ask for their zip code to help you ascertain what locale your customers are coming from.)
- How did you find out about our store? (A very critical question!)
- How else might we be of service to you?
- How might we serve you better?

Listen to their answers and value the information for what it is: primary market research data. Write down the customer's exact words and take them into consideration as you determine your promotional mix.

Choosing Your Promotional Strategies

As you plan your promotional mix, attach price tags to each potential strategy. Every promotional strategy costs money. Seek to concentrate your efforts on one or two strategies that work well for your business.

Consider the following promotional strategies.

Point-of-purchase displays. Use in-store units provided by the franchisor or the manufacturer/distributor of the product to highlight a special promotion on an impulse item such as a movie tie-in product. Just keep in mind that products pushed in point-of-purchase displays are often loss leaders. Less profit is accepted in exchange for pushing the item through the distribution channel.

Publicity. Use free ink and free air to your advantage by using press releases to publicize activities in your store. Alert the media to your grand opening events. Develop "evergreen" stories about your business that you can supply to the local media. Visit the marketing department of your local newspaper for information on targeting its readers. Use this information to angle your release. Make sure you catch the reader's attention. Keep the message simple. Be sure to include the five Ws (who, what, where, when, and why) and the noble H (how) of journalism.

Community events. Can you support the local high school football team or band? A young soccer team? Look for ways to tie into what is happening in your market area.

Personal selling. Locate appropriate clubs or organizations in your area and start building a network of contacts. Figure your salary and expenses as a promotional cost. Use advertising to make your selling efforts more effective. It may make customers more receptive to your sales presentation or even tell part of the message, thus saving much of your time.

Tours and seminars. Look for ways to bring groups into your store. Consider sponsoring a tour for a local Brownie troop, or an educational seminar. Exposing visitors to your business will pay off in the long run.

Frequent buyer coupons. An inexpensive way to encourage repeat business is to reward customers for their loyalty. Offer a free cup of coffee for every ten purchased; $25 worth of framing free for every $250 spent; a free UPS delivery for every ten packages sent; and so on.

Registries. Are your products suitable for new couples, new parents, or new home owners? What about birthdays, anniversaries, graduations, bar and bat mitzvahs, and other milestones acknowledged with gifts? Look for unique ways to encourage purchases.

Storefront displays. Change your window or storefront display frequently to attract attention. Car lots are experts at this. They'll do anything to get customers to look at them as they drive by: streamers, hot air balloons, raised hoods, or stuffed animals in cars. They want passersby to notice what's on the lot and stop when they see a car that interests them.

Freebies. Freebies are a tremendously effective promotional gimmick. Use them to get the customer's attention, to create interest in a new product or service, or to gather market research. Freebies don't have to be expensive to help you connect with customers.

Discount coupons. Coupons build traffic as they reveal the effectiveness of a particular medium. Code them so you can tell whether the customer received it in a local newspaper ad, a door-to-door flyer, or some other medium. As they are redeemed, you will know which medium got the most response. Be sure to include an expiration date and multiple-use disclaimers that say the coupon cannot be used in conjunction with other promotions or discounts. Always test coupons in small quantities before you roll them out. Consider using them as part of your grand opening celebration, to introduce a new product, or to stimulate business during slow times.

Newsletters. Place ads in community newsletters within a two-mile radius of your franchise. The ads don't cost much and help keep your visibility high. Study the community newsletter and develop your own format. Consider sending out your own newsletter every couple of months.

Paid media advertising. This choice assumes that you know what your target customer reads or listens to. Ask the display ad department of the magazine or newspaper for its media kit, a reader profile, and the rates for their mailing lists for the geographic areas you want to reach. Many magazines will sell lists by zip code. Contact local radio stations for demographic statistics about their listeners.

Direct mail. Direct mail doesn't work in every market—but when it does, it takes you straight to the heart of your target market and is worth every penny it costs. Work with mailing-list brokers (find them in the Yellow Pages) to identify list possibilities. Ask for sample names so you can check mailing list accuracy against your target customer profiles. Then prepare a self-mailer or mailing package that is attractive and makes an offer that people will want to respond to.

Flyers. Have flyers printed and distribute them in your community.

Develop a database. An accurate and up-to-date database of information about your customers can mean money in the bank. Develop one by capturing names through a guest log, orders, warranty cards, feedback forms, or other vehicles that let you gather name, address, phone number, and pertinent demographic information. Database software is so easy to use that you may even want to start separate databases for the media, competitors, and vendors and suppliers. It's much easier to have this information in a single computer file instead of scattered on paper scraps all over your office.

Network. Everybody networks. In school, you networked for information about teachers and courses. When you moved into a new community, you networked for information about doctors, dentists, car repair service, baby-sitters, and bargains. On the job, you networked your way to sales leads, brainstormed your way to better designs, or solved problems with coworkers. As a franchisee, you can network your way to a surprising number of new customer connections. Develop your network and build core groups of people within it. A network grows naturally from the loose association of people you already know and can be broadened as you participate in local business and community organizations. Networking can spell success in big letters.

Handling Taxes, Banks, Insurance, and Recordkeeping

Janice Dwyer and Ronald L. Noll, MS, CPA

No matter how much service and support a franchisor offers, there are still many responsibilities that are yours to execute as a franchise business owner. It's up to you to purchase enough insurance to protect yourself and your family in case of a disaster and to keep records that let you monitor the health of your business. It's also your job to pay income and employment taxes and to collect and transfer state and local sales taxes correctly.

Each one of these areas is essential to your success. As you create your franchise's organization and delegate responsibilities, be sure that these are assigned to someone who can meet the challenge. In the early years, it may well be you.

Registering Your Business with Tax Authorities

Before you ever collect or pay a cent of tax, you will have to register your business with federal and state tax authorities.

Obtain a Federal Employee Identification Number

Whether your business is a sole proprietorship, a corporation, or a partnership, you must apply with the Internal Revenue Service (IRS) for a federal employer identification number (EIN). An EIN is to a business entity what a Social Security number is to an individual. This is the number you use for all of your tax filings.

Once your entity is formed, you must complete and file IRS Form SS-4 with the Internal Revenue Service. Send a cover letter with the form by certified mail, return receipt requested, so you know the IRS has received it. In several weeks, the IRS will acknowledge receipt of the letter and send you your EIN. You can obtain the number over the phone by calling the IRS (the Atlanta office number is 404-455-2360). You must have the completed form in front of you at the time of the call, and you still must send or fax in the form.

State Sales Tax Number

If you are required to collect sales taxes on the products or services you offer, you must apply for a sales tax dealer number. In Florida, a sales tax dealer must collect sales tax and remit it monthly with a sales tax return. You are allowed to keep a small portion of the tax to cover your administrative and accounting costs. Check your state's laws and requirements and discuss this issue with your accountant.

State Unemployment Compensation Returns

In certain states you need to file a report to determine status with the appropriate state department that oversees employment and labor. The state then assigns you an account number to use when filing quarterly state unemployment returns. Discuss this with your accountant.

Opening a Bank Account

Opening a business bank account requires several items. Unless you are a sole proprietor, you will be asked for a copy of your filed organizational document (for example, articles of incorporation, certificate of limited partnership). If you are operating a business under a different name, you will also have to show proof of compliance with your state's fictitious name, trade name, or assumed name statute. A federal employer identification number is also a prerequisite for opening a business account.

The bank will give you a document of "corporate resolutions" specifying who has authority to sign checks, borrow money, and so on. This document must be completed and signed by an authorized person and the company seal affixed. If you are organized as a corporation, the resolutions should be included in the minutes of the organizational or first meeting of the board of directors.

Consult your accountant about the best type of bank account for your business as well as cash management options like credit card merchant accounts and overdraft protection.

Insuring Your Business

Because you will be required to purchase and carry several types of insurance, insurance will be a big percentage of your start-up costs and continuing operations. Both your franchisor and your landlord will require you to carry insurance to protect their interests, and you will need to purchase additional insurance to protect your investment, your equity, and your personal assets.

Work with an agent who specializes in business insurance. Tell the agent about the requirements of your franchise and lease agreements, and ask about other types of coverage that may be appropriate. If your franchisor offers insurance through a national insurance agency, compare its quotes with quotes from your local agent.

To fully protect yourself, your assets, and your family, consider the following types of insurance:

- *Property.* This insurance covers damage to buildings you own or lease and are responsible for insuring.
- *Contents, inventory, and equipment.* This insurance protects and reimburses you in case of theft.
- *Loss of income and/or business interruption.* Often overlooked but very important, this coverage protects you from loss of earnings if you cannot operate your business because property and contents are damaged.
- *Business liability, including products and completed operation.* This insurance protects your business from lawsuits resulting from bodily injury or property damage sustained by customers from your operations.
- *Automobile.* Even if you don't own and operate a business vehicle, you should purchase liability coverage for hired and nonowned automobiles to protect employees running errands on your behalf or vehicles rented for business use.
- *Workers' compensation.* Mandatory in most states if you employ a certain number of employees, this insurance protects your business from claims arising from injury to your employees while they're working. It can also protect you if you choose to purchase the coverage. Check with your agent on the rules in your particular state.
- *Umbrella.* This insurance provides a coverage limit for your business insurance and automobile needs above that which you purchase under primary coverage.
- *Employee dishonesty.* Also often overlooked, this insurance covers losses from employee theft of funds or inventory.
- *Buy/sell agreement insurance:* Proceeds can be used to fund agreement in case of partner's death.

Your franchisor may require you to list it as an additional insured on many of these policies to protect it from claims brought against it from your business operations. Most insurance carriers will provide this extension readily.

When purchasing insurance, ask for the broadest payment terms available. Most insurance can be paid monthly, which frees up valuable cash reserves. As you compare quotes and companies, also keep in mind that what you are really purchasing is the insurance carrier's promise to pay if you do have a claim. Make sure the carrier you select is financially solvent. Look for companies that have been rated A, XII, or better by A.M. Best Rating.

Assuming that your new franchise is not a highly hazardous operation, your biggest obstacle to purchasing insurance will be your lack of experience in your new business. Just as automobile insurers like drivers with clean driving records, business insurers like to see companies with established track records. Your new business won't have one, but your franchisor will. Ask your franchisor to recommend insurers that are familiar with its system, or introduce your agent to the franchisor to collect historical information about the system. If you are buying business interruption insurance, your franchisor will be able to tell your agent what kinds of interruptions can be expected.

If you purchase adequate amounts of the right kind of insurance, you'll be amply protected should the inevitable happen. Don't skimp on insurance. It is an important financial partner in your business.

Keeping Financial Records

Carefully tracking "money in" and "money out" is the first step toward the profitable management of your franchise. Without adequate records, your franchise won't be able to efficiently handle buying, inventory control, credit and collections, expense control, personnel, production control, and most other aspects of management. Without proper accounting and recordkeeping, it will be impossible to know how your business is doing and impossible to correct problems in a timely fashion.

Failure to maintain adequate records may also land you in hot water with the Internal Revenue Service. Although the IRS does not prescribe specific accounting methods, records, or systems, it does require you to maintain accurate, permanent books of account that clearly show taxable and nontaxable income, expenses, and allowable deductions. Records also must be kept so that they are available for inspection by IRS officers. Because part of your job is to keep government records, it is considered a breach of your trust (fiduciary) duty if you fail to properly remit government monies that you have collected. In such a case, you may be held personally liable for unpaid taxes even if you operate under a corporate entity. The IRS has even been known to hold bookkeepers—not just business owners—responsible for failure to pay monies to the government resulting from a breach of trust.

You can elect to use cash accounting or accrual accounting to report your franchise's income and expenses. The differences between the two are shown in the box below. Discuss the matter with your bookkeeper or accountant before making your choice.

Cash Accounting versus Accrual Accounting

The Cash Method	The Accrual Method
The cash method of accounting is used by individuals and small businesses that do not have inventories.	The purpose of the accrual method of accounting is to match the income and expenses in the correct year.
All items of income received during the year are included in gross income.	All items of income are included in gross income when earned even though they may be received in another tax year.
You must usually deduct expenses in the tax year that you actually pay them.	You deduct business expenses when you become liable for them whether or not you pay them in the same year. All events that set the amount of the liability must have happened, and you must be able to figure the amount of the expense with reasonable accuracy.

Business records can be kept manually or on a computerized system. Manual systems like OneWrite are designed for use in any retail or service establishment, whereas systems like McBee Systems for Photographers are designed for specific retail and service trades. Trade associations often provide guidelines on accounting records tailored to a particular business.

Recordkeeping systems vary in their cost and their degree of sophistication. Let's look at the most common types available.

Manual Systems

Manual recordkeeping systems, such as the series available from the Dome Publishing Company, are designed to record inflows and outflows of money. Similar to a home checkbook but more detailed, manual systems require no technical expertise and are easy to understand. Initially, they are less expensive than computerized systems because they don't require any investment in computer hardware or software.

Among the least expensive and easiest to use manual systems are the Dome Simplified Monthly Bookkeeping Record #612 and Dome Simplified Weekly Bookkeeping Record #600, which are priced at around $10 and available at stationery stores and chain stores. (You can also order a copy by calling 800-432-4352). Dome records contain the following forms sufficient for recording the results of one year's business:

- a monthly record of income and expenses
- an annual summary sheet of income and expenditures
- a weekly payroll record covering 15 employees
- individual employee compensation records

They also contain general instructions, a sample filled-in record of income and expenses, and a list of 276 expenses that are legally deductible for federal income tax purposes.

Designed by a certified public accountant (CPA) over 50 years ago, the Dome system fits every type and kind of business. Like a personal checkbook, the record can be carried around and filled out after the checks have been written. Dome handles cash-basis accounting very efficiently.

Accrual-basis accounting is better served by the OneWrite system, one of the most common recordkeeping systems used by small businesses. OneWrite has a time-saving feature that allows three records to be posted simultaneously at one entry, thus reducing errors. A hot carbon strip creates the check stub as you write the check, and ledger balances in various categories are carried forward. This recordkeeping system has three combinations: accounts payable, accounts payable/payroll, and accounts receivable. At a cost of approximately 20 to 30¢ cents per check, OneWrite is more costly than Dome, whose checks cost less than 10¢ cents each.

OneWrite is manufactured by a number of companies. Its original manufacturer was Burroughs Business Systems and Forms; you may request brochures and catalogs by writing to the Burroughs Corporation at P.O. Box 27, Claymont, DE 19703, or visiting its Web site at www.burroughs.com. Other major suppliers of OneWrite are McBee Systems and Safeguard Business Systems. The McBee Systems catalog is free on request from the company, a division of Litton Industries, 151 Cortland Street, Belleville, NJ 07109, or from its Web site at www.mcbeesystems.com. You can learn about Safeguard Business Systems services and products at www.safe-guard.com.

Computerized Systems

Many software programs are designed to keep computerized records for small businesses. As with everything, you get what you pay for when it comes to recordkeeping software. The less expensive packages have limitations and may need various "work arounds" to meet your needs. Even with the better low-end software packages, we highly recommend that you purchase software support in every case. Call or write the following companies for information on the better low-end recordkeeping software:

- DacEasy Instant Accounting: DacEasy, Inc., 17950 Preston Road, Suite 800, Dallas, Texas 75252; 800-322-3279; Web: www.daceasy.com.
- OneWrite Plus: NEBS Software, Inc., 500 Main Street, Groton, MA 01471; 800-388-8000.
- Peachtree Complete Accounting: Peachtree Software, Inc., 1505 Pavilion Place, Norcross, GA 30093; 800-247-3224; Web: www.peachtree.com.
- QuickBooks: Intuit, P.O. Box 3014, Menlo Park, CA 94026; 800-446-8848; Web: www.intuit.com.

Higher-end software offers recordkeeping systems that are specifically tailored to a particular industry, such as day care, fast food, or construction. These sophisticated recordkeeping programs may cost several thousand dollars per module. Here again, your trade association can provide guidelines for selecting an appropriate system for your type of franchise.

One caveat to keep in mind is that all of these programs require an understanding of accounting theory as well as an accountant who is familiar with your particular software.

You can get the best of both worlds—low-end and high-end—by using an accountant who can supply low-cost software that you can use daily and that is integrated with the sophisticated package used by the accounting firm for your quarterly and year-end reporting. And even though a software company can only handle your computer questions, an accountant can answer all of your bookkeeping and accounting questions at one time as well as dial into your computer and fix any problems you may be having.

Two major national accounting software firms whose accountants provide this type of low-cost bookkeeping solution are Creative Solutions and UBCC. Find out about Creative Solutions and its 200 products by calling 800-968-8900 or by visiting www.csisolutions.com. To contact UBCC, call 800-762-8222.

Hiring a Professional

We highly recommend that you hire a competent bookkeeper *and* a professional accountant. Take time to find the right accountant. Get referrals from others in your business as well as from trade associations, management consultants, business associates, and friends.

It's not necessary to hire an accountant to do your day-to-day bookkeeping, but your bookkeeper must have adequate experience and qualifications to handle the recordkeeping needs of your franchise. Even if you feel that you can handle your own monthly bookkeeping, it is still advisable to have an accountant review your work monthly for at least three months to ensure that you are completely competent in your recordkeeping method of choice.

A professional accountant can offer important advice and help you determine what records to keep, the most economical way of maintaining those records, techniques for avoiding unnecessary taxes, and the most efficient system for cashflow management. An accountant's advice is helpful in keeping track of inventory so that your business will always have enough on hand for customers—not too much or too little. An accountant will also suggest methods for depreciating assets and maintaining up-to-date balance sheets and income statements. It may be more efficient, easier, and less costly overall to engage both bookkeeping and accounting professionals through an accounting firm.

No matter how you decide to keep your records, be sure to keep them up to date to accurately manage the financial status of your franchise.

Essential Cash Records

Daily records

- Cash on hand
- Bank balance (Keep business and personal funds separate.)
- Daily summary of sales and cash receipts
- Correction of all errors in recording collections on accounts
- Maintenance of a record of all monies paid out by cash or check

Weekly records

- Accounts receivable
- Accounts payable
- Payroll
- Taxes and reports to state and federal government

Monthly

- All journal entries classified and posted to general ledger according to like elements for both income and expenses
- Profit and loss statement for the month

Monthly *(continued)*

- Balance sheet accompanying profit and loss statement showing assets and the investment of the owner
- Reconciled bank statement (i.e., owner's books agree with bank's record of cash balance)
- Balanced petty cash account
- All federal tax deposits, withheld income, FICA taxes (Form 501), and state taxes
- Age (i.e., 30, 60, 90 days, etc.) of accounts receivable past due
- Inventory control to remove dead stock and order new stock

The double funnel shown in Figure 17.1 illustrates the types of activities that constitute the major categories of a cash-based business. The control point at the funnel's neck represents your recordkeeping activities and your bank reconciliation, which ensures that your books agree with the bank's figures and that any discrepancies are resolved and understood by both parties.

FIGURE 17.1 Double Funnel Model of Cash-Based Businesses

MONEY IN

Sales of product
Sales tax collected to be remitted
Initial capital or bank loans
Refunds or adjustments

CONTROL POINT

MONEY OUT

Rent, utilities, phones, etc.
Salaries and taxes on salaries
Insurance, i.e., fire, health, liability
Retirement plans

CHAPTER 18

Building a Profitable Relationship with Your Franchisor

Lance Winslow III

Now that you have invested time, energy, and money in buying a franchise, you need to master the secrets of working within the system and taking advantage of everything your franchisor and fellow franchisees have to offer.

A franchise is like a marriage. When communication is good, so is the marriage. But when communication lines shut down, the franchisor-franchisee relationship can become adversarial, hostile, and aggressive—and everyone suffers.

This chapter offers tips on creating and maintaining positive relationships that will help you and the franchisor achieve your mutual goals.

Why Communication Is Important

Good communication is vital to any franchise organization, whether it is large or small, corporate or down-to-earth.

In a very small franchise system with fewer than 30 units, your input is vital. A small system can't afford many franchisee failures. Because your failure could affect future sales, your success matters a great deal. Your problems and suggestions take precedence over all other aspects of the business. You and other franchisees may be able to give the president or founder your feedback on how the franchised model works in different locations with varying demographics and local economic environments. If the franchisor can solve these problems at a unit level now, it will ensure the success of future units 100-fold. Pass along your observations and help the founder work out administrative and organizational bugs in the system.

In medium-sized franchises (those with up to 100 units) you will meet, but not develop a first-name relationship with, the founder or president. Instead, your closest relationship will be with a master franchise operator or a regional director—a relationship that is easy to cultivate. Either of these people will be concerned about your outlet because a regional director may receive incentives for your performance and a master franchisee actually receives part of your royalty payments. The more money you generate, the more money they make.

A large franchisor (those with over 100 units) will have layers of corporate management as well as an intricate web of master franchises, international franchises, and regional directors or master franchisees assigned to different areas. In these companies the founder may have sold most of his or her stake in the company and no longer be actively involved in the operation. Many large franchisors are publicly traded companies that buy and own other franchise systems and may even choose to sell their interest in your franchise to another company. To maintain stability, stay on good terms with your master franchise operator or regional director, who will still be there tomorrow no matter who buys, sells, or trades stock ownership or rights at corporate headquarters.

The Benefits of Good Communication

When you're friendly, helpful, upbeat, and honest in your dealings with your franchisor, you will accrue many benefits that are rarely enjoyed by problem franchisees. For starters, you may be asked to assume extra duties when your system expands quickly. When growth is fast, a franchisor may "outsource" certain functions "in-house" by recruiting and paying franchisees to train new franchisees, sell new units, develop new products, streamline systems, or market services. Both you and the franchisor benefit from this arrangement because

- it costs less than hiring consultants or new franchisor staff;
- it improves your profit when franchisees are paid for their help;
- secrets are not lost to industrywide consultants;
- franchisees do a better job because they have a vested interest in making sure the system succeeds; and
- it builds system teamwork and lets franchisor and franchisee move fast in the marketplace.

Franchisees who are regarded as positive partners are likely to be on good terms with the corporate office staff and regional director, and may come to mind when the franchisor looks for outlets in which to test a new product.

Franchisors take product tests very seriously. They invest generously in local marketing, signage, new menus, new brochures, and other collateral materials to support the product. All these activities help you attract new business to your store. Even if the new product or service is never implemented systemwide (a real possibility as over 50 percent of new products fail), you still win because you now have a larger customer base and greater local awareness of your business.

Testing new products is a benefit of belonging to a franchised system. A new product failure can put a small nonfranchised company out of business. But a franchise can absorb the loss, learn lessons from the experience, and move on—all at the expense of the franchisor, not you!

Of course, if you are a chronic complainer and a problem franchisee, none of these extra perks will be available to you. So how do you maintain a positive relationship with your franchisor and promote a win-win situation? The answer is very simple—yet too few franchisees practice it.

Be Nice—to Everyone

To your franchisor's regional directors, office staff, vendors, and consultants, you are a customer. That's why it's essential to treat everyone associated with your franchisor the way you want your customers to treat you. Always treat them with respect. If you have ever gone out of your way to help a good customer, then you have an idea of why you should be on good terms with these professionals.

At your franchisor's headquarters, days are hectic and people are busy—just like you. When you are sincere, polite, upbeat, and appreciative, you will stand out positively among callers who are overstressed and short-tempered. But join the ranks of those who are abrupt, rude, or arrogant, and your request may be placed at the bottom of the pile. At a franchisor's headquarters, that may be a long way down.

What if you ask headquarters to fax something to your bank so you can buy a new piece of equipment for your store? Ask nicely, and the staff person may simply walk down the hall and pull out your file and fax it right then. Treat the person rudely and your request might take a week. Either way probably complies with the franchise agreement. Make things easy on yourself. Try to get on the unspoken, unwritten list of "good" franchisees.

Likewise, be respectful of your franchisor's vendors. They may have bid low to land your franchisor's account and take advantage of the guaranteed volume and sales that come with a captured market. Because they profit from volume, they may lose money if you demand too much personal service. This doesn't mean you shouldn't get what you pay for. It *does* mean you should demand in a nice way. Invite them to your store. Explain your situation in detail. Show them the problem. But be organized so the vendor or consultant can work efficiently.

When consultants contact you, help them in their search for knowledge. Remember, whatever they recommend to the franchisor might be implemented. If you deny them reasonable access to your business or purposely hide things from them, you run up consulting costs and risk rendering their recommendations worthless. Worse yet, if their recommendations become franchisor policy, you will surely pay for not participating in the process.

Let's say your franchisor has hired a computer consultant to look over the computer system and its use—at $200 per hour. Before the consultant visits, prepare for your meeting. Set aside time to talk without being interrupted. Have your computer turned on and booted up and a cup of coffee ready for your guest. Tell the consultant what you like and dislike about the current system and what you think should be improved. Being organized will save time, enhance the value of your comments, and make a big difference in the consultant's recommendations. Cooperating with vendors and consultants is not only ethical, it also demonstrates the attitude you need to prosper within a franchise system.

How to Complain Effectively

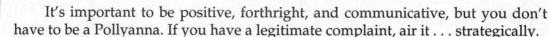

It's important to be positive, forthright, and communicative, but you don't have to be a Pollyanna. If you have a legitimate complaint, air it . . . strategically.

Start off with praise. Single out something that is being done right and tell the franchisor how happy you are. *Then* mention the little something that is causing stress. Mention your solution or offer to sit down and brainstorm for solutions with a regional director or company representative.

It's effective to discuss problems during a meeting at your store. It's your point of power and will enable you to negotiate from a stronger position. Schedule the meeting for peak business hours so the franchisor or regional director can see how efficient and clean your store is and how closely you are following system standards. Treat the visit like a military inspection. When the inspection is over, explain the problem, offer your suggestions, and ask what you should do. Remember: The art of diplomacy is letting someone else get your way.

Your regional director has probably encountered your problem in other outlets and can tell you what other franchisees did to improve the problem. The director can identify which solutions worked best and which not at all as well as which solutions were approved by the company and why. Your solutions will also be of interest. Even if your solution doesn't work now, it may be a missing puzzle piece to a long-term solution that will work systemwide.

If you have really bad news—say you're in default on your franchise agreement—don't lie low. Talk with your franchisor. Develop a time line that you can live with to return to compliance. Franchisors don't want to terminate good franchisees.

More Communication Strategies That Benefit You

Here are more ways to communicate to your advantage!

- *Generate extra public relations.* If you sponsor a Little league team that wins the county championship or a contestant in a citywide beauty contest who becomes Miss Any Town, pass along the good news. Your franchisor will include it in its franchisee newsletter so other franchisees can see an example of good local public relations.

- *Improve efficiency.* If you design a form that helps you increase efficiency, fax it to the vice president of operations with a note: "Bob: This form helps us run more efficiently. Perhaps other franchisees might like it. Do you want me to mail you a disk with the file on it? I used Microsoft Excel 7.0."
- *Help with your expansion.* If you want to expand your area and add another store, do some preliminary demographic work and a finance study that includes a schedule of the franchisor's estimated increased income from royalties and purchases. Ask your franchisor to review it and call you to talk. You'll improve your chances of being approved.
- *Volunteer to help with teamwork.* If your franchisor has a franchisee advisory board, offer to join and help franchisor-franchisee relations.

Relating with Other Franchisees

If your franchise system is a team, then your franchisor is the coach and the other franchisees are your teammates. Good relationships among teammates are essential to the health of the entire system and every one of its members. Some effective ways to build a solid network among your fellow franchisees are described below.

Remember: TEAM is an acronym.

T E A M = Together Everyone Accomplishes More

Call and Say Hi

It's great to have colleagues you can share with. Make a quick call now and then to say hi and remind your fellow franchisees that you're always there. There's no telling what a short phone call can yield: a good lead, a novel way to attract customers, or a strategy for training new employees. Swap stories about the worst customer or the most ridiculous complaint of the year—or just listen sympathetically. For every story you have about the customer from hell, a fellow franchisee will have one to match. You can both laugh and be thankful you own your own business and that it isn't the boss who's giving you a hard time.

Monthly Meetings

Round up the nearest four or five franchisees and have a monthly meeting. Invite your regional director to join you and take notes. Invite a franchisor representative—the higher up the better. Keep the meeting low-key. Meet over pizza or arrange some other casual meeting to ensure a happy atmosphere. Talk shop. Brainstorm. Keep it light with few complaints and lots of solutions and ideas. The company representative will take your concerns to the top.

Speak Highly of Other Franchisees

Whenever you hear anything said about a fellow franchisee, say something positive. Try, "Bob is one of the top producers in the company," "Betty runs a tight ship," "Everyone loves Bill, he's such a great guy," or "Linda's store is so well kept up that you can tell she is on top of things." When you hear something negative, downplay its importance unless it happens a lot. If it does, call the franchisee and say, "You know, Bob, I thought I'd call you directly. I'm sure it's nothing, but Mrs. Smith, one of your customers, said . . . " If what you hear indicates that the problem is persisting, call your regional director or mention it the next time the director comes to visit.

Vacation Management

Franchisees can relieve one another when they want to take a vacation, especially if they don't have a manager who is capable of handling every aspect of the business. Set up an arrangement with neighboring franchisees to help keep an eye on things while they are away. Work out a trade so they can help you when you want a break. Alert your regional director when you're going on vacation. Between your manager, regional director, and the franchisee who is pitching in for you, your business will be safe while you're on vacation.

Joint Accounts

When you have orders you can't fill or an account that's too big to handle, call a fellow franchisee and spread the wealth. Your fellow franchisee will be thankful for the extra business and you will have satisfied customers.

Referrals

When customers want service outside your exclusive territory or are too far away to shop in your store, refer them to another franchisee in your system. Referrals strengthen your company's goodwill and name recognition. They also make someone just like you very happy. And because what goes around comes around, you'll get referrals, too.

Clubs and Organizations

Joining at least one service club helps your business become part of the town. If your neighboring franchisees belong to certain groups, you should belong to a group to which they don't. If one belongs to the Rotary, another to Kiwanis, and a third to the Optimist Club, join the Elks or the Lions or the board of directors for the hospice, the YMCA, the Boy Scouts, or another civic group. That way, each of you will be meeting new people, assisting with service projects, and strengthening your referral network by pooling information about new contacts.

Chamber of Commerce Meetings

Attend chamber of commerce meetings with your fellow franchisees. When more than one franchisee of a system participates in chamber of commerce meetings or mixers, you can answer virtually any question about your system under the sun.

Cooperative Marketing

If you have a countywide newspaper and want to place an advertisement, see if other franchisees are interested. You can put each phone number and location at the bottom of the ad and divide the costs. If you're on good terms with your vendors, they may share in the costs; if you're on your franchisor's "good list," your advertising request will surely be approved.

As a franchisee, you are in business for yourself—but not by yourself. Use this fact to your advantage. Use the resources of your franchisor, your vendors, your fellow franchisees. Make your business great. Enjoy your American Dream. And no matter what you do, don't ever give up. You're "gonna" do fine.

Resource List

Associations

American Association of Franchisees and Dealers (AAFD), PO Box 81887, San Diego, CA 92138-1887; 800-733-9858.

Association of Small Business Development Centers (ASBDC), 3108 Columbia Pike, Suite 300, Arlington, VA 22204; 703-271-8700

International Franchise Association (IFA), 1350 New York Ave., N.W., Suite 900, Washington, DC 20005-4709; 202-662-0763.

Society of Franchising, University of St. Thomas, MPL100 LaSalle Ave., Minneapolis, MN 55403-2005; 612-962-4402

The Franchise Center, University of Texas at El Paso, Miners Hall, Suite 108, El Paso, TX 79968

Franchise Market and Research Services

American Marketing Association, 250 S. Wacker Dr., Suite 200, Chicago, IL 60606; 312-648-0536; www.ama.org/hmpage.htm

BetheBoss: www.betheboss.com/btb

Bison: www.bisonl.com

Expertise Center: www.expertcenter.com

FRANCORP, 2020 Governors Dr., Olympia Fields, IL 60461; 708-481-2900

FRANDATA, 1155 Connecticut Ave., N.W., Suite 275, Washington, DC 20036; 202-659-8640

FRANNET, 4901 Morena Blvd., Suite 122, San Diego, CA 92117; 800-FRANNET

Sales Marketing Network: www.info-now.com

The Internet 800/888 Directory: inter800.com/search.htm

Trade Show Central: www.tscentral.com

Women's Franchise Network: www.franchise.org.wfn

Sample Franchise Agreement

BOBBY RUBINO'S RIBS n MORE FRANCHISE AGEEEMENT

between

SALLY CORPORATION

a Florida corporation

and

_____

Dated: _____, 199____

Location: _____

_____

_____

© 1996 Keith J. Kanouse, P.A.
Lake Wyman Plaza, Suite 353
2424 North Federal Highway
Boca Raton, Florida 33431

BOBBY RUBINO'S RIBS n MORE FRANCHISE AGREEMENT

THIS BOBBY RUBINO'S RIBS n MORE FRANCHISE AGREEMENT is signed on
_____, 199____, between SALLY CORPORATION, a Florida corporation and
_____.

This Agreement has been written in an informal style to make it easier to read and to make sure that you become thoroughly familiar with all of the important rights and obligations that the Agreement covers before you sign it. In this Agreement, we refer to Sally Corporation as "we," "us" or "our." We refer to you as "you" or "your." If a corporation, partnership or other entity is going to own your Bobby Rubino's Ribs n More Franchise, you will notice certain provisions applicable to its shareholders, partners or members, upon whose business skill, financial capability and personal character we are relying in entering into this Agreement. Those individuals will be referred to in this Agreement as "Franchise Owners."

This Franchise Agreement is intended to comply with the Fair Franchising Standards of the American Association of Franchisees and Dealers ("AAFD"). We are seeking provisional accreditation as a "Fair Franchisor" from the AAFD.

All capitalized terms are defined in ARTICLE 19.

BACKGROUND

A.   We are in the business of granting franchise rights for others to operate delivery/take-out/eat-in bar-b-que restaurants called "Bobby Rubino's Ribs n More" featuring the main menu items of ribs, chicken and related items, using certain Secret Recipe Products, procedures and business methods and policies we have developed.

B.   The distinguishing characteristics of the system include: Secret Recipe Products, uniform standards and procedures for business operations; special graphics package; training in the operation, management and promotion of the Bobby Rubino's Ribs n More Franchise; promotional programs; customer development and service techniques; and other technical assistance.

C.   You recognize the benefits from receiving a Bobby Rubino's Ribs n More Franchise and desire to enter into this Agreement subject to the terms in this Agreement and to receive the benefits provided by us under this Agreement.

D.   We have reviewed your application and have decided to award a Bobby Rubino's Ribs n More Franchise to you evidenced by this Agreement.

The parties agree as follows:

ARTICLE 1

APPOINTMENT

Section 1.1. Grant of Franchise.

We grant to you, subject to the terms of this Agreement, the right and you undertake the obligation, to operate 1 Bobby Rubino's Ribs n More Franchise under the System only at the location described in Section 1.2.

Section 1.2. Location of Your Bobby Rubino's Ribs n More Franchise.

You agree that you will operate your Bobby Rubino's Ribs n More Franchise only at the location described in Exhibit A; or, if none is stated, the Premises will be designated and Exhibit A completed after you select a site in accordance with Section 4.1. The location cannot be changed without our written consent and compliance with our relocation procedures. You will not solicit business outside your ADI through the use of an 800 number, catalog, direct mail or other advertising or solicitation method without our consent. We will be responsible for implementing and coordinating these types of solicitation methods to maximum sales for the System and to afford you the right to sell to customers located within your Protected Territory.

Section 1.3. Protected Territory.

During the Term, if you are not in default, we agree not to open or franchise another Bobby Rubino's Ribs n More Franchise within your Protected Territory. However, we reserve for ourselves the rights stated in Section 5.7, that are superior to your rights under this Agreement.

Section 1.4. Relocation of Your Bobby Rubino's Ribs n More Franchise.

(a) **Loss of Lease**. If the Premises is leased by you and the lease or sublease expires or is terminated (provided termination is not due to your default) before the expiration or termination of this Agreement, you then have 90 days to secure a new location within your Protected Territory but not within the protected territory of a Company Unit or another Franchise Unit of the System. The new location must be approved in writing by us. You have 90 days from the date the new lease or new sublease is signed to open and begin full operation of the new Bobby Rubino's Ribs n More Franchise in compliance with this Agreement unless we otherwise agree in writing. The failure to secure a new location and begin operation within the specified times is an Event of Default on your part.

(b) **Casualty**. If the Premises is damaged or destroyed by fire or other casualty, or is required by any governmental authority, to be repaired or constructed you will, at your expense, repair or reconstruct the Premises within a reasonable time under the circumstances. The minimum acceptable appearance for the restored Premises will be as existed just before the casualty. However, every reasonable effort must be made to have the restored Premises reflect the then current Trade Dress of the newest Bobby Rubino's Ribs n More Franchises within the System. If the Premises is substantially destroyed by fire or other casualty, you may, with our written agreement, terminate this Agreement instead of reconstructing the Premises or relocating your Bobby Rubino's Ribs n More Franchise under the terms in Subsection 1.4(c).

(c) **Condemnation.** You will, as soon as possible, give us notice of any proposed taking by eminent domain. If we agree that your Bobby Rubino's Ribs n More Franchise or a substantial portion is to be taken, we will give prompt consideration to transferring your Bobby Rubino's Ribs n More Franchise to a nearby location you select within your Protected Territory but not within the protected territory of a Company Unit or another Franchise Unit as quickly as reasonably possible, within 90 days of the taking. If the new location is accepted and we authorize the transfer, and if you open a new Bobby Rubino's Ribs n More Franchise at the new location in accordance with our specifications within 90 days after obtaining the new location, your new Bobby Rubino's Ribs n More Franchise will be deemed to be your Bobby Rubino's Ribs n More Franchise under this Agreement. If a condemnation takes place and a new Bobby Rubino's Ribs n More Franchise does not, for any reason, become your Bobby Rubino's Ribs n More Franchise under this Agreement, this is an Event of Default on your part.

(d) **Site Relocation Fee**. If you must relocate your Bobby Rubino's Ribs n More Franchise, you will pay a site relocation fee to us sufficient to cover our reasonable and necessary direct costs associated with approving the relocation; for example, site location and/or lease negotiation assistance, legal and accounting fees, travel expenses and other out-of-pocket costs.

Section 1.5. Your Right of First Refusal.

(a) **Within Same County**. If we want to open a Company Unit or Franchise Unit in the county where your Bobby Rubino's Ribs n More Franchise is located but outside your Protected Territory and there is 1 or more existing franchisees in the county, the existing franchisee who is closest to the proposed location of the new Company Unit or Franchise Unit has the right of first refusal for 30 days to purchase another Bobby Rubino's Ribs n More Franchise for the proposed location on the terms substantially similar to those stated in this Agreement. Unless otherwise agreed by the parties, the closing of purchase of the additional Bobby Rubino's Ribs n More Franchise by you will be held at our principal office no later than 60 days after the right of first refusal is exercised. If you do not timely elect to exercise your right of first refusal by written notice to us within 30 days of receipt of notice from us, we may open the Company Unit, or sell the Franchise to another franchisee for the location without any further obligation or liability to you.

(b) **Within Protected Territory**. If we desire to open a Company Unit or a Franchise Unit within your Protected Territory under the reservation stated in Subsection 5.7(a), you have the right of first refusal for 30 days to open and operate the additional unit on substantially similar terms as stated in this Agreement. Unless otherwise agreed by the parties, the closing of purchase of the additional Bobby Rubino's Ribs n More Franchise by you will be held at our principal office no later than 30 days after the right of first refusal is exercised. If you do not timely elect to exercise your right of first refusal by written notice to us within 30 days of receipt of notice from us, we may open the Company Unit, or sell the Franchise to another franchisee for the location without any further obligation or liability to you.

ARTICLE 2

OUR DUTIES

We will provide you with the following assistance and services:

Section 2.1.   Site Selection Assistance.

We must approve the proposed site for your Premises in writing. We will supply to you our site selection criteria. We will also provide all on-site evaluation in response to your request for site selection assistance and approval. However, we will not provide on-site evaluation for any proposed site before receipt of the materials required in the Manuals. We will not unreasonably withhold approval of any site that meets our standards for demographic characteristics, traffic patterns, parking, the predominant character of the neighborhood, competition from other businesses providing similar services within the area, the proximity to other businesses, the nature of other businesses in proximity to the site and other commercial characteristics, the size, appearance and other physical characteristics of the site, and any other factors that we consider relevant in approving or disapproving a site. We will review site approval submissions on a first-in basis. If we do not approve the selected site, you have 30 days from the date of disapproval to submit a new site within the Reserved Area for our written approval.

Section 2.2.   Lease Assistance; Subleasing From Us.

Our Designee, will lease the Premises and sublease them to you at cost, however, you are responsible to pay any security deposit required by the landlord. The landlord may require the Franchise Owners to sign a personal guaranty securing the lease. While we or our Designee will attempt to secure a fair rent for the Premises, no representation is or will be made that the rent will represent the best available rent in the area. We will then construct and equip your Franchise Business to the specifications contained in the Operations Manual and open for business in accordance with Section 2.3.

Section 2.3.   Turn-Key Franchise.

You understand and agree that we are responsible for the construction of your Bobby Rubino's Ribs n More Franchise. You are not permitted to direct, supervise or otherwise take part in any decision regarding the construction and installation of equipment. If you interfere with the construction of your Bobby Rubino's Ribs n More Franchise, you will not be permitted access to the Premises until construction is completed.

Section 2.4.   Business Planning Assistance.

After this Agreement is signed by the parties, we will review and comment upon any business plan and pro forma financial projections you prepare and will also give you leads for securing a working capital line of credit, term loan and/or equipment lease financing.

Section 2.5.   Accounting, Cost Control, Portion Control and Inventory Control Systems.

We will provide standardized accounting, cost control, portion control and inventory control systems.

Section 2.6.   Lists, Forms and Schedules.

We will loan to you:

(a) A list of required supplies, materials, inventory and other items necessary to operate your Franchise and a list of approved suppliers of these items;

(b) An initial set of forms, including the standard brochure and various operational forms, standardized periodic reporting forms for reporting accounting information, cost analysis and purchase order forms;

(c) A schedule of items that must be purchased from us or our Affiliates, including inventory business forms, brochures and other items; and

(d) A schedule of recommended equipment and supplies that can be purchased from third-party suppliers.

Section 2.7.   Employee Information and Assistance.

We will give to you employee hiring information including pay scale guidelines and a standardized interviewing/selection system. You are solely responsible for the hiring, disciplining, supervising, promoting and firing of your employees and the establishment of their salaries.

Section 2.8.   Basic Management Training.

(a) **Basic Management Training**. We will provide 2 weeks of Basic Management Training for up to 3 Trainees at our training facilities in Boca Raton, Florida, or at any other location closer to your Bobby Rubino's Ribs n More Franchise as we specify in writing. Unless otherwise agreed in writing, at least 1 Trainee must be the Franchise Owner. You may designate another person who will be active in the day-to-day activities of your Bobby Rubino's Ribs n More Franchise to be another Trainee. All Trainees must be acceptable to us. In addition to a written test, Basic Management Training includes instruction in marketing, promotion and advertising, sales techniques and computer applications. Training programs may differ for Franchise Owners or employees depending upon their responsibilities at the Bobby Rubino's Ribs n More Franchise. Basic Management Training will be provided approximately 30 days before the Opening Date at a time we schedule. We will provide, at our expense, instructors, facilities, training materials and technical training tools for Basic Management Training. You are responsible for all expenses of the Trainees in attending Basic Management Training including all travel, lodging and meal expenses. You will pay all expenses incurred to have your additional employees or agents attend Basic Management Training, including reasonable training fees.

(b) **Failure to Complete Basic Management Training**. If any Trainee fails to complete satisfactorily Basic Management Training, as reasonably determined by us, we may: a. at your expense, retrain the Trainee or allow you to hire another Trainee; or b. elect to terminate this Agreement and refund the Initial Franchise Fee and other fees collected under this Agreement to you without interest, less our out-of-pocket costs and our standard fees for training (currently $1,500 per person).

Section 2.9. Loan of the Manuals.

We will loan to you 1 registered copy of each volume of the Manuals (with revisions as required). Our practice is to deliver the Manuals to you at or shortly before Basic Management Training.

Section 2.10. Pre-Opening On-Site Training; Opening Supervisor.

We will make available to you pre-opening, on-site training of a minimum of 5 Business Days, in most instances to be conducted at your Bobby Rubino's Ribs n More Franchise shortly before the Opening Date and during the first 3 days of operation, as we deem appropriate. The on-site training program will cover material aspects of the operation of the Bobby Rubino's Ribs n More Franchise including financial control, marketing techniques, maintenance of quality standards, employee hiring and motivation, inventory control, security standards, merchandising techniques, promotional techniques, operations, purchasing and sales. We will also provide an opening supervisor to assist in the grand opening of your Bobby Rubino's Ribs n More Franchise and in the on-site training of your employees. Our opening supervisor will begin assistance on a day we and you mutually agree upon and will remain at your Bobby Rubino's Ribs n More Franchise for a time (not to exceed 5 consecutive Business Days) we, in our sole discretion, deem necessary. We will pay the expenses of the opening supervisor.

Section 2.11. Continued Assistance and Support.

Upon the opening of your Bobby Rubino's Ribs n More Franchise, we will or may provide to you the following:

(a) **Field Visits**. We will provide assistance to you in the development and operation of your Bobby Rubino's Ribs n More Franchise by means of periodic visits by one of our field representatives.

(b) **Telephone Hotline**. We will maintain a telephone "hotline" for informational assistance.

(c) **Advertising and Public Relations Campaigns**. We will generally promote franchisees through advertising and public relations campaigns.

(d) **Local Advertising**. We will provide advice on Local Advertising.

(e) **Promotional Methods and Materials**. We will provide you with promotional methods and materials that we develop.

(f) **Radio and Television Commercials**. We will provide a preapproved radio script and camera-ready television commercials (not including airtime) for your use in your ADI.

(g) **Periodic Assistance**. We may provide advisory assistance in the operation and promotion of the Bobby Rubino's Ribs n More Franchise as we deem advisable. Advisory assistance may include additional training and assistance, communication of new developments, improvements in equipment and supplies, and new techniques in advertising, service and management relevant to the operation of the Bobby Rubino's Ribs n More Franchise.

(h) **Refresher or Additional Training**. We may provide refresher training programs, seminars or advanced management training for you and your employees at our principal training facility (or any other location we designate provided the other location is closer to your Bobby Rubino's Ribs n More Franchise), that may be required at our option. Training is not required more often than once a year. However, if you receive unsatisfactory inspection reports from us and fail to promptly remedy the deficiencies, we may require your Manager and designated employees to attend refresher training as soon as reasonably possible. You are solely responsible for all expenses associated with these programs including the then prevailing standard training fee we charge for these programs and all travel, meals and lodging costs of your attendees.

(i) **Special Assistance**. If you request, we will furnish non-routine guidance and assistance to address your unusual or unique operating problems at reasonable per diem fees, charges and out-of-pocket expenses we establish.

(j) **Research and Development**. We will continue to research and develop new menu items, introductions and techniques as we deem appropriate in our sole discretion. We may conduct market research and testing to determine consumer trends and the salability of new menu items. If you are chosen by us, and if you agree, you will participate in our market research programs, in test marketing new menu items in the Bobby Rubino's Ribs n More Franchise and by providing us with timely reports and other relevant information regarding that market research. If you participate in any test marketing, you agree to purchase a reasonable quantity of the products or services being tested and to effectively promote and make a good faith effort to sell them.

Section 2.12. License of Proprietary Property.

Subject to this Agreement, we license to you the right to use the "Ribs n More" trade name and the other Proprietary Property.

Section 2.13. Our Temporary Operation of Your Unit.

At our option, if:

(a) You fail to keep your Bobby Rubino's Ribs n More Franchise open for business during normal business hours;

(b) You are absent from your Bobby Rubino's Ribs n More Franchise more than 5 days or abandon the Premises;

(c) You or the Franchise Owner dies or becomes permanently incapacitated and the franchise or the ownership interest in the Franchisee is not assigned promptly under Section 11.3;

(d) You materially breach any of our standards and specifications for the operation of your Bobby Rubino's Ribs n More Franchise; or

(e) Your Bobby Rubino's Ribs n More Franchise is terminated and we elect to purchase your business assets as provided in Section 11.4; then, we are entitled (but have no obligation) to enter your Premises and to operate and manage your Bobby Rubino's Ribs n More Franchise for your (or your estate's) account until the Ribs n More Franchise is terminated, transferred to a party under Subsection 11.2(f), purchased by us, or until you resume control over your Bobby Rubino's Ribs n More Franchise and operate it in accordance with this Agreement. Our operation and management will not continue for more than 90 days without your written consent or the consent of the representatives of your estate. If we operate your Bobby Rubino's Ribs n More Franchise, we will account to you or your estate for all net income from the operation less its reasonable expenses incurred in, and a reasonable management fee for, its operation of your Bobby Rubino's Ribs n More Franchise.

Section 2.14. Duties Solely to You.

All of our obligations under this Agreement are only to you. No other party is entitled to rely on, enforce, or obtain relief for breach of the obligations either directly or by subrogation.

Section 2.15. Our Right to Delegate Duties.

You agree to our right to delegate our duties under this Agreement to a Designee. You must discharge your duties with the Designee to the extent we request, as you must do with us. We remain responsible for our obligations under this Agreement even if delegated to the Designee.

ARTICLE 3

FEES AND PAYMENTS

Section 3.1. Types of Fees.

In consideration of our signing this Agreement, you must pay to us the following fees, in addition to any others required under this Agreement, all payable in United States currency at our principal office:

(a) **Initial Franchise Fee**. You must pay to us an Initial Franchise Fee of $20,000, payable at the same time as signing this Agreement. The Initial Franchise Fee is fully earned by us on receipt and, except as expressly provided otherwise in this Agreement is non-refundable upon signing this Agreement. The Initial Franchise Fee is uniform as to all franchisees currently purchasing a Bobby Rubino's Ribs n More Franchise.

(b) **Turn Key Fee**. You will pay a Turn Key Fee of $150,000 for new equipment and construction of your Bobby Rubino's Ribs n More Franchise within 3 Business Days of receipt of a written notice to do so by us. Payment must be made by cashier's check or other cleared funds. These funds will be deposited into our general operating account and will be commingled with our other funds. THE TURN KEY FEE INCLUDES ANY BROKER'S COMMISSION, NEW EQUIPMENT, FIXTURES, SIGNAGE AND LEASEHOLD IMPROVEMENTS AND **DOES NOT INCLUDE** OTHER SUPPLIES, TELEPHONE EQUIPMENT, GOODS, FOOD, BEVERAGES, LICENSES, PERMITS, OPENING INVENTORY, WORKING CAPITAL, LEGAL OR ACCOUNTING FEES AND LABOR NEEDED TO OPERATE THE FRANCHISE FOR WHICH YOU WILL BE ADDITIONALLY RESPONSIBLE.

(c) **Royalty Fee**. You will pay a continuing weekly non-refundable Royalty Fee during the Term equal to 5% of weekly Gross Revenues. All Royalty Fees are derived from each individual Bobby Rubino's Ribs n More Franchise operated by you.

(d) **Advertising Contributions**. Once the Marketing Fund is established pursuant to Section 7.4, you must also pay a continuing weekly Advertising Contribution to the Marketing Fund during the Term in an amount equal to 2% of weekly Gross Revenues. We have the sole right to enforce your obligations and all other franchisees who make Advertising Contributions. Neither you, nor any other franchisee obligated to make Advertising Contributions, is a third party beneficiary of the funds or has any right to enforce any obligation to contribute the funds. We reserve the right to increase the Advertising Contributions paid by you provided: a. the increase is approved by us and a majority of the existing Franchisees; b. that all other Franchise Units and Company Units are subject to the same relative percentage increase in the Advertising Contributions; and c. the Advertising Contributions do not exceed 5% of weekly Gross Revenues.

Section 3.2.   Payment Schedule.

The Royalty Fee and Advertising Contribution must be paid to us, together with any required weekly reports, by Saturday for the previous week. All other amounts due to us from you will be paid as specified in this Agreement. If no time is specified, these amounts are due upon receipt of an invoice from us. Any payment or report not actually received by us on or before the due date is overdue.

Section 3.3.   Payment System.

(a)   All payments by you to us or our Affiliates, upon our request, will be effectuated by a Payment System by the use of pre-authorized transfers from your operating account through the use of special checks or electronic fund transfers, that we will process at the time any payment is due or through the use of any other payment system we designate. You will cooperate with us to implement the Payment System within 15 days before the Opening Date. You agree to cooperate with us in maintaining the efficient operation of the Payment System, including depositing all Gross Revenues you receive in your operating account accessed by the Payment System within 1 Business Day of receipt.

(b)   You will give your financial institution instructions in a form we provide or approve and will obtain the financial institution's agreement to follow these instructions. You will provide us with copies of these instructions and agreement. The financial institution's agreement may not be withdrawn or modified without our written approval and approval is within our sole discretion. You will also sign all other forms for funds transfer as we or the financial institution may request.

(c)   We may require your financial institution to send a monthly statement of all activity in the designated account to us at the same time as it sends these statements to you, and any other reports of the activity in the operating account as we reasonably determine and request.

(d)   If you maintain any other bank accounts for your Bobby Rubino's Ribs n More Franchise, you must identify these accounts to us and provide to us copies of the monthly statements for all these accounts and the details of all deposits and withdrawals to them.

(e) You will pay all charges imposed by your financial institution. We will pay the charges imposed by our financial institution for the Payment System.

(f) You agree that your obligations to make payments under this Agreement and any other agreement entered into with us or our Affiliates for your Bobby Rubino's Ribs n More Franchise, and our rights and those of our Affiliates, if any, to receive these payments, are absolute and unconditional, and are not subject to any abatement, reduction, setoff, defense, counterclaim or recoupment due or alleged to be due to, or by reason of, any past, present or future claims that you have or may have against us, any of our Affiliates, any of our Designees, or against any other person for any reason.

Section 3.4.   Interest on Late Payments.

Although each failure to pay monies when due is an Event of Default, to encourage prompt payment and to cover the costs involved in processing late payments, if any payment under this Agreement or any other agreement between us or our Affiliates and you for your Bobby Rubino's Ribs n More Franchise is overdue for any reason, you must pay to us, on demand, in addition to the overdue amount, interest on the overdue amount from the date it was due until paid equal to the lesser of: a. 18% per annum; or b. the maximum rate of interest permitted by law. If we owe you money, we will pay the same late charge, if we pay you late.

Section 3.5.   Application of Payments.

We have sole discretion to apply any payments you make to your past due indebtedness including the Royalty Fee, Advertising Contribution, purchases from us or our Affiliates, interest or any other indebtedness of you to us or our Affiliates in any manner we choose regardless of your designation.

Section 3.6.   Security Interest.

As security for your monetary and other obligations to us or our Affiliates, you grant to us a first priority security interest in all your business assets, including all furniture, fixtures, machinery, equipment, inventory and all other property, (tangible or intangible), you now own or later acquire used in your Bobby Rubino's Ribs n More Franchise and wherever located, and all your contractual and related rights under this Agreement and all other agreements between the parties. You will sign all financing statements, continuation statements, notices of lien, assignments, or other documents as required to perfect and maintain our security interest, including a UCC-1 Financing Statement in substantially the same form attached as Exhibit B. We agree to subordinate our security interest to: a. the landlord's lien; b. the security interest of a reputable institutional lender for a loan to you for working capital purposes; c. the purchase money security interest of an approved equipment vendor for any equipment you purchase or lease and use in the operation of your Bobby Rubino's Ribs n More Franchise; or d. the purchase money security interest of a supplier of approved products sold at your Bobby Rubino's Ribs n More Franchise. You pay all filing fees and costs for perfecting our security interest.

Section 3.7.   No Withholding.

You agree that under no circumstances will you withhold or suspend payment of, or reduce the amount of the Royalty Fee or Advertising Contribution payable under this Agreement. Notwithstanding the foregoing, if you dispute in good faith the amount of an individual payment due under this Agreement, you may pay only the amount you believe is due, provided that you give us prompt notice of the reasons you dispute the amount of the payment and proceed to make good faith efforts to resolve the dispute.

ARTICLE 4

YOUR DUTIES

Section 4.1. Acquisition of the Site.

You are solely responsible for selecting the site. If a site for your Bobby Rubino's Ribs n More Franchise has not been selected on the Agreement Date, you must complete the sublease arrangements for your Premises located in the Reserved Area, at your expense within 3 months of the Agreement Date, after obtaining our written approval under Section 2.1. If a site has not been approved within 3 months of the Agreement Date, we may terminate this Agreement and refund the Initial Franchise Fee to you without interest, less our out-of-pocket costs and our standard fees and expenses for any training and other assistance provided under this Agreement (including site location and lease negotiation assistance).

Section 4.2. Opening.

You agree not to open your Bobby Rubino's Ribs n More Franchise for business until: 1. all your obligations under Section 4.1 have been fulfilled; 2. the training of the Trainees has been completed to our reasonable satisfaction; 3. the Initial Franchise Fee and all amounts due to us and our Affiliates under this Agreement have been paid in full; 4. we have been furnished with certificates of insurance and copies of all insurance policies or all other evidence of insurance coverage as we reasonably request; 5. you have obtained a certificate of occupancy for your Premises; and 6. you have obtained all necessary licenses and permits to operate your Bobby Rubino's Ribs n More Franchise. Final approval by us of the opening of your Bobby Rubino's Ribs n More Franchise will be given in writing. You agree to comply with these conditions and be prepared to open your Bobby Rubino's Ribs n More Franchise for business within 9 months after the Agreement Date.

Section 4.3. Use of the Premises.

You must use your Premises only for the operation of your Bobby Rubino's Ribs n More Franchise. You must keep your Bobby Rubino's Ribs n More Franchise open for business and in normal operation for the minimum hours and days as we reasonably require in the Manuals or otherwise in writing except as may be limited by local law or the landlord's rules and regulations.

Section 4.4. Maintenance and Repairs.

(a) You must maintain your Bobby Rubino's Ribs n More Franchise in the highest and most uniform degree of sanitation, repair, appearance, condition and security as stated in the Manuals and as a modern, clean, adequately lighted and efficiently operated Bobby Rubino's Ribs n More Franchise providing high quality menu items with efficient, courteous and friendly customer service as we require. You must make all additions, alterations, repairs and replacements to your Bobby Rubino's Ribs n More Franchise (but no others without our written consent) as reasonably required for that purpose, including all periodic repainting, changes in appearance, repairs to impaired equipment and replacement of obsolete signs as we direct subject to Capital Expenditure Limitation stated in Section 4.20. You must meet and maintain the highest safety standards and ratings applicable to the operation of your Bobby Rubino's Ribs n More Franchise as we reasonably require, including the maintenance of the highest sanitation rating.

(b) You must maintain contracts with reputable firms for the maintenance of the Premises and the machinery and equipment and, if we determine to be appropriate or necessary, for the landscaped areas of the Premises. Contracts for maintenance of the Premises and the machinery and equipment must provide for the performance of services, including preventative maintenance services, and be with financially responsible firms, that: a. maintain adequate insurance and bonding; b. have personnel who are factory trained to service equipment of the type in the Premises; and c. maintain an adequate supply of parts for the machinery, equipment and tools. Contracts for landscape maintenance must be with financially responsible firms. You will provide us, upon our request, with a copy of any contract for maintenance that you enter into with any outside maintenance firm. If you fail to keep these contracts in full effect, we may do so at your expense.

Section 4.5.   Operational Requirements.

You agree to operate your Bobby Rubino's Ribs n More Franchise in conformity with all uniform methods, standards and specifications reasonably required in the Manuals or otherwise, to ensure that the highest degree of quality and service is uniformly maintained. You agree to:

(a)   Record all Gross Revenues on the approved P.O.S. System;

(b)   Comply with the procedures and systems we reasonably institute on a System-wide basis both now and in the future, including those on sales, good business practices, advertising and other obligations and restrictions;

(c)   Maintain in sufficient supply (as we may reasonably prescribe in the Manuals or otherwise in writing) and use at all times, only inventory, equipment, materials, advertising methods and formats, and supplies that conform with our standards and specifications, if any, at all times sufficient to meet the anticipated volume of business, and to refrain from deviating from these requirements without our written consent;

(d)   Use menu boards and menus that comply with our specifications for materials, finish, style, pattern and design;

(e)   Adhere to the highest standards of honesty, integrity, fair dealing and ethical conduct in all dealings with customers, suppliers, employees, independent contractors, us and the public;

(f)   Sell or offer for sale only the menu items that meet our reasonable uniform standards of quality and quantity; have been expressly approved for sale in the Manuals or otherwise in writing by us at retail to consumers only from your Bobby Rubino's Ribs n More Franchise including take-out and delivery; not sell any items for redistribution or resale; sell or offer for sale all approved menu items; refrain from any deviation from our standards and specifications for providing or selling the menu items without our written consent; and discontinue selling and offering for sale any menu items that we reasonably disapprove on a System-wide basis in writing at any time;

(g) Maintain all equipment, fixtures, furnishings and signs in a condition that meets the operational standards specified in the Manuals. As equipment becomes obsolete or inoperable, you will replace the equipment with the equipment that is then approved for use in the Bobby Rubino's Ribs n More Franchise. If we determine that additional or replacement equipment is needed on a System-wide basis because of a change in menu items or method of preparation and service, a change in technology, customer concerns or health or safety considerations, you will install the additional equipment or replacement equipment within the time we specify, subject to the Capital Expenditure Limitation in Section 4.20.

(h) Refrain from selling, or offering for sale, any alcoholic beverages without our written approval, which approval may be conditioned upon all requirements as we deem necessary for the protection of the Proprietary Marks and the System, including the requirement that you comply with all laws and regulations applicable to the sale of alcoholic beverages and obtain appropriate insurance coverage for your benefit and our benefit.

Section 4.6.   P.O.S. System; E-Mail.

(a) Before the Opening Date you must procure and install at your Bobby Rubino's Ribs n More Franchise the P.O.S. System we specify in the Manuals or otherwise. You will provide any assistance we require to bring the P.O.S. System "on-line" with our computer. You agree that we have the right to retrieve all data and information from your P.O.S. System as we, in our sole discretion, deem necessary, with the telephonic cost of retrieval to be paid by you. All of the items specified to be installed or purchased, or activities specified to be accomplished by you, and the delivery of all hardware and software, are at your sole expense.

(b) You must install and maintain, at your own expense, an E-mail link with us and all other Bobby Rubino's Ribs n More Franchisees. Reasonable minimum hardware and software standards for these connections will be set by us from time to time, and you will have reasonable time to upgrade when standards change. Standards will include current uniform communications software in use by the System; word processing and spreadsheet software which is either the same as that in use at our office or capable of reading and converting files created by our office; and a computer capable of running the software and containing reasonable minimums for memory and data storage and a modem connected via network links to our System. You will be responsible for all normal communications charges from the networks making connection to our System such as phone bills or bills from an on-line service. Important System-wide information will be sent to your computer address electronically. In order to stay informed on developments affecting the System and your Bobby Rubino's Ribs n More Franchise, you agree to check your electronic mailbox for system communications on a regular basis.

(c) You agree that computer systems are designed to accommodate a certain maximum amount of data and terminals, and that, as limits are achieved, and/or as technology and/or software is developed in the future, we in our sole discretion may require you to add memory, ports and other accessories and/or peripheral equipment and/or additional, new or substitute software to the original P.O.S. System you purchased. You agree that at a certain point in time it may become necessary for you to replace or upgrade the entire P.O.S. System with a larger system capable of assuming and discharging all of those computer-related tasks and functions as we specify. You agree that computer designs and functions change periodically and that we may be required to make substantial modifications to our computer specifications, or to require installation of entirely different systems, during the Term. To ensure full operational efficiency and communication capability between our computers and your computers, you will keep the P.O.S. System in good maintenance and repair and to install all additions, changes, modifications, substitutions and/or replacements to its computer hardware, software, telephone and power lines and other computer-related facilities as we direct on those dates and within those times we specify, in our sole discretion, in the Manuals or otherwise on a System-wide basis subject to the capital expenditure limitation in Section 4.20. Upon termination or expiration of this Agreement, all software, disks, tapes and other magnetic storage media provided to you by us must be returned to us in good condition (reasonable wear and tear excepted). You will delete all software and applications from all memory and storage.

Section 4.7.   Hiring, Training and Appearance of Employees.

You will maintain a competent, conscientious staff and employ the minimum number of employees necessary to meet the anticipated volume of business and to achieve the goals of the System. You will take all steps necessary to ensure that your employees meet the employment criteria and keep a neat appearance and comply with any dress code we require, subject to the requirements of landlords. You are solely responsible for the terms of their employment and compensation and, except for training required under this Agreement, for the proper training of the employees in the operation of your Bobby Rubino's Ribs n More Franchise. You are solely responsible for all employment decisions and functions, including hiring, firing, establishing wage and hour requirements, disciplining, supervising and record keeping. You will not recruit or hire any employee of a Bobby Rubino's Ribs n More Franchise operated by us or another franchisee within the System without obtaining the employer's written permission.

Section 4.8.   Management of Your Bobby Rubino's Ribs n More Franchise.

(a)   The Manager must devote his or her best full-time efforts to the management and operation of your Bobby Rubino's Ribs n More Franchise. You agree that your Bobby Rubino's Ribs n More Franchise requires the day-to-day supervision of the Manager at all times your Bobby Rubino's Ribs n More Franchise is open for business. The Manager, and all successive Managers, if any, are required to complete Basic Management Training before managing your Bobby Rubino's Ribs n More Franchise, unless we otherwise agree in writing.

(b)   If we have permitted the Manager to be an individual other than the Franchise Owner, and the Manager fails to satisfy his or her obligations provided in Subsection 4.8(a) due to death, disability, termination of employment or for any other reason, the Franchise Owner will satisfy these obligations until you designate a new Manager of your Bobby Rubino's Ribs n More Franchise acceptable to us who has successfully completed Basic Management Training. You are solely responsible for the expenses associated with Basic Management Training, including the then-prevailing standard training fee we charge (currently $1,500).

Section 4.9.   Approved Specifications and Sources of Supply.

(a) **Purchases from Us**. You must purchase from us the Secret Recipe Products and other items that we require if implemented on a System-wide basis. You will be charged the same price then being charged to all franchisees equal to our cost plus 10%.

(b) **Authorized Specifications and Suppliers**. You must purchase or lease equipment, supplies, inventory, advertising materials, menu items, and other products and services used for the operation of your Bobby Rubino's Ribs n More Franchise solely from authorized manufacturers, contractors and other suppliers who demonstrate, to our continuing reasonable satisfaction: the ability to meet our standards and specifications for these items; possess adequate quality controls and capacity to supply your needs promptly and reliably; and have been approved in writing by us and not later disapproved. We will use our best reasonable efforts to negotiate agreements with suppliers that, in our good faith belief, are in the best interest of all Bobby Rubino's Ribs n More Franchisees. We may approve a single supplier for any brand and may approve a supplier only as to a certain brand or brands. In approving suppliers for the System, we may take into consideration factors like the price and quality of the products or services and the supplier's reliability. We may concentrate purchases with 1 or more suppliers to obtain the lowest prices and/ or the best advertising support and/or services for any group of Franchise Units or Company Units within the Chain. Approval of a supplier may be conditioned on requirements on the frequency of delivery, standards of service, warranty policies including prompt attention to complaints, and concentration of purchases, as stated above, and may be temporary, pending our additional evaluation of the supplier.

(c) **Approval of New Specifications and Suppliers**. If you propose to purchase or lease any equipment, supplies, inventory, advertising materials, menu items, or other products or services from an unapproved supplier, you must submit to us a written request for approval, or request the supplier to do so. We will have the right to require, as a condition of its approval, that its representatives be permitted to inspect the supplier's facilities, and that samples from the supplier be delivered, at our option, either to us or to an independent, certified laboratory designated by us for testing. We are not liable for damage to any sample that results from the testing process. You will pay a charge not to exceed the reasonable cost of the inspection and the actual cost of the testing. We reserve the right, at our option, to reinspect the facilities and products of any approved supplier and continue to sample the products at the supplier's expense and to revoke approval upon the supplier's failure to continue to meet our standards and specifications. We may also require as a condition to our approval, that the supplier present satisfactory evidence of insurance, for example, product liability insurance, protecting us and our franchisees against all claims from the use of the item within the System.

Section 4.10. Secret Recipe Products.

You agree that we have already developed the Secret Recipe Products and may continue to develop for use in the System certain additional products that are all highly confidential, secret recipes and are our trade secrets. Due to the importance of quality control and uniformity of these products and the significance of the proprietary products to the System, it is to the mutual benefit of the parties that we closely control the production and distribution of the Secret Recipe Products. Accordingly, you will use the Secret Recipe Products and will purchase from us or from an approved source we designate and license, all of your supplies of the Secret Recipe Products, all in accordance with our requirements then in effect. All Secret Recipe Products sold by or through us or our Affiliates to you will be sold in accordance with the terms we or the manufacturer expressly states.

Section 4.11. Sales of Menu Items to Your Affiliates.

All sales of menu items to your affiliates, if any, must be on terms regularly applicable to your nonaffiliated customers, and in all cases must be arm's-length.

Section 4.12. Credit Cards and Other Methods of Payment.

You will maintain credit card relationships with VISA, MasterCard, American Express, Diners Club, Discover and all other credit and debit card issuers or sponsors, check verification services, financial center services, and electronic fund transfer systems as we designate in order that you may accept customers' credit and debit cards, checks, and other methods of payment. We reserve the right to require the addition or deletion of credit card relationships and other methods of payment is implemented on a System-wide basis. You will subscribe to an approved credit verification service. You will comply with all our credit card policies including minimum purchase requirements for a customer's use of a credit card as stated in the Manuals.

Section 4.13. Telephones and Answering Service.

You will:

(a) Maintain continuously the number of operating telephone lines and telephone numbers to be used exclusively for the operation of your Bobby Rubino's Ribs n More Franchise as we reasonably require, with sufficient staff to handle telephone calls in an efficient and courteous manner at all times during normal business hours;

(b) Maintain continuously a dedicated operating telephone line and telephone number at your Bobby Rubino's Ribs n More Franchise that only we can use, and that permits us to monitor accounting and operational information via a modem; and

(c) Have a pay telephone installed in the public area of the Premises.

Section 4.14. Compliance with Laws, Rules and Regulations.

You will comply with all federal, state, and local laws, rules and regulations, and will timely obtain, maintain and renew when required all permits, certificates, licenses or franchises necessary for the proper conduct of your Bobby Rubino's Ribs n More Franchise under this Agreement, including qualification to do business, fictitious, trade or assumed name registration, building and construction permits, occupational licenses, sales tax permits, health and sanitation permits and ratings, fire clearances and environmental permits, and liquor licenses to dispense alcoholic beverages at the Premises. You will provide copies of all inspection reports, warnings, certificates and ratings, issued by any governmental entity during the Term on the conduct of your Bobby Rubino's Ribs n More Franchise that indicates your material non-compliance with any applicable law, rule or regulation, to us within 2 days of your receipt of these items.

Section 4.15. Tax Payments; Contested Assessments.

You will promptly pay when due all taxes required by any federal, state or local tax authority including unemployment taxes, withholding taxes, sales taxes, use taxes, income taxes, tangible commercial personal property taxes, real estate taxes, intangible taxes and all other indebtedness you incur in the conduct of your Bobby Rubino's Ribs n More Franchise. You will pay to us an amount equal to any sales tax, goods and services taxes, gross receipts tax, or similar tax imposed on us for any payments to us required under this Agreement, unless the tax is measured by or involves the net income or our corporate status in a state. If we pay any tax for You, you will promptly reimburse us the amount paid. If there is any bona fide dispute as to liability for taxes assessed or other indebtedness, you may contest the validity or the amount of the tax or indebtedness in accordance with procedures of the taxing authority or applicable law. However, you will not permit a tax sale or seizure by levy or execution or similar writ or warrant, or attachment by a creditor, to occur against the Premises or any assets used in your Bobby Rubino's Ribs n More Franchise.

Section 4.16. Customer Surveys; Customer List.

You will present to customers any evaluation forms we require and will participate and/or request your customers to participate in any marketing surveys performed by or for us. You will maintain a current customer list containing each customer's name, address, telephone number and zip code (9 digits) and supply a copy of the list to us on a quarterly basis. You must participate in any process we develop to record all customer information. You retain ownership of its customer lists. We will not use your customer list for any profit or in any activity adverse to, or in competition with, you.

Section 4.17. Inspections.

You will permit us and/or our representatives to enter your Premises or office at any time during normal business hours upon reasonable notice, for purposes of conducting inspections. You will cooperate fully with us and/or our representatives in inspections by rendering assistance as they may reasonably request and by permitting them, at their option, to observe how you are preparing, selling and delivering the menu items, to monitor sales volume, to conduct a physical inventory, to confer with your employees and customers and to remove samples of any products, supplies and materials in amounts reasonably necessary to return to our office for inspection and record-keeping. A portion of a sample we take will be given to you for safe-keeping in a tamper-proof container. The inspections will be performed in a manner that minimizes interference with the operation of your Bobby Rubino's Ribs n More Franchise. We and/or you may videotape the inspections. Upon notice from us, and without limiting our other rights under this Agreement, you will take all steps necessary to correct immediately any deficiencies detected during inspections, including immediately stopping use of any equipment, advertising, materials, products, supplies or other items that do not conform to our then-current requirements. If you fail or refuse to correct any deficiency, we have the right, without any claim to the contrary by you, to enter your Premises or office without being guilty of trespass or any other tort, for the purposes of making or causing to be made all corrections as required, at your expense, payable by you upon demand.

Section 4.18. Notices to Us.

(a) You must notify us in writing within 5 days of any of the following events:

(i)   The start of, any action, suit, implemented or other proceeding against you or any of your employees that may have a material adverse effect on the Franchise Business or the System;

(ii)   You or any of your employees receive any notice of noncompliance with any law, rule or regulation that may have a material adverse effect on the Franchise Business or the System; or

(iii) The issuance of any order, writ, injunction, award or decree of any court, agency or other governmental instrumentality against you or any of your employees that may have a material adverse effect on the Franchise Business or the System.

(b) You will provide us with any information we request, within 5 days of request, about the progress and outcome of events.

Section 4.19. Operational Suggestions.

You are encouraged to submit suggestions in writing to us for improving elements of the System, including products, services, equipment, service format, advertising and any other relevant matters, that we consider adopting or modifying standards, specifications and procedures for the System. You agree that any suggestions you make are our exclusive property. We have no obligation to use any suggestions. If any suggestion is implemented by us, we will negotiate with you on a reasonable fee for your suggestions based on its value to the System. You may not use any suggestions inconsistent with your obligations under this Agreement without our written consent.

Section 4.20. Renovation and Upgrading.

You will abide by our requirements for alterations, remodeling, upgrading or other any improvements to your Bobby Rubino's Ribs n More Franchise to achieve the strategic marketing goals of the System. Generally, the standards to comply satisfactorily will not exceed those applicable to new Franchise Units and new Company Units. These requirements will not impose an undue economic burden or occur more frequently than every 5 years. You will bear the entire cost of changes or additions, for any changes in, or additions of, equipment, furnishings, fixtures, lighting, carpeting, painting or the taking of other actions we specify to satisfy our then-current standards for image, positioning, marketing strategy, cleanliness or appearance but not to exceed total capital expenditures of $50,000 every 5 years (the "Capital Expenditure Limitation").

ARTICLE 5

PROPRIETARY PROPERTY

Section 5.1.   Our Representations As to the Proprietary Marks.

We represent to you that:

(a) Bobby Rubino's U.S.A., Inc. (an unaffiliated entity) is the sole owner of the Proprietary Marks;

(b) We have rights to license the Proprietary Marks to you;

(c) We have not licensed the Proprietary Marks to any others except other Bobby Rubino's Ribs n More Franchisees;

(d) We will take all steps necessary to preserve and protect the ownership and validity of the Proprietary Marks; and

(e) We will take no action that causes a dilution in the value of the Proprietary Marks.

Section 5.2.   Your Use of the Proprietary Property.

You may use the Proprietary Property only in accordance with standards and specifications we reasonably determine and implement on a System-wide basis. You agree that:

(a) You will use the Proprietary Property only for the operation of your Bobby Rubino's Ribs n More Franchise at the Premises;

(b) You agree not to employ any of the Proprietary Marks in signing any contract, check, purchase agreement, negotiable instrument or legal obligation, application for any license or permit, or in a manner that may result in liability to us for any indebtedness or obligation of yours;

(c) You have no right to pre-package or sell pre-packaged food products or beverages using the Proprietary Marks unless approved in writing by us;

(d) You will use the Proprietary Marks as the sole service mark identifications for your Bobby Rubino's Ribs n More Franchise and will display prominently the Proprietary Marks on and/or with all materials we designate and authorize, and in the manner we require;

(e) You will not use the Proprietary Property as security for any obligation or indebtedness;

(f) You will comply with our instructions in filing and maintaining any required fictitious, trade or assumed name registrations for the "Bobby Rubino's Ribs n More" trade name, and will sign all documents we or our counsel deem reasonably necessary to obtain protection for the Proprietary Property and our interest in the Proprietary Property, for example, John Jones d/b/a "Bobby Rubino's Ribs n More" or ABC, Inc. d/b/a "Bobby Rubino's Ribs n More;"

(g) You will maintain a suitable sign or graphics package at, or near the front of the Premises, on any pylon sign, building directory or other area identifying the Premises only as "Ribs n More." The signage must conform in all respects to our requirements except to the extent prohibited by local governmental restrictions or landlord regulations;

(h) All materials including place mats, menus, matchbook covers, order books, plastic or paper products and other supplies and packaging materials used in the System will bear our Proprietary Marks, as required by us; and

(i) You will exercise caution when using the Proprietary Property to ensure that the Proprietary Property is not jeopardized in any manner.

Section 5.3. Infringement by You.

You acknowledge that the use of the Proprietary Property outside the scope of this Agreement, without our written consent, is an infringement of our rights in the Proprietary Property. You agree that during the Term, and after the expiration or termination of this Agreement, you will not, directly or indirectly, commit an act of infringement or contest or aid in contesting the validity of, or our right to, the Proprietary Property, or take any other action in derogation of our rights.

Section 5.4. Claims Against the Proprietary Property.

If there is any claim of infringement, unfair competition or other challenge to your right to use any Proprietary Property, or if you become aware of any use of, or claims to, any Proprietary Property by persons other than us or our franchisees, you will promptly (within 7 days) notify us in writing. You will not communicate with anyone except us and our counsel on any infringement, challenge or claim except under judicial process. We have sole discretion as to whether we take any action on any infringement, challenge or claim, and the sole right to control any litigation or other proceeding arising out of any infringement of, challenge or claim to any Proprietary Property. You must sign all documents, render all assistance, and do all acts that our attorneys deem necessary or advisable in order to protect and maintain our interest in any litigation or proceeding involving the Proprietary Property or otherwise to protect and maintain our interests in the Proprietary Property.

Section 5.5. Your Indemnification.

We indemnify you against and will reimburse you for all damages you are held liable in any proceeding from your use of any Proprietary Property in accordance with this Agreement, but only if you: 1. have timely notified us of the claim or proceeding in accordance with Section 5.4; 2. have otherwise complied with this Agreement; and 3. allow us sole control of the defense and settlement of the action in accordance with Section 5.4.

Section 5.6. Our Right to Modify the Proprietary Marks.

(a) If we deem it advisable to modify or discontinue the use of any of the Proprietary Marks and/or use 1 or more additional or substitute names or marks, including due to the rejection of any pending registration or revocation of any existing registration of any of the Proprietary Marks, due to the rights of senior users, due to our negligence or due to a radical change in direction of the Systems unilaterally caused or mandated by us, you are obligated to do so at your expense within 30 days of our request. In this event, we will only be liable to reimburse you for your reasonable direct printing and signage expenses in modifying or discontinuing the use of the Proprietary Marks and substituting different Proprietary Marks (these expenses will not include any expenditures made by you to promote a modified or substitute Proprietary Marks).

(b) If the modification or discontinuation of the use of any of the Proprietary Marks is due to a continuing need to modernize the System, you will be liable for all expenses in substituting the modified or new Proprietary Marks in your Bobby Rubino's Ribs n More Franchise.

Section 5.7. Our Reservation of Rights.

You agree that the license of the Proprietary Marks granted to you has limited exclusivity and that, in addition to our right to use and grant others the right to use the Proprietary Marks outside the Protected Territory, all rights not expressly granted in this Agreement to you concerning the Proprietary Marks or other matters are expressly reserved for us, including the right to:

(a) Establish, develop, license or franchise other systems, different from the System licensed by this Agreement in or outside the Protected Territory, without offering or providing you any rights under any other systems; and

(b) Sell any similar Ribs n More menu items authorized for the Bobby Rubino's Ribs n More Franchise using the Proprietary Marks through dissimilar channels of distribution including supermarkets, catalogs and mail order and under any terms that we deem appropriate within or outside the Protected Territory without offering or providing you the right to participate. We will not sell or otherwise distribute any product or service bearing any of the Proprietary Marks without first determining through appropriate market research that the sale or distribution of the product or service, as offered under the proposed marketing plan, is not likely to have a material negative effect on Gross Revenues for Franchisees generally. We will fairly compensate you for any sales made within the Protected Territory.

If we acquire a Competitive Business and units of the Competitive Business encroach upon your Protected Territory, we will have 1 year from the date of acquisition of the Competitive Business to sell the encroaching units without being in default under this Agreement.

Section 5.8. Ownership; Inurement Solely to Us.

You agree that: 1. you have no ownership or other rights in the Proprietary Property, except as expressly granted in this Agreement; and 2. we are the owner or authorized licensor of the Proprietary Property. You agree that all good will associated with the Bobby Rubino's Ribs n More Franchise inures directly and exclusively to our benefit and is our sole and exclusive property except through profit received from the operation or possible permitted sale of your Bobby Rubino's Ribs n More Franchise during the Term. You will not in any manner prohibit, or do anything which would restrict, us or any existing or future franchisee of a business either similar or dissimilar to the Franchise Business from using the names or the Proprietary Marks or from filing any trade name, assumed name or fictitious name registration with respect to any business to be conducted outside the Protected Territory or any business within the Protected Territory that is permitted by this Agreement. If you secure in any jurisdiction any rights to any of the Proprietary Marks (or any other Proprietary Property) not expressly granted under this Agreement, you will immediately notify us and immediately assign to us all of your right, title and interest to the Proprietary Marks (or any other Proprietary Property).

ARTICLE 6

THE MANUALS AND OTHER
CONFIDENTIAL INFORMATION

Section 6.1. In General.

To protect our reputation and good will and to maintain uniform standards of operation under the Proprietary Marks, you will conduct your Bobby Rubino's Ribs n More Franchise in accordance with the Manuals. The Manuals are deemed an integral part of this Agreement with the same effect as if fully stated in this Agreement.

Section 6.2. Confidential Use.

(a) You will treat and maintain the Confidential Information as our confidential trade secrets. The Manuals will be kept in a secure area within the Premises. You will strictly limit access to the Confidential Information to your employees, to the extent they have a "need to know" in order to perform their jobs. You will report the theft, loss or destruction of the Manuals immediately to us. Upon the theft, loss or destruction of the Manuals, we will loan to you a replacement copy at a fee of $200 for each Manual. A partial loss or failure to update any Manual is considered a complete loss.

(b) You agree that, during and after the Term, you, your owners and employees will:

(i) Not use the Confidential Information in any other business or capacity, including any derivative or spin-off of the Ribs n More concept;

(ii) Maintain the absolute secrecy and confidentiality of the Confidential Information during and after the Term;

(iii) Not make unauthorized copies of any portion of the Confidential Information disclosed or recorded in written or other tangible form; and

(iv) Adopt and implement all procedures that we prescribe to prevent unauthorized use or disclosure of, or access to, the Confidential Information.

(c) All persons whom you permit to have access to the Manuals or any other Confidential Information, must first be required by you to sign our form of confidentiality agreement.

Section 6.3. Periodic Revisions.

We may change the contents of the Manuals. You will comply with each new or changed provision beginning on the 30th day (or any longer time as we specify) after our written notice. Revisions to the Manuals will be based on what we, in our sole discretion, deem is in the best interests of the System, our interest and the interest of our Franchisees, including to promote quality, enhance good will, increase efficiency, decrease administrative burdens, or improve profitability subject to the capital expenditure limitation stated in Section 4.20. You agree that because complete and detailed uniformity under many varying conditions may not be possible or practical, we reserve the right, in our sole discretion and as we may deem in the best interests of all concerned in any specific instance, to vary standards for any franchisee due to the peculiarities of the particular site or circumstances, density of population, business potential, population of trade area, existing business practices or any condition that we deem important to the successful operation of a Bobby Rubino's Ribs n More Franchise. You are not entitled to require us to grant to you a similar variation under this Agreement. You will ensure that your copy of the Manuals contains all updates you receive from us. In any dispute as to the contents of the Manuals, the terms contained in our master copy of each of the Manuals we maintain at our home office is controlling.

ARTICLE 7

ADVERTISING

Recognizing the value of advertising, and the importance of the standardization of advertising programs to the good will and public image of the System, the parties agree:

Section 7.1. Local Advertising.

(a) You must spend during each month during the Term, beginning on the Opening Date, at least 2% of monthly Gross Revenues for Local Advertising.

(b) You must submit to us for approval, all materials to be used for Local Advertising, unless they have been approved before or they consist only of materials we provide. All materials on which the Proprietary Marks are used must include the applicable designation service mark^{RM} , trademark^{TM}, registered$^{®}$ or copyright$^{©}$, or any other designation we specify. If you have not received the written or oral disapproval of materials submitted within 10 days from the date we received the materials, the materials are deemed approved. We may require you to withdraw and/or discontinue the use of any promotional materials or advertising, even if previously approved, if in our judgment, the materials or advertising may injure or be harmful to the System. This requirement must be made in writing by us, and you have 5 days after receipt of notice to withdraw and discontinue use of the materials or advertising, unless otherwise agreed in writing. The submission of advertising to us for our approval does not affect your right to determine the prices at which you sell your products or services.

(c) Subject to any legal restrictions, you must include in all advertisements and promotions, and on a sign in a conspicuous place within the Premises, substantially the following statement: "Bobby Rubino's Ribs n More Franchise Opportunities Available." All responses will be immediately referred to us at (800) 339-2184 or any other number we designate and include our corporate address. You have no authority to act for us in franchise sales.

(d) You will maintain a listing or listings in The Real Yellow Pages of the telephone directories servicing the location of the Bobby Rubino's Ribs n More Franchise under the "Restaurant" section, in the form and size we specify in the Manuals or otherwise in writing.

Section 7.2. Regional Cooperative Advertising.

You agree that we have the right, in our discretion, to establish a regional advertising cooperative in any ADI. You will immediately upon request by us become a member of the Cooperative for the ADI where some or all of the Protected Territory is located. Your Bobby

Rubino's Ribs n More Franchise is not required to be a member of more than 1 Cooperative. The Cooperative will be governed in the manner required by us. The Cooperative has the right to require each of its members to make contributions to the Cooperative, not to exceed 1% of that member's weekly Gross Revenues. The following provisions apply to each Cooperative:

(a) The Cooperative will be organized and governed in a form and manner, and will begin operation on a date, approved in advance by us in writing;

   (i) The Cooperative will be organized for the exclusive purpose of administering advertising programs and developing, subject to our approval, standardized promotional materials for use by the members in Local Advertising in the Cooperative's ADI;

   (ii) The Cooperative may adopt its own rules and procedures, but the rules or procedures must be approved by us and will not restrict nor expand your rights or obligations under this Agreement. Except as otherwise provided in this Agreement, and subject to our approval, any lawful action of the Cooperative at a meeting attended by 2 of the members, including assessments for Local Advertising, is binding upon you if approved by 3 of the members present, with each Bobby Rubino's Ribs n More Franchise and Company Unit having 1 vote; however no franchisee (or controlled group of franchisees) has more than 25% of the vote in the Cooperative regardless of the number of Bobby Rubino's Ribs n More Franchises you own;

   (iii) No advertising or promotional plans or materials may be used by the Cooperative or furnished to its members without our written approval. All plans and materials must be submitted to us in accordance with the procedure stated in Section 7.1;

   (iv) The Cooperative has the right to require its members to make a contribution to the Cooperative in any amount the Cooperative determines. This amount will be credited against your obligation for Local Advertising as provided by Section 7.1; but you are not required to contribute to the Cooperative in excess of 1% of your weekly Gross Revenues;

   (v) Each member will submit to the Cooperative, no later than Saturday of each week, his or her contribution as provided in Subsection 7.2(a)(iv), together with all other statements or reports required by us or by the Cooperative with our written approval;

   (vi) If an impasse occurs owing to the inability or failure of the Cooperative members to resolve within 45 days any issue affecting the establishment or effective functioning of the Cooperative, the issue will, upon request of a member of the Cooperative, be submitted to the Advisory Council (or us, if the Advisory Council does not exist) for consideration and its resolution of the issue will be final and binding on all members of the Cooperative; and

   (vii) The Cooperative will render quarterly reports to us of its advertising expenditures.

(b) We, in our sole discretion, may grant to any franchisee an exemption for any length of time from the requirement of membership in the Cooperative, upon written request of the franchisee stating reasons supporting the exemption. Our decision concerning the request for exemption is final. If an exemption is granted to a franchisee, that franchisee must expend on Local Advertising the full amount provided in Section 7.1.

Section 7.3.   Special Advertising Expenditures.

If you fail to meet your requirements for Local Advertising during any period specified in this Agreement, upon our request and in addition to our rights and remedies for failure of you to make the proper expenditures, you will contribute the amount that you failed to spend on Local Advertising directly to the Marketing Fund.

Section D.   Marketing Fund.

(a) We reserve the right to create a special fund called the "Ribs n More Marketing Fund" (the "Marketing Fund") for the benefit of all Franchise Units and Company Units who contribute to the Marketing Fund, when there are a sufficient number of Franchise Units and Company Units, as determined by the Franchisor and a majority of its Franchisees.

(b) The Marketing Fund will be administered by the Marketing Fund Committee. The Franchisee will elect or appoint 2 members and we will appoint 2 members to the Marketing Fund Committee to serve for a one-year term corresponding to the calendar year. The 4-member committee will by a majority vote determine the selection and placement of national and regional advertising. Each committee member has one vote. The Marketing Fund where Advertising Contributions will be deposited is maintained and operated by the Marketing Fund Committee as a fiduciary to you and used to meet the costs of conducting regional and/or national advertising and promotional activities on a regional or national scale (including the cost of advertising campaigns, test marketing, marketing surveys, public relations activities and marketing materials) we deem beneficial to the System. We are authorized to charge the Marketing Fund fees at reasonable market rates for advertising, marketing or promotional services actually provided by us, in lieu of engaging third party agencies to provide these services. No funds will be used by us to offer to sell, or sell, Bobby Rubino's Ribs n More Franchises to prospective franchisees.

(c) All expenditures are at the sole discretion of the Marketing Fund Committee. They may spend in any calendar year more or less than the total Advertising Contributions to the Marketing Fund in that year. The Marketing Fund may borrow from us or other lenders to cover deficits of the Marketing Fund or cause the Marketing Fund to invest any surplus for future use by the Marketing Fund. You authorize us to act as your sole agent to enter into contracts with parties offering promotion, discount or other programs whereby you would receive rebates or marketing allowances ("Rebates") from handling items offered for sale by the parties. All Rebates will be paid to us and we will contribute them to the Marketing Fund. By signing this Agreement, you assign all of your right, title and interest in all Rebates to us, and authorize us to furnish any proof of purchase evidence as may be required in accordance with the contracts. All Rebates received by us from our Company-Units will also be contributed to the Marketing Fund.

Section 7.5. Content and Concepts.

(a) The Marketing Fund Committee retains sole discretion over all advertising, marketing and public relations programs and activities financed by the Marketing Fund, including the creative concepts, materials and endorsements used and the geographic market, media placement and allocation. You agree that the Marketing Fund may be used to pay the costs of preparing and producing associated materials and programs as the Marketing Fund Committee determines, including video, audio and written advertising materials employing advertising agencies; sponsorship of sporting, charitable or similar events, administering regional and multi-regional advertising programs including purchasing direct mail and other media advertising, and employing advertising agencies to assist with marketing efforts; and supporting public relations, market research and other advertising, promotional and marketing activities.

(b) You grant us the right to freely use, without your consent, any pictures, financial information, or biographical material relating to you or your Bobby Rubino's Ribs n More Franchise for use in promotional literature or in any other way beneficial to the Ribs n More organization as a whole. You will cooperate in securing photographs, including obtaining consents from any persons appearing in photographs. If we publish anything you feel reflects unfairly or inaccurately on your Bobby Rubino's Ribs n More Franchise or yourself, we will take all reasonable steps in our power to retract the material.

(c) You acknowledge that the Advertising Contributions are intended to maximize general public recognition of and the acceptance of the Proprietary Marks for the benefit of the System as a whole. The Marketing Fund Committee undertakes no obligation, in administering the Marketing Fund, to make expenditures for you that are equivalent or proportionate to your contribution, or to insure that any particular franchisee or Company Unit benefits directly or pro rata from advertising or promotion conducted with the Advertising Contributions.

Section 7.6. Advertising Contributions Not Our Asset.

The Advertising Contributions are not our asset. A report of the operations of the Marketing Fund as shown on the books of the Marketing Fund will be prepared annually by an independent certified public accountant that the Marketing Fund Committee selects at the expense of the Marketing Fund, and mailed to all franchisees.

Section 7.7. Termination of Expenditures.

We maintain the right to terminate the collection and disbursement of the Advertising Contributions and the Marketing Fund. Upon termination, the remaining funds will be disbursed by us for the purposes authorized under this Agreement.

Section 7.8. Advertising Contributions by Us.

Company Units are required to contribute to the Marketing Fund and any Cooperative on the same basis as you are required to contribute.

ARTICLE 8

ACCOUNTING AND RECORDS

Section 8.1. Records.

You will maintain complete and accurate records for the operations of your Bobby Rubino's Ribs n More Franchise. Records must be segregated from all other not concerning your Bobby Rubino's Ribs n More Franchise. You must preserve the records for at least 6 years from the dates of their preparation (including after the termination, transfer or expiration of this Agreement).

Section 8.2. Reports and Statements; Confidentiality.

(a) **Weekly Reports**. You will report Gross Revenues by telephone within 2 days after the end of the business week (currently Tuesday) and submit written weekly summaries showing results of operations by the following Saturday. If you fail to report your Gross Revenues on a timely basis, we may estimate your Gross Revenues.

(b) **Monthly Reports**. You will submit to us by the 10th day of each month during the Term, in the form we require, accurate records reflecting all Gross Revenues of the previous month and all other information we require. If you must collect and remit sales taxes, you must also supply to us copies of your sales tax returns.

(c) **Annual Financial Statements**. You must also submit, an annual balance sheet and income statement, within 90 days of the end of your fiscal year prepared in accordance with Generally Accepted Accounting Principles and compiled by an independent certified public accountant acceptable to us, and must be signed by you or by your treasurer or chief financial officer attesting that the financial statements are true and correct and fairly present your financial position at and for the times indicated. You will also supply to us copies of your federal and state income tax returns at the time these returns are filed with the appropriate tax authorities. The financial statements and/or other periodic reports described above must be prepared to segregate the income and related expenses of your Bobby Rubino's Ribs n More Franchise from .those of any other business that you may conduct.

(d) **Confidentiality**. We agree to maintain the confidentiality of all financial information we obtain about your operations, and will not disclose this financial information to any third party who is not bound to maintain the confidentiality of the information; provided however, that a. we may use the information in preparing any earnings claims or other information required by federal or state franchise law; and b. we may prepare a composite list of financial performances by our franchisees for dissemination among the franchisees, identifying your Gross Revenues and advertising expenditures.

Section 8.3. Review and Audit.

We and our representatives have the right at all reasonable times to examine and copy, at our expense, your records and inspect all cash control devices and systems and conduct a physical inventory. We have the right to access your P.O.S. System to determine, among other things, sales activity and Gross Revenues. We also have the right, at any time, to have an independent audit made of your records but no more frequently than 2 times a year. If an inspection reveals that any financial information reported to us (including Gross Revenues or payments owed to us) has been understated in any report to us, you must immediately pay to us, upon demand, the amount understated in addition to interest at the maximum rate permitted by law beginning from the time the required payment was due. If any inspection discloses an intentional understatement of 2% or more of Gross Revenues you must, in addition, reimburse us for the expenses for the inspection (including reasonable accounting and attorneys' fees and costs). In addition, we reserve the right to require that all your future year-end financial statements be audited by an independent certified public accountant reasonably acceptable to us at your expense. These remedies are in addition to any other remedies we have under this Agreement or under applicable law. If the audit discloses an overpayment in any amount you paid to us, we will promptly pay you the amount of the overpayment or offset the overpayment against any amounts owed to us.

Section 8.4. Your Name, Home Address and Telephone Number.

You agree that, under federal and state franchise laws and other applicable laws, we may be required to disclose your name, home address and telephone number and you agree to the disclosure of your name, home address and telephone number. You must notify us of any change in your name, home address and telephone number within 10 days of the change. You release us and our officers, directors, stockholders, agents and legal successors and assigns from all causes of action, suits, debts, covenants, agreements, damages, judgments, claims and demands, in law or in equity, that you ever had, now have, or that you later may have, from our disclosure of your name, home address and telephone number.

ARTICLE 9

INSURANCE

Section 9.1. Types and Amounts of Coverage.

You must obtain and maintain insurance, at your expense, as we require, in addition to any other insurance that may be required by applicable law, your landlord, lender or otherwise. All policies must be written by an insurance company reasonably satisfactory to us with a Best rating of "A" or better and include the types and amounts of insurance as stated in the Manuals. We may periodically adjust the amounts of coverage required under the insurance policies and require different or additional kinds of insurance at any time, including excess liability insurance, to reflect inflation, identification of new risks, changes in law or standards of liability, higher damage awards, or other relevant changes in circumstances, if the changes are required throughout the System including any Company Units.

Section 9.2. Evidence of Insurance.

At least: a. 30 days before the date any construction is begun; b. 10 days from the Agreement Date if the Premises is constructed and presently owned or leased by you; or c. 10 days after a sublease of the Premises is signed, whichever is applicable, a certificate of insurance issued by an approved insurance company showing compliance with these requirements and a paid receipt showing the certificate number you must furnish to us. The certificate of insurance must include a statement by the insurer that the policies will not be canceled, subject to nonrenewal or materially altered without at least 30 days' written notice to us. Copies of all insurance policies and proof of payment will be submitted promptly upon our request to you. You will send to us current certificates of insurance and copies of all insurance policies on an annual basis.

Section 9.3.   Requirements for Renovation.

For any renovation, refurbishment, or remodeling of the Premises, you must require the general contractor to maintain with a reputable insurer commercial general liability insurance (with comprehensive automobile liability coverage for both owned and non-owned vehicles, builder's risk, product liability, and independent contractor's coverage) for at least $1,000,000, with you and us as additional named insureds, as their interests may appear, together with workers' compensation and employer's liability insurance required by law.

Section 9.4.   Our Right to Participate in Claims Procedure.

We, or our insurer, has the right to participate in discussions with your insurance company or any claimant (with your insurance company) regarding any claim. You agree to adopt our reasonable recommendations to your insurance carrier regarding the settlement of any claims.

Section 9.5.   Waiver of Subrogation.

Insofar as and to the extent that this Section may be effective without invalidating it or making it impossible to secure insurance coverage obtainable from responsible insurance companies doing business in the state where your Bobby Rubino's Ribs n More Franchise is located (even though an extra premium may result), the parties agree that, for any loss that is covered by insurance then being carried by them, their respective insurance companies have no right of subrogation against the other.

Section 9.6.   Effect of Our Insurance.

Your obligation to maintain the policies in the amounts required is not limited by reason of any insurance we maintain, nor will our performance of your obligations relieve you of liability under the indemnity provisions in this Agreement.

Section 9.7.   Failure to Maintain Insurance.

If either party fails to maintain the insurance required by this Agreement, the other party has the right and authority (without any obligation to do so) immediately to procure the insurance and to charge the cost of the insurance to the party obligated to maintain the insurance, plus interest at the maximum rate permitted by law, which charges, together with a reasonable fee for the party's expenses in so acting, the other party agrees to pay immediately upon notice.

Section 9.8.   Group Insurance.

If we make available to you insurance coverage through group or master policies we arrange including property and casualty, workers' compensation, liability and health, life and disability insurance, you may participate, at your expense, in this group insurance program.

ARTICLE 10

INDEPENDENT ASSOCIATION OF BOBBY RUBINO'S RIBS n MORE FRANCHISEES

Section 10.1. Your Right to Join the Independent Association of Bobby Rubino's Ribs n More Franchisees

We recognize your right and the other franchisees' right to freely associate. You and the other franchisees have the right to create an independent franchise association to be known as the "Independent Association of Bobby Rubino's Ribs n More Franchisees" (the "Franchisee Association"). The decision to join the Franchisee Association is solely your decision.

Section 10.2. Our Dealings with the Franchisee Association.

Once at least 10 franchisees, representing at least 75% of the total Franchisees within the System, are members of the Franchisee Association, we will recognize the Franchisee Association as the official body representing the franchisees as a group. Any renewal to this Agreement must be collectively negotiated with the Franchisee Association with both parties agreeing to negotiate in good faith.

Section 10.3. Annual Convention.

We and the Franchisee Association will coordinate and conduct an Annual Convention of the Ribs n More System when we and the Franchisee Association deem it appropriate. We will pay 50% of the cost of the Annual Convention and the Franchisee Association will pay 50%. Each Franchisee will pay their own travel, lodging and meal costs to the extent not paid for by us, the Franchisee Association or sponsors. Representatives of the Franchisor and the Franchisee Association will coordinate in the planning and agenda of each Annual Convention.

ARTICLE 11

TRANSFER OF INTEREST

Section 11.1. Transfer by Us.

We have the right to assign this Agreement to any person without your consent provided the transfer is part of a merger or sale of the entire System and the transferee has sufficient business experience, aptitude and financial resources to competently assume our obligations under this Agreement.

Section 11.2. Transfer by You.

(a) **Personal Rights**. You agree that, unless otherwise expressly permitted by this Agreement, you will not sell, assign, transfer, convey or give voluntarily, involuntarily, directly or indirectly, by operation of law or otherwise (collectively "transfer") any direct or indirect interest in this Agreement, in the Franchise or in you without our written consent. However, our written consent is not required for: a. a transfer of less than a 5% interest in a publicly-held corporation; b. a transfer of all or any part of any interest in you to one of your other original shareholders or partners; or c. a transfer to another existing franchisee of the System. A transfer of 50% or more of the voting or ownership interests in your corporation, partnership or limited liability company, individually or in the aggregate, directly or indirectly, is, for all purposes of this Agreement, considered a transfer of an interest in this Agreement by you. Any purported transfer by you, by operation of law or otherwise in violation of this Agreement, is void and is an Event of Default on your part.

(b) **Transfer to Your Corporation**. This Agreement may be assigned to a corporation where you own a majority of the issued and outstanding capital stock if:

(i) You or a Manager approved by us actively manages the corporation and continues to devote his or her best efforts and full and exclusive time to the day-to-day operation of your Bobby Rubino's Ribs n More Franchise. You must advise us of the name of the Manager and the Manager must meet our standards including training;

(ii) The corporation cannot use the trade name "Ribs n More" in any derivative or form in the corporate name;

(iii) An authorized officer of the corporation signs a document in a form we approve, agreeing to become a party bound by all the provisions of this Agreement;

(iv) All stock certificates representing shares bear a legend that they are subject to this Agreement.

(c) **No Subfranchising Rights**. You have no right to grant a subfranchise.

(d) **No Encumbrance**. You agree that your rights under this Agreement and any voting or ownership interest of more than 50% in you (or any Franchise Owner) may not be pledged, mortgaged, hypothecated, given as security for an obligation or in any manner encumbered. Any attempted encumbrance is void and is an Event of Default on your part.

(e) **"For Sale" Restrictions**. You will not permit to be placed upon the Premises a "Business For Sale" or "For Sale" sign, or any sign of a similar nature or purpose, nor in any manner use the Proprietary Marks to advertise the sale of your Bobby Rubino's Ribs n More Franchise or the sale or lease of the Premises. These prohibitions apply to any activities under a listing agreement that you may enter into with a real estate or business broker.

(f) **Permitted Transfer**. We will consent to a transfer of this Agreement if the following requirements are satisfied or waived by us in our sole discretion:

(i) We have not exercised our right of first purchase as provided in Section 11.4;

(ii) You are not in default of any term of this Agreement or any other agreement between you and us or our Affiliates;

(iii) The transferee interviews at our principal office without expense to us and demonstrates to our reasonable satisfaction that the transferee has the business and personal skills, reputation and financial capacity we require;

(iv) The transferee satisfactorily completes our application procedures for new franchisees;

(v)   The transferee demonstrates to our reasonable satisfaction that he or she has properly assumed your obligations under this Agreement and will be able to comply with all of his or her obligations to the Bobby Rubino's Ribs n More Franchise, including an assumption of the Sublease. You will remain liable for all obligations to us under this Agreement before the effective date of the transfer and will sign all instruments we reasonably request to evidence these liabilities;

(vi)   At the transferee's expense, the transferee or transferee's Manager completes Basic Management Training then in effect for new franchisees upon all terms as we reasonably require; and

(vii)   You pay a transfer fee of $5,000 to reimburse us for our direct out-of-pocket costs in approving the transfer and in training the transferee. If the transferee is a wholly-owned corporation, spouse or child of the transferor, or another Franchisee within the System, no transfer fee will be charged.

No disapproval of the transferee for failure to satisfy the transfer conditions described in this Subsection, or of any other condition to transfer stated in this Agreement causes any liability of us to the transferee.

Our consent to a transfer is not a waiver of any claims we may have against you, nor is it a waiver of our right to demand the transferee's exact compliance with this Agreement. No transfer (even if we approve) relieves you of liability for your conduct before the transfer, including conduct in breach of this Agreement.

Section 11.3. Transfer Upon Death or Disability.

(a)   If any Franchise Owner becomes disabled from any cause and is unable to perform his or her obligations under this Agreement for a continuous period in excess of 3 consecutive months, or on the death of the Franchise Owner, you (or your legal representative) will within 30 days after the 3 months of disability or death, provide and maintain a replacement satisfactory to us to perform the obligations. If a replacement is not provided or maintained as required, we may hire and maintain your replacement. You will compensate the replacement for his or her services at the rate we establish in the reasonable exercise of its discretion. For all purposes of this Agreement, any period of disability that is interrupted by a return to active work and proper performance of duties under this Agreement for 14 days or less is deemed continuous.

(b)   If: a. any individual who holds a 50% or greater voting or ownership interest in the Franchisee (or in any Franchise Owner); or b. you die during the Term, your interests in the Franchisee (or in any Franchise Owner) or in this Agreement are required to be transferred within 12 months of the death to an approved transferee in accordance with the terms of this ARTICLE.

Section 11.4. Our Right of First Purchase.

(a)   If during the Term you or any person who owns at least a 50% ownership or voting interest in a corporation or other entity that owns your Bobby Rubino's Ribs n More Franchise (or in any entity with an ownership interest in a corporation or other entity that owns your Bobby Rubino's Ribs n More Franchise) desire to sell your Bobby Rubino's Ribs n More Franchise, (whether as a sale of assets or a sale of stock or other equity interests), you must first approach us with a specific price and terms and offer us the opportunity to purchase your Bobby Rubino's Ribs n More Franchise. We have 30 days to accept or reject your offer at the designated price. If we reject your offer and you and we cannot otherwise reach agreement within the 30-day period, you then have the right to list the Bobby Rubino's Ribs n More Franchise and offer it for sale to third parties (either in or outside the System) at or above the designated price and on terms no less favorable than offered to us, for a period of 120 days, with a closing to take place within 60 days after the date of the purchase agreement. If a third party purchases your Bobby Rubino's Ribs n More Franchise at a price or terms equal or more favorable than rejected by us; the sale can proceed, provided you and the third party comply with the terms of Subsection 11.2(f).

(b) If you decide within the 120-day period to offer your Bobby Rubino's Ribs n More Franchise or accept an offer from a third party (the "Offeror") at a lower price and/or terms less favorable to you (the "Offer") than offered to us, you must then give us a right of first refusal.

(c) If we give notice of acceptance of the Offer, then you will sell the Bobby Rubino's Ribs n More Franchise to us and we will purchase the Bobby Rubino's Ribs n More Franchise for the consideration and upon the terms stated in the Offer. Our creditworthiness is deemed at least equal to the creditworthiness of any proposed purchaser. If we are, our Affiliate is, a public company at that time having shares traded on a national securities exchange, the Offeror must accept a quantity of stock at our then-current value or our, or our Affiliate's, registered shares in lieu of cash or Unique Consideration.

(d) If an independent third party's written Offer (and the Offeror's corresponding offer to us) provides for the purchaser's payment of a Unique Consideration that is of a nature that cannot reasonably be duplicated by us, we may, in our notice of exercise, in lieu of the Unique Consideration, substitute cash or stock (if a public company with registered shares) consideration determined by mutual agreement of you and us within 45 days after the Offer is made or, failing agreement, by an independent appraiser selected by us.

(e) If the proposed sale includes assets of the Offeror that are not part of the operation of the Bobby Rubino's Ribs n More Franchise, we may, at our option, elect to purchase only the assets that are part of the operation of the Bobby Rubino's Ribs n More Franchise and an equitable purchase price will be determined in our reasonable discretion and allocated to each asset included in the sale.

(f) We will purchase your Bobby Rubino's Ribs n More Franchise subject to all customary warranties given by a seller of the assets of a business or voting stock of a corporation, as applicable, including warranties as to ownership, condition and title to the shares and/or assets, liens and encumbrances on the shares and/or assets, validity of contracts and liabilities of the corporation whose stock is purchased and affecting the assets, contingent or otherwise.

(g) Unless otherwise agreed by you and us, the closing of the purchase of your Bobby Rubino's Ribs n More Franchise will be held at our then principal office or other location designated by us, no later than the 60th day after the Offer is delivered to us. The closing of any purchase where a cash or stock consideration is determined in accordance with Subsection 11.4(d) will be held on the 15th day after the cash or stock consideration is finally determined. At any closing, the Offeror must deliver to us an assignment and other documents reasonably requested by us representing a transfer of ownership of your Bobby

Rubino's Ribs n More Franchise free and clear of all liens, claims, pledges, options, restrictions, charges and encumbrances, in proper form for transfer and with evidence of payment by the Offeror of all applicable transfer taxes. We will simultaneously make payment of any cash consideration for your Bobby Rubino's Ribs n More Franchise by a cashier's check drawn on a bank or thrift doing business in the county of our principal place of business or payment by the issuance of our or our Affiliate's registered shares, after set off against the amount due to the Offeror for all amounts you owe us, if any. The remaining terms of the purchase and sale will be stated in the Offer.

(h) If we do not accept the Offer, you are free, for 90 days after we have elected not to exercise our option, to sell your Bobby Rubino's Ribs n More Franchise to the prospective purchaser for the consideration and upon the terms stated in the prospective purchaser written Offer, subject to full compliance with all terms of transfer required under this Agreement, including those in Section 11.2. Before any sale of the shares to a prospective purchaser, there must be delivered by the prospective purchaser an acknowledgment that the shares purchased by the prospective purchaser is subject to the terms of this Agreement and that the prospective purchaser agrees to be bound to the terms of this Section on transferring the shares, in the same manner as the Offeror. If you do not sell your Bobby Rubino's Ribs n More Franchise within the 90-day period, then any transfer by you of your Bobby Rubino's Ribs n More Franchise is again subject to the restrictions stated in this Agreement.

(i) If a proposed transferee is your corporation or the spouse or child of the Offeror, we will not have any right of first purchase.

(j) All transferees are subject to all of the restrictions on transfer of ownership imposed on you under this Agreement.

ARTICLE 12

DEFAULT AND TERMINATION

Section 12.1. Termination by You.

If you have substantially complied with this Agreement and we materially breach this Agreement, you have the right to terminate this Agreement if we do not cure the breach within 30 days after we receive a written notice of default from you. However, if the breach cannot reasonably be cured within 30 days, you have the right to terminate this Agreement if, after our receipt of a written notice of default from you, we do not within 30 days undertake and continue efforts to cure the breach until completion. You may also terminate this Agreement upon the mutual written agreement with us. Any termination of this Agreement by you other than as stated above, is a wrongful termination by you.

Section 12.2. Termination by Us - Without Notice.

(a) Subject to applicable law, this Agreement automatically terminates without notice to you or your having an opportunity to cure on the date of the occurrence of any of the following Events of Default: if you damage the Ribs n More System through violation of federal, state or local environmental laws; if you make a general assignment for the benefit of creditors; a petition in bankruptcy is filed by you or a petition is filed against or consented to by you and the petition is not dismissed within 45 days; you are adjudicated as bankrupt; a bill in equity or other proceeding for the appointment of your receiver or other custodian for your business or assets is filed and consented to you; a receiver or other custodian (permanent or temporary) of your business or assets is appointed by any court of competent jurisdiction; proceedings for a composition with creditors under federal or any state law is begun by or against you; a final judgment in excess of $25,000 remains unsatisfied or of record for 30 days or longer (unless a *supersedeas* bond is filed); execution is levied against your operation or property, or suit to foreclose any lien or mortgage against the Premises or your assets is begun against you and not dismissed within 45 days; or a substantial portion of your real or personal property used in your Bobby Rubino's Ribs n More Franchise is sold after levy by any sheriff, marshal or constable.

(b) You will notify us within 3 days of the occurrence of any of the events described in Subsection 12.2(a).

Section 12.3. Termination by Us - After Notice.

You are in default and we may, at our option, terminate all rights granted to you under this Agreement, without affording you any opportunity to cure the default, effective immediately upon notice to you, upon the occurrence of any of the following Events of Default:

(a) If you cease to do business at the Premises for more than 14 days in any calendar year or for more than 7 consecutive days, or lose the right to possession of the Premises after the expiration of all redemption periods and has not satisfied the provisions of Section 1.4, if applicable, or otherwise forfeit the right to do or transact business in the jurisdiction where your Bobby Rubino's Ribs n More Franchise is located;

(b) If a serious or imminent threat or danger to public health or safety results from the construction, maintenance or operation of your Bobby Rubino's Ribs n More Franchise and the threat or danger remains uncorrected for 5 days after your receipt of written notice from us or a governmental authority. If a cure cannot be reasonably completed in this time, then all reasonable steps to cure must begin within this time, but a cure must be completed promptly within 30 days after receipt of written notice;

(c) If you fail or refuse to comply with any mandatory specification, standard or operating procedure required by us in this Agreement, in the Manuals or otherwise in writing, on the cleanliness or sanitation of your Bobby Rubino's Ribs n More Franchise or violate any health, safety, or sanitation law, ordinance, or regulation and do not correct the failure or refusal within 3 days after written notice from us or a governmental authority. If a cure cannot be reasonably completed in this time, then all reasonable steps to cure must begin within this time, but a cure must be completed within 30 days after receipt of written notice;

(d) If you, or your officer, director, owner or managerial employee are convicted of a felony, a crime of moral turpitude or any other crime or offense that we reasonably believe is likely to have a material adverse effect on the System, the Proprietary Property, the good will associated with the Proprietary Property, or our interest in any of the Proprietary Property, unless you immediately and legally terminate the individual as your officer, director, owner and employee;

(e)   If you deny us the right to inspect your Bobby Rubino's Ribs n More Franchise or to audit your Records;

(f)   If you engage in conduct that is deleterious to or reflects unfavorably on you or the System in that the conduct exhibits a reckless disregard for the physical or mental well being of employees, customers, our representatives or the public at large, including battery, assault, sexual harassment or discrimination, racial harassment or discrimination, alcohol or drug abuse or other forms of threatening, outrageous or unacceptable behavior as determined in our sole discretion;

(g)   If you, contrary to this Agreement, purport to encumber or transfer any rights or obligations under this Agreement (including transfers of any interest in a corporation or other entity which owns your Bobby Rubino's Ribs n More Franchise), without our written consent;

(h)   If any breach occurs under Sections 6.2 or 14.1 concerning confidentiality and non-competition covenants;

(i)   If you knowingly maintain false records, or knowingly submit any false reports to us; or

(j)   If you misuse or make any unauthorized use of the Proprietary Property or otherwise materially impairs the good will associated with the Proprietary Property or our rights in the Proprietary Property.

Section 12.4. Termination by Us - After Notice and Right to Cure.

Except as otherwise provided above, you have 30 days after delivery from us of a written Notice of Default specifying the nature of the default to remedy any default other than as stated above, and provide evidence of cure satisfactory to us. If any default is not cured within that time, or any longer time as applicable law may require, an Event of Default has occurred by you and all your rights under this Agreement terminate without additional notice to you effective immediately upon the expiration of the 30 days or any longer time as applicable law may require. In addition to the Events of Default specified in Sections 12.2 and 12.3, an Event of Default by you occurs if you fail to comply with any of the requirements imposed by this Agreement, as it may be revised or supplemented by the Manuals, or the Sublease, or to carry out this Agreement in good faith. You have the burden of proving that you properly and timely cured any default, to the extent a cure is permitted under this Agreement.

ARTICLE 13

YOUR OBLIGATIONS UPON TERMINATION DUE TO YOUR DEFAULT

Upon the termination of this Agreement due to your default, the Sections of this ARTICLE apply to the rights and obligations of the parties.

Section 13.1. Cease Operations.

You will immediately cease to operate your Bobby Rubino's Ribs n More Franchise. You will not, directly or indirectly, use any of the Proprietary Property nor represent yourself as a present or former franchisee of us or in any other way affiliate yourself with the System. You will immediately cease using all stationery, signage and other materials containing the Proprietary Marks. You will also immediately cease using all telephone numbers for the Bobby Rubino's Ribs n More Franchise used at any time before termination or expiration, and empowers us to take whatever actions are necessary to comply with this Section.

Section 13.2. Payment of Outstanding Amounts.

We may retain all fees paid under this Agreement except for refunds expressly required in this Agreement. In addition, within 10 days after the effective date of the termination or any later dates as we determine that amounts are due to us, you must pay to us all Royalty Fees, Advertising Contributions, amounts owed for products or services you purchased from us or our Affiliates, and all other amounts owed to us, our Affiliates and your other creditors that are then unpaid.

Section 13.3. Discontinuance of Use of Trade Name.

You will cancel any fictitious, trade or assumed name registration that contains our trademark, trade name or service mark or colorable imitation of our trademark, trade name or service mark. You will furnish us with evidence of compliance with this obligation to cancel the registration within 30 days after termination or expiration of this Agreement. If you fail to cancel, you appoint us as your attorney-in-fact to do so.

Section 13.4. Our Option to Purchase Your Bobby Rubino's Ribs n More Franchise.

(a) We have the option, exercisable by giving written notice within 30 days from the date of termination, to purchase from you all the assets used in your Bobby Rubino's Ribs n More Franchise. As used in this Section, "assets" means leasehold improvements, equipment, vehicles, furnishings, fixtures, signs, inventory (non-perishable products, materials and supplies) and the lease or sublease for the Premises. We have the unrestricted right to assign this option to purchase. We or our assignee are entitled to all customary warranties given by a seller of a business, including: a. ownership, condition and title to the assets; b. the absence of liens and encumbrances on the assets; and c. validity of contracts and liabilities, inuring to us or affecting the assets, contingent or otherwise. The purchase price for the assets of your Bobby Rubino's Ribs n More Franchise is their fair market value, determined as of the effective date of purchase in a manner consistent with reasonable depreciation of your leasehold improvements and the equipment, vehicles, furnishings, fixtures, signs and inventory of your Bobby Rubino's Ribs n More Franchise. The purchase price will take into account the termination of the Bobby Rubino's Ribs n More Franchise granted under this Agreement and will not contain any factor or increment for any trademark, service mark or other commercial symbol used in the operation of your Bobby Rubino's Ribs n More Franchise.

(b) If the parties cannot agree on the fair market value of the assets within 30 days after your receipt of our notice exercising its option, the fair market value will be determined by an independent appraiser the parties selected. If they are unable to agree on an independent appraiser within 10 days after expiration of the 30-day period, the parties will each select one independent appraiser, who will select a third independent appraiser (the "Third Appraiser"), and the fair market value will be the value determined by the Third Appraiser. If either party fails to select an appraiser and give notice to the other of the identity of the appraiser within the 10-day period, the appraiser selected by the other party will select the Third Appraiser. The Third Appraiser will be given full access to your Bobby Rubino's Ribs n More Franchise, the Premises and your records during customary business hours to conduct the appraisal and must value the leasehold improvements, equipment, furnishings, fixtures, signs and inventory in accordance with the standards of this Section. The Third Appraiser's costs will be paid equally by the parties.

(c)   The purchase price will be paid in cash equivalent, or our marketable securities or the marketable securities of an Affiliate of equivalent value at the closing of the purchase, which will take place no later than 90 days after your receipt of notice of exercise of the option to purchase. At the closing, you will deliver instruments transferring to us or our assignee: a. good and merchantable title to the assets purchased, free and clear of all liens and encumbrances (other than liens and security interests acceptable to us or our assignee), with all your sales and other transfer taxes paid; b. all licenses and permits of your Bobby Rubino's Ribs n More Franchise that may be assigned or transferred; and c. the lease or sublease for the Premises. If you cannot deliver clear title to all of the purchased assets, or if there are other unresolved issues, the closing of the sale will be accomplished through an escrow. The parties will comply with all applicable legal requirements, including the bulk sales provisions of the Uniform Commercial Code of the state where your Bobby Rubino's Ribs n More Franchise is located and the bulk sales provisions of any applicable tax laws and regulations. You will, before or simultaneously with the closing of the purchase, pay all tax liabilities incurred in the operation of your Bobby Rubino's Ribs n More Franchise. We have the right to set off against and reduce the purchase price by all amounts you owe to us, and the amount of any encumbrances or liens against the assets or any obligations we assume.

(d)   If we or our assignee exercise the option to purchase, pending the closing of the purchase, we have the right to appoint a manager to maintain the operation of your Bobby Rubino's Ribs n More Franchise under Section 2.13. Alternatively, we may require you to close your Bobby Rubino's Ribs n More Franchise during this time period without removing any assets. You will maintain in force all insurance policies required in this Agreement until the date of closing. If the Premises is leased, we agree to use reasonable efforts to effect a termination of the existing lease for the Premises and enter into a new lease on reasonable terms with the landlord. If we are unable to enter into a new lease and your rights under the existing lease are assigned to us or we sublease the Premises from you, we indemnify you from any ongoing liability under the lease occurring after the date we assume possession of the Premises. If you own the Premises, upon purchase of the assets, you, at your option, may enter into a new lease with us under a standard lease on terms comparable to those for similar commercial properties in the area that are then being leased, for a term of at least 10 years and for a rental equal to the fair market rental value of the Premises. If the parties cannot agree on the fair market rental value of the Premises, then the rental value will be determined by the Appraiser (selected in the manner described above).

Section 13.5. Distinguishing Operations.

(a)   If we do not exercise our option under Section 13.4 and you desire to remain in possession of the Premises and operate a noncompetitive business, you must make all modifications or alterations to the Premises immediately upon termination of this

Agreement as necessary to distinguish the appearance of the Premises from that of other Bobby Rubino's Ribs n More Franchisees operating under the System. You will make all specific additional changes to the Premises as we reasonably request for that purpose including a change of use of the Premises. You agree to refrain from taking any action to reduce the good will of your customers or potential customers toward us, our franchisees or any other aspect of the System.

(b) You must remove immediately all identifying architectural superstructure and signage on or about the Premises bearing the name or logos of Ribs n More (or any name or logo similar to Ribs n More), in the manner we specify. All property belonging to us will be held by you for delivery to us, at our expense, upon request. Any signage that you are unable to remove within 1 Business Day of the termination of this Agreement must be completely covered by you until the time of its removal. If you fail or refuse to comply with this obligation, we have the right to enter upon the Premises, without being guilty of trespass or any other tort for the purpose of removing the signage and storing it at another location, at a reasonable expense (for signage not owned by us) payable by you on demand.

(c) Until all modifications and alterations required by this Section are completed, you must: a. maintain a conspicuous sign at the Premises in a form specified by us stating that your business is no longer associated with our System; and b. advise all customers or prospective customers telephoning your business that the business is no longer associated with our System.

(d) If you fail or refuse to comply with the requirements of this Section, we have the right to enter upon the Premises for the purpose of making or causing to be made, all changes as may be required, at a reasonable expense (which expense you must pay upon demand) and at your sole risk and expense, without responsibility for any actual or consequential damages to your property or others, and without liability for trespass or other tort or criminal act. You agree that your failure to make these alterations will cause irreparable injury to us.

Section 13.6. Unfair Competition.

You agree, if you continue to operate or later begin to operate any other business, not to use any reproduction or colorable imitation of the Proprietary Marks, Trade Dress, methods of operation or undertake any other conduct either in any other business or the promotion of any other business, that is likely to cause confusion, mistake or deception, or that is likely to dilute our rights in and to the Proprietary Marks. In addition, you agree not to utilize any designation of origin or description or representation that falsely suggests or represents an association or connection with us, or any of our Affiliates. This Section does not relieve, directly or indirectly, your obligations under ARTICLE 14.

Section 13.7. Return of Materials.

You will immediately deliver to us all tangible Proprietary Property in your possession or control, and all copies and any other forms of reproductions of these materials. You agree that all these materials are our exclusive property.

Section 13.8. Our Purchase Rights of Items Bearing Proprietary Marks.

Even if we do not exercise our option under Section 13.3, we have the option (but not the obligation) to be exercised by notice of intent to do so within 30 days after termination to purchase any items bearing the Proprietary Marks owned by you including signs, advertising materials, supplies, inventory or other items at a price equal to the lesser of your cost or fair market value. If the parties cannot agree on fair market value within a reasonable time, we will designate an independent appraiser whose cost will be paid equally by the parties, and the appraiser's determination will be binding. The fair market value of tangible assets will be determined without reference to good will, going concern value, or other intangible assets. If we elect to exercise our option to purchase, we will have the right to set off all amounts due from you under this Agreement, and ½ the cost of the appraisal, if any, against any payment to you. If you fail to sign and deliver the necessary documents to transfer good title to your assets to us or our nominee, we are entitled to apply to any court of competent jurisdiction for a mandatory injunction to compel you to comply with the rights granted in this Agreement. All expenses, including our reasonable attorneys' fees, you will pay to us and may be credited by us to the agreed purchase price.

Section 13.9. Liquidated Damages for Premature Termination.

If termination is the result of your default, you will pay to us a lump sum payment (as liquidated damages for causing the premature termination of this Agreement and not as a penalty) equal to the total of all Royalty Fees for: a. the 36 calendar months of operation of your Bobby Rubino's Ribs n More Franchise preceding your default; b. the period of time your Bobby Rubino's Ribs n More Franchise has been in operation preceding the notice, if less than 36 calendar months, projected on a 36-calendar month basis; or c. any shorter period as equals the unexpired Term at the time of termination. The parties agree that a precise calculation of the full extent of the damages that we will incur on termination of this Agreement as a result of your default is difficult and the parties desire certainty in this matter in the extreme, and agree that the lump sum payment provided under this Section is reasonable in light of the damages for premature termination that we will incur in this event. This payment is not exclusive of any other remedies that we have.

ARTICLE 14

YOUR INDEPENDENT COVENANTS

Section 14.1. Diversion of Business; Competition and Interference With Us.

You agree that we would be unable to protect the Confidential Information against unauthorized use or disclosure and would be unable to encourage a free exchange of ideas and information among the franchisees within the System if franchisees were permitted to hold interests in any Competitive Business.

(a) **In-Term**. You covenant that during the Term, except as we otherwise approve in writing, you will not:

(i) Directly or indirectly, solicit or otherwise attempt to induce, by combining or conspiring with, or attempting to do so, or in any other manner influence any Business Associate to terminate or modify his, her or its business relationship with us or to compete against us;

(ii) Directly or indirectly, as owner, officer, director, employee, agent, lender, broker, consultant, franchisee or in any other capacity be connected with the ownership, management, operation, control or conduct of a Competitive Business (this restriction will not apply to a 5% or less beneficial interest in a publicly-held corporation); or

(iii) Interfere with, disturb, disrupt, decrease or otherwise jeopardize our business or the business of any of our franchisees.

(b) **Post-Term**. You also covenant that, for 24 months after the termination of this Agreement due to your default or for 24 months after you transfer your Bobby Rubino's Ribs n More Franchise, except as we otherwise approve in writing, you will not:

(i) Directly or indirectly, solicit or otherwise attempt to induce, by combining or conspiring with, or attempting to do so, or in any other manner influence any Business Associate to terminate or modify his, her or its business relationship with us or to compete against us;

(ii) Directly or indirectly, as owner, officer, director, employee, agent, lender, broker, consultant, franchisee or in any other capacity be connected with the ownership, management, operation, control or conduct of a Competitive Business within 5 miles of any Bobby Rubino's Ribs n More Franchise or Company-Owned Unit then in operation or under construction (this restriction will not apply to a 5% or less beneficial interest in a publicly-held corporation); or

(iii) Interfere with, disturb, disrupt, decrease or otherwise jeopardize our business or the business of any of its franchisees.

If you violate this Subsection and compete with us, we have the right to require that all sales made by the Competitive Business be reported to us. You will also pay to us, on demand, a weekly fee of $15,000 plus 5% of all sales made by the Competitive Business without being deemed to revive or modify this Agreement. These payments are liquidated damages to compensate us for our damages from your violation of the covenant not to compete and are not a penalty.

(c) You agree that the length of the term and geographical restrictions contained in this Section are fair and reasonable and not the result of overreaching, duress or coercion of any kind. You agree that your full, uninhibited and faithful observance of each of the covenants in this Section will not cause any undue hardship, financial or otherwise, and that enforcement of each of the covenants in this Section will not impair your ability to obtain employment commensurate with your abilities and on terms fully acceptable to you or otherwise to obtain income required for the comfortable support of yourself and your family, and the satisfaction of your creditors. You agree that your special knowledge of the business of a Bobby Rubino's Ribs n More Franchise (and anyone acquiring this knowledge through you) would cause us and our franchisees serious injury and loss if you (or anyone acquiring this knowledge through you) were to use this knowledge to the benefit of a competitor or were to compete with us or any of our other franchisees.

(d) If any court finally holds that the time or territory or any other provision in this Section is an unreasonable restriction upon you, you agree that the provisions of this Agreement are not rendered void, but apply as to time and territory or to any other extent as the court may judicially determine or indicate is a reasonable restriction under the circumstances involved.

Section 14.2. Independent Covenants; Third Party Beneficiaries.

(a)   The parties agree that the covenants in this ARTICLE are independent of any other provision of this Agreement. You agree that the existence of any claim you may have against us or any of our Affiliates, regardless of whether under this Agreement, is not a defense to our enforcement of these covenants.

(b)   The parties agree that all other Franchisees are third party beneficiaries of the terms of Section 14.1 and have the right to separately enforce these covenants, if we are unwilling or unable to enforce these covenants.

ARTICLE 15

INDEPENDENT CONTRACTOR AND INDEMNIFICATION

Section 15.1. Independent Status.

You are an independent contractor and unless expressly provided to the contrary, nothing in this Agreement is intended to designate either party an agent, legal representative, subsidiary, joint venturer, partner, employee, affiliate or servant of the other party for any purpose. The parties agree that nothing in this Agreement authorizes either party to make any agreement, warranty or representation for the other party, nor to incur any debt or other obligation in the other party's name. You will take all affirmative action as we request to indicate that you are an independent contractor, including placing and maintaining a plaque in a conspicuous place within the Premises and a notice on all stationery, business cards, sales literature, contracts and similar documents that states that your Bobby Rubino's Ribs n More Franchise is independently owned and operated by you. The content of any plaque and notice is subject to our written approval.

Section 15.2. Indemnification.

You are responsible for all losses or damages from contractual liabilities to third persons from the possession, ownership and operation of your Bobby Rubino's Ribs n More Franchise and for all claims and demands for damages to property or for injury, illness or death of persons directly or indirectly resulting from your actions. You indemnify us from all costs, losses and damages (including reasonable attorneys' fees and costs, even if incident to appellate, post-judgment or bankruptcy proceedings) from claims brought by third parties involving the ownership or operation by you of your Bobby Rubino's Ribs n More Franchise unless caused by our negligence or intentional misconduct. This indemnity obligation continues in full effect even after the expiration, transfer or termination of this Agreement. We will notify you of any claims and you will be given the opportunity to assume the defense of the matter. If you fail to assume the defense, we may defend the action in the manner it deems appropriate and you will pay to us all costs, including attorneys' fees, we incur in effecting the defense, in addition to any sum that we may pay by reason of any settlement or judgment against us. Our right to indemnity under this Agreement arises and is valid regardless of any joint or concurrent liability that may be imposed on us by statute, ordinance, regulation or other law.

ARTICLE 16

REPRESENTATIONS AND WARRANTIES

Section 16.1. Our Representations.

We make the following representations and warranties to you that are true and correct upon the signing of this Agreement:

(a) **Organization**. We are a corporation duly organized, validly existing and in good standing under the laws of the State of Florida.

(b) **Authorization**. We have the corporate power to sign, deliver, and carry out the terms of this Agreement. We have taken all necessary action for proper authorization. This Agreement has been duly authorized, signed and delivered by us and is our valid, legal and binding agreement and obligation in accordance with this Agreement, except as may be limited by applicable bankruptcy, insolvency, reorganization and other laws and equitable principles affecting creditors' rights generally.

(c) **No Violation**. Our performance of our obligations under this Agreement will not result in: a. the breach of any term of any contract or agreement to which we are a party to or bound by, or be an event that, with notice, lapse of time or both, would result in a breach or event of default; nor b. result in the violation by us of any statute, rule, regulation, ordinance, code, judgment, order, injunction or decree.

Section 16.2. Your Representations.

You make the following representations and warranties to us, that are true and correct upon signing this Agreement and throughout the Term:

(a) **Organization**. If you are a corporation, limited liability company or a general or limited partnership, you are duly organized, validly existing and in good standing under the laws of its state of organization.

(b) **Authorization**. You have the power to sign, deliver, and carry out this Agreement. You have taken all necessary action for proper authorization. This Agreement has been duly authorized, signed and delivered by you and is your valid, legal and binding agreement and obligation in accordance with this Agreement, except as may be limited by applicable bankruptcy, insolvency, reorganization and other laws and equitable principles affecting creditors' rights generally.

(c) **No Violation**. The performance by you of your obligations under this Agreement will not result in: a. the breach of any term of, or be a default under, any term of any contract, agreement or other commitment in which you are a party to or is bound by, or be an event that, with notice, lapse of time or both, would result in a breach or event of default; nor b. result in the violation by you of any statute, rule, regulation, ordinance, code, judgment, order, injunction or decree.

(d) **No Speculative Intent**. You are not obtaining this Bobby Rubino's Ribs n More Franchise for speculative or investment purposes and have no present intention to sell or transfer or attempt to sell or transfer any part of this Agreement or the Bobby Rubino's Ribs n More Franchise.

(e) **True Copies**. Copies of all documents you are required to furnish to us are correct copies of the documents, including all amendments or modifications and contain no misleading or incorrect statement or material omissions.

Section 16.3. Receipt of FOC.

You agree that you received from us an FOC for the state where your Bobby Rubino's Ribs n More Franchise will be located and your state of residence, with all exhibits and supplements to the FOC, on or before the first personal meeting with our representatives and at least 10 Business Days before: 1. signing this Agreement and any other agreement imposing a binding obligation on you; and 2. any payment by you of any consideration for the sale or proposed sale, of a franchise.

Section 16.4. Receipt of Completed Franchise Agreement.

You agree that you received from us a completed copy of this Agreement and all related agreements, containing all material terms, (except for the date, signatures and any minor matters not material to the agreements), with all blanks filled in, at least 5 Business Days before signing this Agreement.

Section 16.5. Acknowledgment of Risk.

You agree to the following:

(a) **YOUR SUCCESS IN OWNING AND OPERATING YOUR BOBBY RUBINO'S RIBS n MORE FRANCHISE IS SPECULATIVE AND DEPENDS ON MANY FACTORS INCLUDING, TO A LARGE EXTENT, YOUR INDEPENDENT BUSINESS ABILITY. NO REPRESENTATIONS OR PROMISES, EXPRESS OR IMPLIED, HAVE BEEN MADE BY US OR ANY OF OUR EMPLOYEES, BROKERS OR REPRESENTATIVES, TO INDUCE YOU TO ENTER INTO THIS AGREEMENT EXCEPT AS INCLUDED IN THIS AGREEMENT. NO OFFICER, DIRECTOR, EMPLOYEE, OFFICER, DIRECTOR, BROKER OR REPRESENTATIVE IS AUTHORIZED TO DO OTHERWISE.**

(b) **YOU AGREE THAT IN ALL OF YOUR DEALINGS WITH US, OUR OFFICERS, DIRECTORS, EMPLOYEES, BROKERS (IF ANY) AND OTHER REPRESENTATIVES ACT ONLY IN A REPRESENTATIVE CAPACITY AND NOT IN AN INDIVIDUAL CAPACITY. YOU AGREE THAT THIS AGREEMENT AND ALL BUSINESS DEALINGS BETWEEN YOU AND ANY INDIVIDUALS AS A RESULT OF THIS AGREEMENT, ARE ONLY BETWEEN YOU AND US.**

(c) **IN ADDITION, WE MAKE NO WARRANTY AS TO YOUR ABILITY TO OPERATE THE BOBBY RUBINO'S RIBS n MORE FRANCHISE IN THE JURISDICTION WHERE YOUR BOBBY RUBINO'S RIBS n MORE FRANCHISE IS TO BE OPERATED. IT IS YOUR OBLIGATION TO SEEK OR OBTAIN ADVICE OF COUNSEL SPECIFICALLY ON THIS ISSUE. IF LEGISLATION ENACTED BY, OR REGULATION OF, ANY GOVERNMENTAL BODY PREVENTS YOU FROM OPERATING YOUR BOBBY RUBINO'S RIBS n MORE FRANCHISE, WE ARE NOT LIABLE FOR DAMAGES NOR REQUIRED TO INDEMNIFY YOU OR TO RETURN ANY MONIES RECEIVED FROM YOU.**

ARTICLE 17

MEDIATION AND ARBITRATION; EQUITABLE RELIEF

Section 17.1. Mediation.

For any dispute involving this Agreement, before any arbitration proceeding taking place, either party may, at his, her or its option, submit the controversy or claim to non-binding mediation before the Center for Public Resources — National Franchise Mediation Program, FAM, the American Arbitration Association, or another mutually agreeable mediator. Both parties will execute a confidentiality agreement reasonably satisfactory to us. Upon submission, the obligation to attend mediation is binding on both parties. Each party will bear his, her or its own costs for the mediation, except the mediation fee and the fee for the mediator will be split equally.

Section 17.2. Arbitration.

(a) Except as specifically modified by this ARTICLE and excepting matters involving remedies in Section 17.3, any controversy or claim under this Agreement, including any claim that this Agreement, or any part of this Agreement, is invalid, illegal or otherwise voidable or void, including any claim of fraud in the inducement or any antitrust claim, must be submitted to arbitration before and in accordance with the arbitration rules of FAM, or if FAM is unable to conduct the arbitration for any reason or if both parties agree, before the American Arbitration Association in accordance with its commercial arbitration rules, or any other mutually agreeable arbitration association.

(b) The terms of this Section are independent of any other term of this Agreement. If a court of competent jurisdiction determines that any term is unlawful in any way, that court will modify or interpret the terms to the minimum extent necessary to have it comply with the law. All issues of the arbitrability or the enforcement of the agreement to arbitrate contained in this Agreement are governed by the United States Arbitration Act (9 U.S.C. §§1 *et seq.*) and the federal common law of arbitration.

(c) All claimants with substantially similar claims may join the proceedings.

(d) All parties who may be legally responsible agree to participate in the arbitration and all potential legal claims can be joined in the arbitration forum.

(e) Limited discovery will be allowed, consistent with Rule 10 of the Commercial Rules of the American Arbitration Association and pursuant to a discovery plan approved by the arbitrators.

(f) The actual hearing on the merits must occur within 6 months of the date of filing of the arbitration proceeding.

(g) A reasoned written opinion of the merits must be issued by the arbitrators within 30 days of the completion of the hearings on the merits.

(h) Judgment on an arbitration award may be entered in any court having competent jurisdiction and is binding, final and non-appealable. If any party to arbitration wishes to appeal any final award (there will be no appeal of interim awards or other interim relief), the party may appeal, within 30 days of the final award, to a 3-arbitrator panel appointed by the same organization that conducted the arbitration. The issues on appeal will be limited to the proper application of the law to the facts found at the arbitration hearing and will not include any trial *de novo* or other fact-finding function. The party requesting the appeal must pay all expense charged by the arbitration appeal panel and/or arbitration organization in the appeal and must post any bond deemed appropriate by the arbitration organization or arbitration appeal panel. In addition, a party requesting appeal that does not prevail on the appeal will pay the other party's (or parties') attorneys' fees and other costs of responding to the appeal.

(i)   Before any arbitration proceeding takes place, either party may elect to have the arbitrator conduct, in a separate proceeding before the actual arbitration, a preliminary hearing, at this hearing testimony and other evidence may be presented and briefs may be submitted, including a brief stating the then applicable statutory or common law methods of measuring damages in respect of the controversy or claim being arbitrated.

(j)   This arbitration provision is self-executing and remains in full effect after the expiration, transfer or termination of this Agreement. If either party fails to appear at any properly noticed arbitration proceeding, an award may be entered against that party by default or otherwise.

Section 17.3. Exceptions to Mediation and Arbitration; Equitable Relief.

(a)   The obligation to mediate or arbitrate is not binding on either party for claims involving the Proprietary Property; claims involving any sublease of real property between the parties or their related entities; your obligations upon the termination, transfer or expiration of this Agreement; any encumbrances or transfers restricted under this Agreement concerning interests in the Franchisee, your Bobby Rubino's Ribs n More Franchise and this Agreement; matters involving actions that may impair the good will associated with the Proprietary Marks; matters involving claims of danger, health or safety involving you, the employees, customers or the public; or requests for restraining orders, injunctions or other procedures in a court of competent jurisdiction to obtain specific performance when deemed necessary by any court to preserve the *status quo* or prevent irreparable injury pending resolution by mediation or arbitration of the actual dispute between the parties.

(b)   You recognize that your Bobby Rubino's Ribs n More Franchise is intended to be one of a large number of businesses identified by the Proprietary Marks in selling to the public the menu items associated with the Proprietary Marks, and that the failure on the part of a single franchisee to comply with the terms of his or her franchise agreement is likely to cause irreparable damage to us and damages at law would be an inadequate remedy. You agree that upon your breach or threatened breach of any of the terms of this Agreement concerning any matters referenced in Subsection 17.3(a), we are entitled to seek an injunction restraining the breach and/or to a decree of specific performance, without showing or proving any actual damage, together with recovery of reasonable attorneys' fees and costs incurred in obtaining equitable relief. This equitable remedy is in addition to all remedies that we have by virtue of your breach of this Agreement. We are entitled to seek this relief without the posting of any bond or security or, if a bond is nevertheless required by a court of competent jurisdiction, the parties agree that the sum of $1,000 is a sufficient bond.

ARTICLE 18

TERM

Section 18.1. Term.

The Term of this Agreement is 10 years from the Agreement Date, unless sooner terminated under ARTICLE 12. The conditions under which you have the opportunity to obtain a Successor Bobby Rubino's Ribs n More Franchise Agreement at the expiration of this Agreement are those stated in Section 18.2.

Section 18.2. Option to Obtain Successor Bobby Rubino's Ribs n More Franchise Agreement.

(a) You are granted unlimited options to obtain a Successor Bobby Rubino's Ribs n More Franchise Agreement for terms of 10 years each provided the following conditions are met at the time the option is exercised and immediately before the beginning of the Succeeding Term, unless another time is specified below:

(i)   You must give us written notice of your intention to exercise the option by submitting your application at least 6 months but not more than 12 months before the end of the Term;

(ii) You cannot be in default of any provision of this Agreement or any other agreement between you and us or our Affiliates;

(iii) You, within 10 days before the end of the Term, must sign and deliver to us a Successor Bobby Rubino's Ribs n More Franchise Agreement that will not vary the material business terms reflected in this Agreement. However, you agree to sign our Successor Bobby Rubino's Ribs n More Franchise Agreement, even if materially different from this Agreement, if the new Agreement was collectively negotiated and approved by 50% of the Franchisees in the System;

(iv) You must comply with all other requirements imposed by us under the Successor Bobby Rubino's Ribs n More Franchise Agreement upon its signing, except that there will be no Initial Franchise Fee; and

(v)   You are entitled to continue to occupy the Premises for the entire Succeeding Term including, if you are then leasing the Premises from us or a third party, you are entitled to renew the lease or obtain our approval of a new location for the Bobby Rubino's Ribs n More Franchise within the Protected Territory, but not within the protected territory of a Company Unit or Franchise Unit, in accordance with our relocation procedures.

(b) If you have not met all of the conditions stated in Subsection 18.2(a), we may elect not to enter into a Successor Bobby Rubino's Ribs n More Franchise Agreement. At your written request within 5 days of notice from us that you have elected not to enter into a Successor Bobby Rubino's Ribs n More Franchise Agreement, for a 180-day period following this notice (this notice will extend the Term, as necessary, to the end of the 180-day period, unless we have grounds to otherwise terminate the Term), we will permit you to sell your Bobby Rubino's Ribs n More Franchise to a purchaser subject to our right of first refusal. This transfer must be in compliance with the provisions of Subsection 11.2(f) and all the other applicable terms of this Agreement.

Section 18.3. Reinstatements and Extensions.

If any termination or expiration of the Term would violate any applicable law, we may reinstate or extend the Term for the purpose of complying with the law, for the duration provided by us in a written notice to you, without waiving any of our rights under this Agreement or otherwise modifying this Agreement.

ARTICLE 19

DEFINITIONS

Section 19.1. Definitions.

As used in this Agreement, the Exhibits attached to this Agreement and any other document signed incidental to this Agreement and any exhibits to those documents, the following terms have the following meanings:

"**ADI**" means an Area of Dominant Influence, and is a geographic survey area created and defined by Arbitron based on measurable patterns of television viewing.

"**Advertising Contributions**" means the payments described in Subsection 3.1(d).

"**Affiliate**" means a company related to us such as a parent corporation, brother/sister corporation or subsidiary corporation.

"**Agreement**" means this Bobby Rubino's Ribs n More Franchise Agreement, as it may be amended, supplemented or otherwise modified by an agreement in writing signed by you and us under Section 20.2.

"**Agreement Date**" means the date of signing this Agreement.

"**Basic Management Training**" means the training described in Subsection 2.8(a).

"**Bobby Rubino's Ribs n More Franchise**" means the bar-b-que restaurant you are authorized to establish and operate under this Agreement.

"**Business Associate**" means any of our employees, officers, directors, agents, consultants, representatives, contractors, suppliers, distributors, franchisees or other business contacts.

"**Business Day**" means a day other than Saturday, Sunday or a U.S. national holiday. Any time period ending on a Saturday, Sunday or U.S. national holiday will be extended until 5:00 p.m. on the next Business Day.

"**Chain**" means the group of Company Units and Franchise Units each operating a Bobby Rubino's Ribs n More bar-b-que restaurant.

"**Company Unit**" means a Bobby Rubino's Ribs n More bar-b-que restaurant operated under the System and owned by us or any Affiliate.

"**Competitive Business**" means a business that is engaged, wholly or partially, directly or indirectly, in the sale of bar-b-que food items.

"**Confidential Information**" means all information, knowledge, know-how and technologies that we designate as confidential, proprietary or trade secrets. Confidential Information includes the Manuals and Secret Recipe Products.

"**Cooperative**" means the regional advertising cooperative described in Section 7.2.

"**Designee**" means 1 or more of our representatives who are independent contractors and are appointed by us to perform certain of our duties under this Agreement as described in ARTICLE 2.

"**Enforcement Costs**" means the costs described in Section 20.9.

"**Event of Default**" means a breach of this Agreement including those situations described in Sections 1.4(a), 1.4(c), 3.4, 11.2(a), 11.2(d) and 12.4 assuming any requirement for the giving of notice, the lapse of time, or both, or any other condition is satisfied.

"**FAM**" means Franchise Arbitration and Mediation, Inc.

"**FOC**" means our current Franchise Offering Circular and all its exhibits and supplements.

"**Franchise**" means the rights granted to you under this Agreement.

"**Franchise Owner**" means: a. if you are an individual, it means you; b. if you are a corporation, the individual who owns a majority of the voting and ownership interests in the corporation; c. if you are a partnership, the individual who is, or owns a majority of the voting and ownership interests in an entity that is a general partner of the partnership; and d. if you are a limited liability company, the individual who owns the majority of the membership interests in the company.

"**Franchise Unit**" means a Bobby Rubino's Ribs n More Franchise owned and operated under the System by a franchisee.

"**Franchisee Association**" means the Independent Association of Bobby Rubino's Ribs n More Franchisees described in Section 10.1.

"**Generally Accepted Accounting Principles**" means those standards, conventions and rules accountants follow in recording and summarizing transactions, and in the preparation of financial statements. Generally accepted accounting principles derive, in order of importance, from: (i) issuances from an authoritative body designated by the American Institute of Certified Public Accountants ("AICPA") Council; other AICPA issuances including AICPA Industry Guides; (iii) industry practice; and (iv) accounting literature in the form of books and articles.

"**Gross Revenues**" means the entire amount of all of your revenues from the ownership or operation of your Bobby Rubino's Ribs n More Franchise or any business at or about the Premises including catering and delivery and also including the proceeds of any business interruption insurance and any revenues received from the lease or sublease of a portion of the Premises, whether the revenues are evidenced by cash, credit, checks, gift certificates, scrip, food stamps, coupons and premiums (unless exempted by us) services, property or other means of exchange, excepting only the amount of any sales taxes that are collected and paid to the taxing authority (based on the cash method of accounting). Cash refunded and credit given to customers and receivables uncollectible from customers will be deducted in computing Gross Revenues to the extent that the cash, credit or receivables represent amounts previously included in Gross Revenues where Royalty Fees and Advertising Contributions were paid. Gross Revenues are deemed received by you at the time the goods, products, merchandise or services from which they derive are delivered or rendered or at the time the relevant sale takes place, whichever occurs first. Gross Revenues consisting of property or services (for example, "bartering" or "trade outs") are valued at the prices applicable, at the time the Gross Revenues are received, to the products or services exchanged for the Gross Revenues.

"**Initial Franchise Fee**" means the fee described in Subsection 3.1(a).

"**Local Advertising**" means advertising and promotion you undertake in media directed primarily in your local market area including television, radio, newspapers, magazines, billboards, posters, handbills, direct mail, yellow pages, sports program booklet advertising, church bulletins, collateral promotional and novelty items (for example, matchbooks, pens and pencils, bumper stickers, calendars) that prominently display the Proprietary Marks, advertising on public vehicles including cabs and buses, the cost of producing materials necessary to participate in these media and agency commissions on the production of the advertising and amounts paid to an approved regional advertising cooperative or to a merchant's association for advertising of which you are a member. Local Advertising does not include payments to the Marketing Fund nor payments for permanent on-premises signs, lighting, purchasing or maintaining vehicles even though the vehicles display in some manner the Proprietary Marks (except the cost of the materials displayed are included), contributions, sponsorships (unless the Proprietary Marks are prominently displayed by the group or activity receiving the contribution or sponsorship), premium or similar offers including discounts, price reductions, special offers, free offers and sweepstake offers (except that the media costs associated with promoting the premium offers are included), employee incentive programs and other similar payments that we may determine in its sole discretion should not be included in determining whether you have met your obligation for Local Advertising.

"**Manager**" means the Franchise Owner, unless we otherwise agree in writing.

"**Manuals**" means all manuals produced by, or for the benefit of, we and loaned to you and any revisions prepared for the internal use of the Bobby Rubino's Ribs n More Franchise.

"**Marketing Fund**" means the fund described in Section 7.4 that Advertising Contributions will be deposited for use in regional and national marketing activities to promote the System.

"**Notice of Default**" means the notices described in Section 12.4.

"**Opening Date**" means the date your Bobby Rubino's Ribs n More Franchise is first opened for business to the general public after being newly constructed.

"**P.O.S. System**" means the computerized cash registers, printer and modem or other computer hardware you are required to purchase in accordance with our specifications contained in the Manuals.

"**Premises**" means the entire real property subleased by you, where your Bobby Rubino's Ribs n More Franchise will be located, as described in Exhibit A.

"**Proprietary Marks**" means the service mark and logo "Bobby Rubino's Ribs n More" and all other trademarks, service marks, trade names, logos and commercial symbols authorized by us as part of the System.

"**Proprietary Property**" means the Proprietary Marks, Confidential Information and copyrighted information of us or our Affiliates that you are entitled to use under this Agreement.

"**Protected Territory**" means an area comprising a 3-mile radius from the Premises.

"**Reserved Area**" means the area where you will undertake your site selection process to submit proposed sites for our approval in accordance with our site approval process. The Reserved Area will be _____, but excluding any protected territory of a Company Unit or another Franchise Unit within the Chain who already has a Bobby Rubino's Ribs n More Franchise in operation or to be operated in the Reserved Area and excluding any protected territory of any unit owned or licensed by Bobby Rubino's U.S.A, Inc.

"**Royalty Fee**" means the fee described in Subsection 3.1(c).

"**Secret Recipe Products**" means the Bobby Rubino's Bar-B-Que Sauce and all other recipes and products created by us and deemed secret.

"**Succeeding Term**" means the term of the Successor Bobby Rubino's Ribs n More Franchise Agreement.

"**Successor Bobby Rubino's Ribs n More Franchise Agreement**" means the form of franchise agreement for new Win-win-Win franchisees at the time you elect to enter into an agreement in accordance with Section 18.2.

"**System**" means our business system for operating a Bobby Rubino's Ribs n More restaurant. The System includes specific standards and procedures and Proprietary Property, that may be changed.

"**Term**" means the term of the Agreement described in Section 18.1.

"**Trade Dress**" means the store design and image we developed and own for Bobby Rubino's Ribs n More restaurant as it may be revised and developed by us. The Trade Dress currently emphasizes a unified earth tone color scheme throughout the Bobby Rubino's

Ribs n More Franchise and includes the following features: Southwest theme and theme pictures.

"**Trainees**" means the persons approved by us who attend Basic Management Training.

"**Transfer Fee**" means the fee described in Subsection 11.2(f)(vii).

"**Unique Consideration**" means the consideration described in Subsection 11.4(d).

"**Unit**" means either a Company Unit or a Franchise Unit.

Section 19.2. Other Definitional Provisions.

(a) All of the terms defined in this Agreement have these defined meanings when used in other documents issued under or delivered under this Agreement unless the context otherwise requires or unless specifically otherwise defined in the other document; and

(b) The term "person" includes any corporation, limited liability company, partnership, estate, trust, association, branch, bureau, subdivision, venture, associated group, individual, government, institution, instrumentality and other entity, enterprise, association or endeavor of every kind.

ARTICLE 20

GENERAL PROVISIONS

Section 20.1. Amendments.

Except as stated in this Agreement, the provisions of this Agreement cannot be amended, supplemented, waived or changed orally, except by a written document signed by the party against whom enforcement of any amendment, supplement, waiver or modification is sought and making specific reference to this Agreement. Only our President has the authority to sign an amendment for us. This Section is expressly limited by the terms of Sections 20.3 and 20.7.

Section 20.2. MODIFICATION OF THE SYSTEM.

YOU AGREE THAT AFTER THE AGREEMENT DATE WE MAY MODIFY THE SYSTEM. YOU AGREE TO ACCEPT AND BE BOUND BY ANY MODIFICATIONS IN THE SYSTEM AS IF THEY WERE PART OF THIS AGREEMENT AT THE TIME OF SIGNING THIS AGREEMENT. YOU WILL MAKE ALL EXPENDITURES AND MODIFICATIONS OF THE SYSTEM AS WE REQUIRE SUBJECT TO THE CAPITAL EXPENDITURE LIMITATION CONTAINED IN SECTION 4.20.

Section 20.3. Binding Effect.

The terms of this Agreement are binding upon, benefit and are enforceable by the parties and their respective personal representatives, legal representatives, heirs, successors and permitted assigns.

Section 20.4. Notices.

All notices, requests, consents and other communications required or permitted under this Agreement must be in writing (including telex, telecopied and telegraphic communication) and must be (as elected by the person giving the notice) hand delivered by messenger or courier service, telecopied, telecommunicated, or mailed (airmail if international) by registered or certified mail (postage prepaid), return receipt requested, addressed to:

If to us: With a copy to:

Sally Corporation   Keith J. Kanouse, Esquire
1200 Building, Suite 200   Keith J. Kanouse, P.A.
1200 N. Federal Highway   Lake Wyman Plaza, Suite 353
Boca Raton, Florida 33431   2424 N. Federal Highway
Attn: Bobby Rubino, President   Boca Raton, Florida 33431

If to You: With a copy to:

_____   _____

_____   _____

Attn: _____   _____

or to any other address any party designates by notice complying with the terms of this Section. Each notice is deemed delivered: 1. on the date delivered if by personal delivery; 2. on the date of transmission with confirmed answer back if by telex, telefax or other telegraphic method; and 3. on the date the return receipt is signed or delivery is refused or the notice is designated by the postal authorities as not deliverable if mailed.

Section 20.5. Headings.

The headings and subheadings in this Agreement are for convenience of reference only, are not to be considered a part of this Agreement and will not limit or otherwise affect in any way the meaning or interpretation of this Agreement.

Section 20.6. Severability.

(a) If any term of this Agreement or any other agreement entered into under this Agreement is contrary to, prohibited by or invalid under applicable law or regulation, that term only will be inapplicable and omitted to the extent so contrary, prohibited or invalid, but the remainder of this Agreement will not be invalidated and will be given full effect so far as possible. If any term of this Agreement may be construed in two or more ways, one that would render the term invalid or otherwise voidable or unenforceable and another that would render the term valid and enforceable, that term has the meaning that renders it valid and enforceable.

(b) If any applicable law of any jurisdiction requires a greater notice of the termination of or non-renewal of this Agreement (if permitted) than is required under this Agreement, or the taking of some other action not required under this Agreement, or if under any applicable law of any jurisdiction, any term of this Agreement or any of our requirements is invalid or unenforceable, the notice and/or other action required by that law will be substituted for the comparable provisions of this Agreement. We have the right, in our sole discretion, to modify any invalid or unenforceable requirement to the extent required to be valid and enforceable. Any modification to this Agreement will be effective only in that jurisdiction, unless we elect to give the modification greater applicability, and this Agreement will be enforced as originally made and entered into in all other jurisdictions.

Section 20.7. Waivers.

The failure or delay of any party at any time to require performance by another party of any term of this Agreement, even if known, will not affect the right of that party to require performance of that provision or to exercise any right or remedy under this Agreement. Any waiver by any party of any breach of any term of this Agreement is not a waiver of any continuing or later breach of that term, a waiver of the term itself, or a waiver of any right or remedy under this Agreement. No notice to or demand on any party in any case, of itself, entitles that party to any other notice or demand in similar or other circumstances.

Section 20.8. Enforcement Costs.

If any arbitration, legal action or other proceeding is begun for the enforcement of this Agreement, or for an alleged dispute, breach, default or misrepresentation under any term of this Agreement, the prevailing party is entitled to recover reasonable pre-institution and post-institution attorneys' fees, court costs and all expenses even if not taxable as court costs (including all fees and expenses incident to arbitration, appellate, bankruptcy and post-judgment proceedings), incurred in the action or proceeding, in addition to any other relief that the party is entitled. Attorneys' fees include paralegal fees, administrative costs, investigative costs, costs of expert witnesses, court reporter fees, sales and use taxes, if any, and all other charges billed by the attorneys to the prevailing party. If we engage a collection agency or legal counsel for your failure to pay when due any monies owed under this Agreement or submit when due any reports, information or supporting records, or for any failure otherwise to comply with this Agreement, you must reimburse us on demand for all of the above-listed expenses we incur. Each party will bear his, her or its own costs in any mediation.

Section 20.9. Jurisdiction and Venue.

(a) The parties irrevocably and unconditionally: a. agree that any mediation, arbitration or suit, action or legal proceeding involving your Bobby Rubino's Ribs n More Franchise or this Agreement and involving just you and us (and no other franchisees) will be conducted where the Franchise Business is located or may be brought in the District Court of the United States, in the district where the Franchise Business is located or, if this court lacks jurisdiction, the courts of record of the state and county where our principal place of business is then located; b. consent to the jurisdiction of each court in any suit, action or proceeding; c. waive any objection that he, she or it may have to the laying of venue of any suit, action or proceeding in any of these courts; and d. agree that service of any court paper may be effected on the party by mail at the last known address, as provided in this Agreement, or in any other manner as may be provided under applicable laws or court rules in the state where the Franchise Business is located.

(b) The parties irrevocably and unconditionally: a. agree that any mediation, arbitration or suit, action or legal proceeding involving your Bobby Rubino's Ribs n More Franchise or this Agreement and involving you and one or more other franchisees and us, will be conducted in the county where our principal place of business is then located or may be brought in the District Court of the United States, in the district where our principal place of business is then located or, if this court lacks jurisdiction, the courts of record of the state and county where our principal place of business is then located; b. consent to the jurisdiction of each court in any suit, action or proceeding; c. waive any objection that he, she or it may have to the laying of venue of any suit, action or proceeding in any of these courts; and d. agree that service of any court paper may be effected on the party by mail at the last known address, as provided in this Agreement, or in any other manner as may be provided under applicable laws or court rules in the state where our principal place of business is then located.

Section 20.10. Remedies Cumulative.

Except as otherwise stated in this Agreement, no remedy in this Agreement for any party is intended to be exclusive of any other remedy. Each remedy is cumulative and is in addition to every other remedy given under this Agreement, now or later existing, at law, in equity, by statute or otherwise. No single or partial exercise by any party of any right or remedy under this Agreement precludes any other exercise of any other right or remedy.

Section 20.11. Effectiveness; Counterparts.

This Agreement is not effective or binding and enforceable against us until it is accepted by us at our home office in Boca Raton, Florida and signed by our President. You are advised not to incur any expenses for opening your Bobby Rubino's Ribs n More Franchise until you have received a final signed copy of this Agreement from our home office . This Agreement may be signed in counterparts, each is deemed an original, but all together are the same instrument. Confirmation of signing by telex, telecopy, or telefax of a facsimile signature page is binding upon any party to the confirmation.

Section 20.12. Reasonableness.

We both agree to act reasonably in all dealings with each other pursuant to this Agreement. Whenever the consent or approval of either party is required or contemplated under this Agreement, the party whose consent is required agrees not to unreasonably withhold or delay the consent.

Section 20.13. Duty of Good Faith and Fair Dealing.

This Agreement imposes upon both parties a duty of good faith and fair dealing in performance of this Agreement. "Good faith and fair dealing" means honesty in fact and the observance of reasonable standards of fair dealing in the restaurant industry.

Section 20.14. Governing Law.

Except to the extent governed by the United States Trademark Act of 1946 (Lanham Act, 15 U.S.C. §§1051 *et seq.* or the United States Arbitration Act, 9 U.S.C. §§1 et seq.), this Agreement and any other agreement between the parties and all transactions contemplated by this Agreement are governed by the laws of the State of Florida without regard to principles of conflicts of laws. If there exists state franchise laws in the state where the Franchise Business is located which provide you with greater protection than the laws of the state set forth above, then that state's franchise laws will also govern and apply in the event of conflict.

Section 20.15. Survival.

All of the parties' obligations that expressly or by their nature survive the expiration or termination of this Agreement continue in full force after the transfer, expiration or termination of this Agreement until they are satisfied or by their nature expire.

Section 20.16. Force Majeure.

Neither party is liable for loss or damage or is in breach of this Agreement if the failure to perform the obligations results solely from the following causes beyond his, her or its reasonable control, specifically: 1. transportation shortages, inadequate supply of equipment, merchandise, supplies, labor, material, or energy; 2. compliance with any applicable law; or 3. war, strikes, natural disaster or acts of God. Any delay resulting from any of these causes extends performance accordingly or excuses performance as may be reasonable, except that these causes do not excuse payments of amounts owed to us for any reason.

Section 20.17. Third Parties.

Except as provided in this Agreement to the contrary for any Affiliates or other Ribs n More franchisees nothing in this Agreement, whether express or implied, is intended to confer any rights or remedies under this Agreement on any persons (including other Ribs n More franchisees) other than the parties and their respective personal representatives, other legal representatives, heirs, successors and permitted assigns. Except as provided in this Agreement to the contrary for any Designee of us, nothing in this Agreement is intended to relieve or discharge the obligation or liability of any third persons to any party to this Agreement, nor will any provision give any third persons any right of subrogation or action over or against any party to this Agreement.

Section 20.18. AAFD Fair Franchising Standards.

This Agreement is intended, by the parties, to comply with and interpreted consistent with the AAFD Fair Franchising Standards. To the extent not in conflict with the terms of this Agreement, the Fair Franchising Standards are incorporated into this Agreement.

Section 20.19. Entire Agreement.

This Agreement, its Exhibits and all other written agreements involving this Agreement and expressly referenced in this Agreement, represent the entire understanding and agreement between the parties on the subject matter of this Agreement and supersede all other negotiations, understandings and representations, if any, made between the parties. No representations, inducements, promises or agreements, oral or otherwise, if any, not embodied in this Agreement, its Exhibits and all other written agreements concerning this Agreement and expressly referenced in this Agreement are of any effect.

IN WITNESS WHEREOF, the parties have duly signed this Agreement.

Witnesses: YOU or YOUR:

_____   _____

_____   By:_____

WE, US, OUR:

SALLY CORPORATION

By: _____

_____   Robert M. Rubino, Sr., President

_____

STATE OF _____

COUNTY OF _____

  This instrument was acknowledged before me on _____, 199____, by _____, who personally appeared before me at the time of notarization.

NOTARY PUBLIC - STATE OF _____

My Commission Expires:

                              sign _____

                              print _____

            Personally Known _____ OR Produced Identification _____
                  Type of Identification Produced:

                  _____

STATE OF FLORIDA

COUNTY OF PALM BEACH

  This instrument was acknowledged before me on _____, 199__, by Robert M. Rubino, Sr., as President of Sally Corporation, a Florida corporation, for the corporation. He personally appeared before me at the time of notarization.

NOTARY PUBLIC - STATE OF FLORIDA:

                              sign _____

                              print _____

            Personally Known _____ OR Produced Identification _____
                  Type of Identification Produced:

                  _____

My Commission Expires:

INDEX